"J. Michael Desmond's book is itself a monument to the architecture of LSU. It is a delightful and engrossing history that delves into the little-known facts about the unique buildings that make Louisiana State University distinctive."

—CHARLES E. SCHWING
former president of the American Institute of Architects

"Desmond's crisp, clear diagrams facilitate our comprehension of campus development, and his knowledge of architectural history helps us read the buildings. After this, you'll want to visit Baton Rouge."

—ROBERT D. LEIGHNINGER JR.
author of *Building Louisiana: The Legacy of the Public Works Administration*

"Desmond has intelligently presented and explicitly detailed how great design personalities, lofty ideals, and classical inspirations were combined to create and sustain a campus where the blend of landscape planning and architecture is unmatched. LSU's campus is an intentional assembly of significant buildings, melted seamlessly into the natural setting, 'that both symbolizes and provides for the aspirations' of the university, its students, and the citizens of the proud state of Louisiana."

—KEVIN HARRIS
Fellow of the American Institute of Architects

LSU Memorial Tower with other early campus buildings, showing the open sally port at its heart and Hill Memorial Library in the distance.
LSU Photograph Collection, RG #A5000, Louisiana State University Archives, LSU Libraries, Baton Rouge, LA.

THE ARCHITECTURE OF LSU

J. Michael Desmond

LOUISIANA STATE UNIVERSITY PRESS
BATON ROUGE

Publication of this book is made possible in part by the support of Mr. and Mrs. Robert L. Galantucci.

Published by Louisiana State University Press

Manufactured in the United States of America
First printing

DESIGNER: Michelle A. Neustrom
TYPEFACE: Vulpa
PRINTER AND BINDER: Walsworth Print Group

FRONT COVER IMAGE: Memorial Tower and the Administration entry group in the late 1920s, photograph colorized by LSU Press, used courtesy of the East Baton Rouge Parish Library.

LIBRARY OF CONGRESS CATALOGING-IN-PUBLICATION DATA
Desmond, John Michael.
The architecture of LSU / J. Michael Desmond.
p. cm.
Includes bibliographical references and index.
ISBN 978-0-8071-4976-8 (cloth : alk. paper) — ISBN 978-0-8071-4977-5 (pdf) — ISBN 978-0-8071-4978-2 (epub) — ISBN 978-0-8071-4979-9 (mobi) 1. Louisiana State University (Baton Rouge, La.) —Buildings. 2. College buildings—Louisiana—Baton Rouge. 3. Baton Rouge (La.) —Buildings, structures, etc. I. Title. II. Title: Architecture of Louisiana State University.
LD3114.6.D47 2013
378.763'18—dc23
2012027901

The paper in this book meets the guidelines for permanence and durability of the Committee on Production Guidelines for Book Longevity of the Council on Library Resources. ♾

CONTENTS

PREFACE

Standing on the wide terrace of the Campanile in the shade of that beautiful spire raised in memory of those citizens of Louisiana who gave their lives during the World War, General Robert Lee Bullard today dedicated the new Louisiana State University to "the service of the state and nation in preparing future citizens for our increasing world-wide relationships and our responsibility to show the world the beauties and benefits of a state of society and government developed under the genial influence of a larger political freedom than any that has yet been enjoyed elsewhere upon our plane."

—*Baton Rouge State Times,* April 30, 1926

Louisiana is blessed with both a richly varied natural landscape and a wonderfully diverse array of creative peoples. The story of its great university is one that brings these two together around the focus provided by a unique group of buildings riding a gentle rising upland overlooking the Mississippi River near the geographical, political, and economic center of the state. Over its 150-year history, Louisiana State University has had four homes. It began with a new building in Pineville constructed just before the Civil War but was forced to relocate after a fire a few years later to an existing facility in Baton Rouge before occupying a campus on the northern edge of the city for almost forty years. Its establishment on its current site began in 1926. In the beginning, the university was conceived as one of many such efforts around the nation to introduce practical science, along with the traditional disciplines of the fine, social, and business arts, into the general education of a populace for the betterment of all. It has evolved into a major teaching and research university with more than 220,000 graduates, most of whom are still working in every corner of the state, the nation, and the world. At the core of this great endeavor lies an assembly of buildings unmatched in their design and planning by those on any other campus in America. For more than eighty years, this campus, with its live oaks, tile roofs, and broad sheltering arches, has provided a home for higher education in Louisiana. Originally modeled after the architecture of the warmer climes of southern Europe, the campus presents a finely textured ensemble of significant buildings that both symbolize and provide for the aspirations of a people to improve themselves and their land and to increase the prosperity of both.

This book grew out of a 2006 historic-preservation study of the current campus funded by the Getty Foundation's Campus Heritage Grants program, a welcome initiative that has made it possible for many colleges and universities around the country to prepare historic-preservation plans. The research team's use of this resource produced an architectural and planning technical report on the campus and its historical development, a survey of existing conditions (gettysurvey.lsu.edu) for the most historic part of the campus, and a public exhibition about the campus and its origins. All of that work focused on the general campus plans of 1921 and 1922 and the core buildings indicated in those plans, which define the Louisiana State University quadrangles. The core area is defined by eighteen of the most historic buildings, which make up the quadrangles of the current campus. This core, along with a number of surrounding buildings dating from the 1920s and 1930s, was designated a National Historic District in 1988.

The technical report detailed the history and development of the university and its various campuses, from Pineville and the downtown Baton Rouge locations to the work of Frederick Law Olmsted Jr., of Brookline, Massachusetts, all leading up to the plan made by the St. Louis architect Theodore C. Link and the initial stages of its execution. In the survey of existing conditions, the state of the exterior of these core buildings, including an inventory of cracks and other surface anomalies, was recorded, and templates were produced for coordinating the replacement of doors and windows throughout this part of the campus. The third part of the grant effort, an exhibition entitled *LSU: Building an American Renaissance,* was mounted in the LSU Union Art Gallery in the fall of 2009. The Louisiana Secretary of State's Office then took the exhibition on a tour of venues across the state, including the Tioga Heritage Park and Museum near Pineville, the Delta Music Museum in Ferriday, the Louisiana State Exhibit Museum in Shreveport, the Imperial Calcasieu Museum in Lake Charles, the Masur Museum in Monroe, Louisiana's Old State Capitol in Baton Rouge, and the Louisiana State Museum at the Cabildo on Jackson Square in New Orleans. The Getty has called this exhibition "hands-down the most successful educational component" of any of its Campus Heritage Grants.

Work on the present book, that exhibition, and the grant effort out of which they grew were bracketed by two important milestones in the history of LSU. On the one hand, they were the result of a planning process that began with the university's preparations for its celebration of seventy-five years on the current campus in 2001. Among the most lasting results of that Diamond Jubilee Celebration was a comprehensive campus master plan in 2003. That effort, first suggested in discussions among the members of the Commission for the History of LSU and supported by former chancellor Paul Murrill and then newly arrived chancellor Mark Emmert, along with a host of others, laid the foundation for a process of continuous physical planning at LSU, something long overdue and crucial to the efficient operation of any institution of its size and scope.

The 2003 Campus Master Plan is only the second significant plan the university has produced in more than seventy-five years in its current location. That plan struggled with how to expand the scope of building on the campus over the coming decades while respecting, learning from, and restoring the core of campus buildings dating from the early 1920s. The 2003 master plan also emphasized the need for a continuing series of planning studies at LSU, specifically noting the need for comprehensive transportation planning and planning for the preservation of the core. Following that initiative, the university completed a series of interrelated master plans for parking and traffic, residential life, recreation and athletic facilities, the student union, and veterinary medicine, while participating in the broader community planning of the University Lakes region. The historic-preservation study that preceded this book was also a result of that 2003 master-planning process.

On the other hand, the year 2010 was the 150th anniversary of LSU's beginnings in Pineville, a year also marked by celebrations. The public exhibition served to introduce a wider segment of the population to the story of the architecture and planning of the university. The present book continues and expands that work, adding a chapter on the growth of the current campus out to Highland Road through the Huey Long years and the New Deal up to the Second World War.

Any effort as broad as a study of this kind must of necessity benefit from the contributions of many hands, and that has certainly been the case here. Van Cox, of the LSU School of Landscape Architecture, provided valuable insight into the evolution of the campus landscape. LSU architectural graduate Anthony Threatt contributed significantly to the research and production of the Getty technical report, the public exhibition, and the survey of existing conditions. Santanu Majumdar designed the exhibition boards while he was a graduate student in the Department of Graphic Design of the LSU School of Art. Andrew Wallace, then a student in the LSU School of Architecture, designed and built a series of illustrative wooden models of key buildings in the Link plan. These were inspired by the models of the buildings of Andrea Palladio produced by architecture students at the University of Venice in the 1970s. The retired architect and historic-preservation professor William Brockway offered valuable advice and counsel. Many LSU graduate and undergraduate students participated in various capacities, including Ivy Johnson, Owen Sketchler, Kristen Kelsch, Melissa Seanard, Stuart Neilson, Andrew Greenwood, Bryce Risher, and Abe Kinney.

Many people in the broader university community also contributed to this effort. Chief among them were members of the Commission for the History of LSU; Laura F. Lindsay, of the Department of Mass Communications, a co-chair of the university's Diamond Jubilee Commission; Paul Hoffman, of the History Department, the unofficial historian of LSU, who has been an invaluable adviser and consultant; and Faye Phillips, of the LSU Library. Marsha Cuddeback, of the LSU School of Architecture, contributed to the design and layout of the exhibition boards and provided insight into the planning logic of Link's General Plan. Emmett David, of LSU Facility Development, and Paul Favoloro, of LSU Facility Management, provided welcome assistance at every turn. The assistance of Farrell Jones, of LSU's CADGIS (Computer-Aided Design & Geographic Information Systems) lab, has been crucial as well.

Lieutenant Governor Jay Dardenne and Lance Harris, of the Louisiana Secretary of State's Office, enabled the people of Louisiana to get a firsthand look at the history and development of the LSU campus through their support and handling of the traveling exhibition throughout 2010. Nancy Little and Aaron Looney, of the LSU Office of Communications and University Relations, were instrumental in making that happen. John Sykes and Tom Riley, of the Louisiana State Museum, provided valued support. Robert Leighninger, now at Arizona State University, provided helpful encouragement and advice in person and through his wonderful books on the architecture of the New Deal era. Shane Bernard, historian and curator for the McIlhenny Company of Avery Island, provided insight and assistance on the material in chapter 5.

Others had a less direct role and deserve mention as well. Chief among these is former chancellor Mark Emmert, whose enthusiasm for LSU and comprehensive vision of its mission were an early inspiration. The work and insight of William Eskew over the years, especially during his time with LSU Facility Development, was a contributing factor. The university photographer Jim Zeitz provided many of the most descriptive pictures. Barry Cowan and Judy Bolton, of the LSU Library, have been a significant resource. This work could not have been produced without the always excellent help of the entire staff of Special Collections at LSU's Hill Memorial Library. Appreciation is due as well to Charlene Bonnette, of the Louisiana Collection at the State Library of Louisiana, and to the Southeast Architectural Archives at Tulane University. David Cronrath, then dean of the College of Art and Design, also provided valuable support and assistance, as did the college's senior development officer, Michael Robinson. The support and encouragement of Rusty Jabour when he was vice chancellor and director of the LSU Office of Communications and University Relations was very helpful and much appreciated. The St. Louis architect Gary Tetley was generous with his knowledge of Theodore C. Link's life and work. I also want to express my debt to the Getty Foundation and to Associate Director Joan Weinstein for her encouragement and advice along the way. The talent, and the courteous and professional attitude, of everyone I have worked with at LSU Press have made a significant contribution to the final outcome of this effort, and I want to extend my appreciation especially to Margaret Lovecraft, Catherine Kadair, and Michelle Neustrom, and for the help of text editor Joanne Allen.

This work is dedicated to my children, Ella and Jacob, both now LSU undergraduates in good standing, and to the many other students with whom I have had the great pleasure of working at this outstanding institution.

THE ARCHITECTURE OF LSU

1

The Downtown Campus

The visitor strolling through the capital of Louisiana finds no more attractive spot than the beautiful grounds of the Louisiana State University. The smooth-shaven lawns, the shaded walks, the flowers, the giant oaks, and the quaint old buildings form an ideal setting for the handsome cadets who gather in groups about the grounds and buildings.

The grounds lie between the northernmost street of the city and the fine artificial lake that was formed some years ago by building a dam across Bayou Gracie. They have a frontage of nearly half a mile on the bluff overlooking the Mississippi river, and extend back more than a mile. The front is occupied by the University proper, and the back by one of the three Experiment Stations of the University, the other two being located at Audubon Park, in New Orleans, and at Calhoun, in Ouachita Parish.

The buildings and grounds were formerly used by the United States as a garrison, but were given to Louisiana in 1886 for the use of the State University. Around this old military post cluster historic associations of greatest interest. Occupied in succession by French, English, Spanish and American garrisons, it has been at some time the temporary home of nearly every man who has become distinguished in the military history of the United States.

—JOHN T. MICHEL, *Report of the Secretary of State . . . 1902*

ORIGINS AND THE MOVE TO BATON ROUGE

The story of the architecture of Louisiana State University begins in 1853 with the establishment of the Louisiana State Seminary of Learning in Pineville. The new institution moved into a freshly built seminary structure there, just across the Red River from Alexandria, in 1860, the year before Louisiana seceded from the Union. Designed by Alexander T. Wood, it was a rather stark Italianate structure of three stories consisting of a central pavilion and four crenellated corner towers projecting from a central mass. The most basic architectural aspects—size, material, and configuration—were used to shape the impression of the building, to make it stand out as something unique. There was also a glimmer of an intentional historical reference in the use of quasi-Gothic detailing. Although unremarkable in its almost vernacular use of popular architectural elements, it must have been among the most imposing and

FIG. 1.1. The "Seminary Building" of the original LSU campus near Pineville. LSU Photograph Collection, RG #A5000, Louisiana State University Archives, LSU Libraries, Baton Rouge, LA.

monumental buildings in the northern and central parts of the state at the time. The building was abandoned during the Civil War and then burned to the ground in 1869 after a brief reoccupation (fig. 1.1).

At this point the Seminary of Learning moved into a temporary home in Baton Rouge, occupying at first a portion of the state's Institution for the Deaf and Dumb and the Blind, on the southern edge of town. This facility, which had been more skillfully designed in the Gothic Revival style, was influenced by James Dakin's use of that style in his design for the Louisiana State Capitol, completed in 1852. These two structures, which would have been the largest and most imposing in Baton Rouge at the time, show up in several sketch views of the city that have survived from the nineteenth century (figs. 1.2–1.4).

The Institution for the Deaf and Dumb and the Blind, completed by 1858, was composed of three main structures, a large central building and two flanking ones to the rear that served as classrooms. These structures enclosed an open space to the rear that was used by the university cadets as a drill ground (fig. 1.5). The central building was divided into five massing units comprising a central body, two outlying side pavilions, and two small connecting pieces. The central portion was the largest, five stories high and five windows across, rising to a towerlike roof structure. The side pavilions, each containing two windows, were connected to the center by wings with three windows each. This was a carefully designed structure, meant to exhibit a precise architectural order following the trend of its day. In keeping with architecture around the world, formal characteristics were used in this building, as they had been in the university's first structure in Pineville, to separate it from the ordinary and make it stand out. The use of a recognized architectural style frequently associated with institutional programs in that period, along with the compositional traits of bilateral symmetry, hierarchy, and monumentality, was intended to bolster the perception and identity of the institution these buildings were meant to house. Many of these architectural features are typical of institutional structures built in the United States in the nineteenth century and would reappear in the core of the present LSU campus with different stylistic references. Over the next several years the Seminary of Learning would become the Louisiana State University, and the institution would absorb the recently formed Louisiana Agricultural & Mechanical College, previously housed in New Orleans.

THE PENTAGON BARRACKS SITE

By the early 1880s, the limited land available for agricultural experiments had become a problem. In response to the growing demands, the university acquired the rights to use the recently decommissioned Pentagon Barracks and old U.S. Arsenal site on the northern side of the city. This tract of land had been assembled over time from several

Baton Rouge, Louisiana.

FIG. 1.2. *Louisiana Institute for the Deaf, Dumb and the Blind,* 1859, by Marie Adrien Persac (Franco-American, 1823–73). Gouache and collage on paper, 18 x 23½ in. LSU MOA 77.4, Gift of the Friends of LSU Museum of Art. Courtesy of LSU Museum of Art. Photograph by David Humphreys.

FIG. 1.3. The Gothic Revival Old State Capitol in Baton Rouge, shown here with the lanterns installed during the late-nineteenth-century renovation. Postcard in author's personal collection.

FIG. 1.4. The Louisiana Institution for the Deaf and Dumb and the Blind and the Old State Capitol were the first imposing institutional buildings in Baton Rouge, clearly visible from the Mississippi River in this nineteenth-century view. Courtesy of Documenting the American South, The University of North Carolina at Chapel Hill Libraries.

FIG. 1.5. The rear court of the Louisiana Institution for the Deaf and Dumb and the Blind, showing its three-part hierarchical composition. Office of Public Relations Records, RG #A0020, Louisiana State University Archives, LSU Libraries, Baton Rouge, LA.

FIG. 1.6. "Plan of Fort Baton Rouge," by Georges Henri Victor Collot, 1796. Reprinted 1826. Fort New Richmond was located on the bluff at what would become Baton Rouge. Bayou Gracie is shown to the left (north). Courtesy of David Rumsey Map Collection, www.davidrumsey.com.

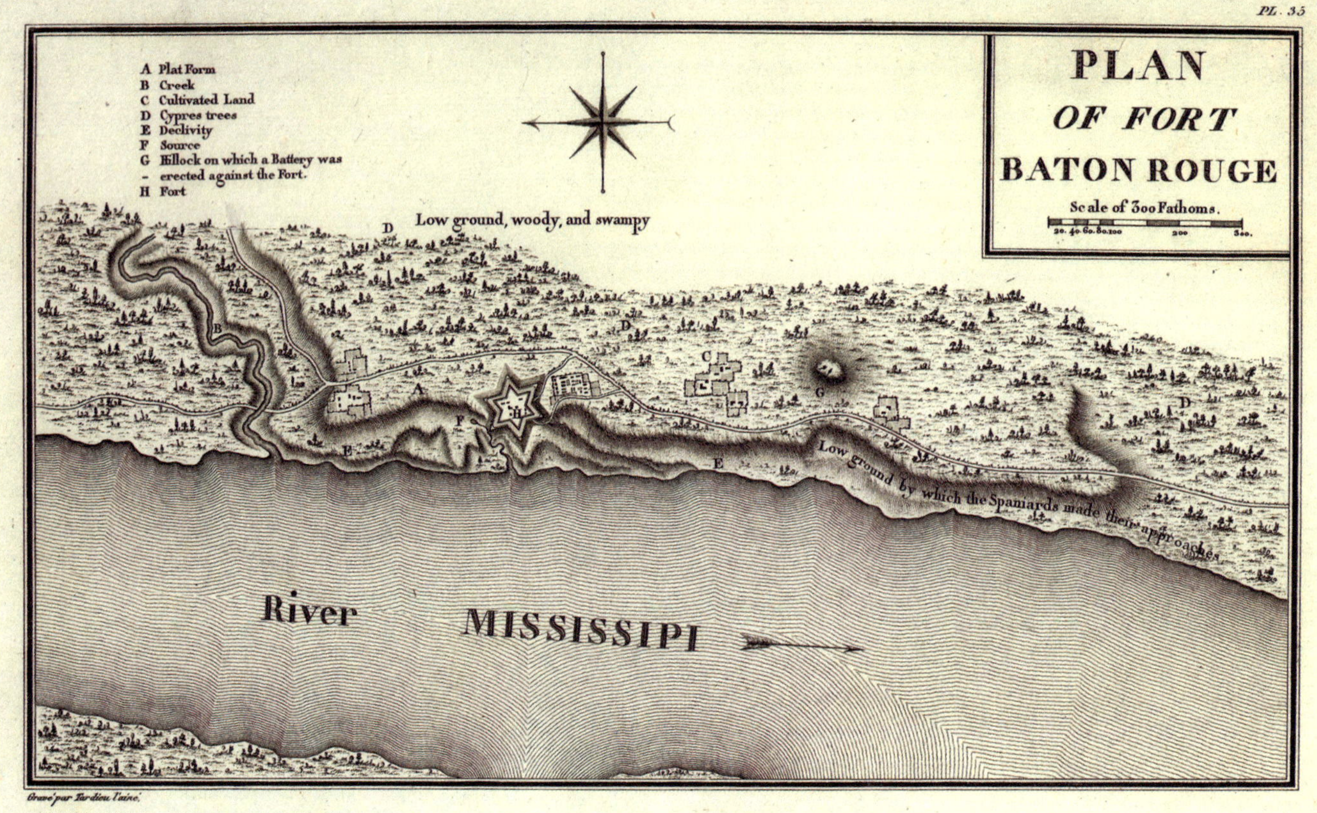

FIG. 1.7. (*facing page*) Surveyor general's plat map from 1895 for the Greensburg District, showing nineteenth-century property divisions along the Baton Rouge Reach. The locations of the downtown and current LSU campuses are noted. Courtesy of Louisiana State Land Office.T7S/R1W.

separate earlier land grants reflecting the French arpent system of land measure. It occupied high ground that was bounded on the north by the dammed Bayou Gracie, which became known as University Lake, and on the west by the railroad that ran along the Mississippi River just below the bluff on which the original fort, and now the barracks, had been built (figs. 1.6 and 1.7). The site was penetrated by Lafayette Street and by Third Street. Third Street came to be known as University Avenue and divided the tract into two sections.

This new location on the northern side of downtown developed somewhat haphazardly into a campus. In the first years, the Pentagon Barracks (1825) and the Arsenal (1838) were the main structures. The Barracks had been built on the site of the older military fortification on the Mississippi River; the Arsenal was an abandoned powder magazine. The five-sided form of the Barracks, with the side parallel to the river unbuilt, defined a central space with a pleasing surround of four buildings that deferred to the order of the open side. Besides the Barracks and the Arsenal, the site contained a nondescript collection of wood-frame buildings of various sizes, as well as open areas for gardening and horticultural research.

Slowly, a relatively unstructured group of largely wood-frame buildings grew up around these two older structures. A house for the commander of the garrison built due east on axis with the Pentagon Barracks was adapted for use by the university president. At first, the house acted as a kind of informal center for a number of buildings that developed around it. The use of this building as the president's house solidified the idea of the university continuing or building upon the representation of order expressed by the better military structures there. By 1895 the university included agricultural, chemical, and mechanical laboratories, an engineering department, dormitories and fraternity buildings, a library (in the former magazine), a gymnasium, a mess hall, and various other residences and auxiliary structures relating to agricultural studies. While there does not appear

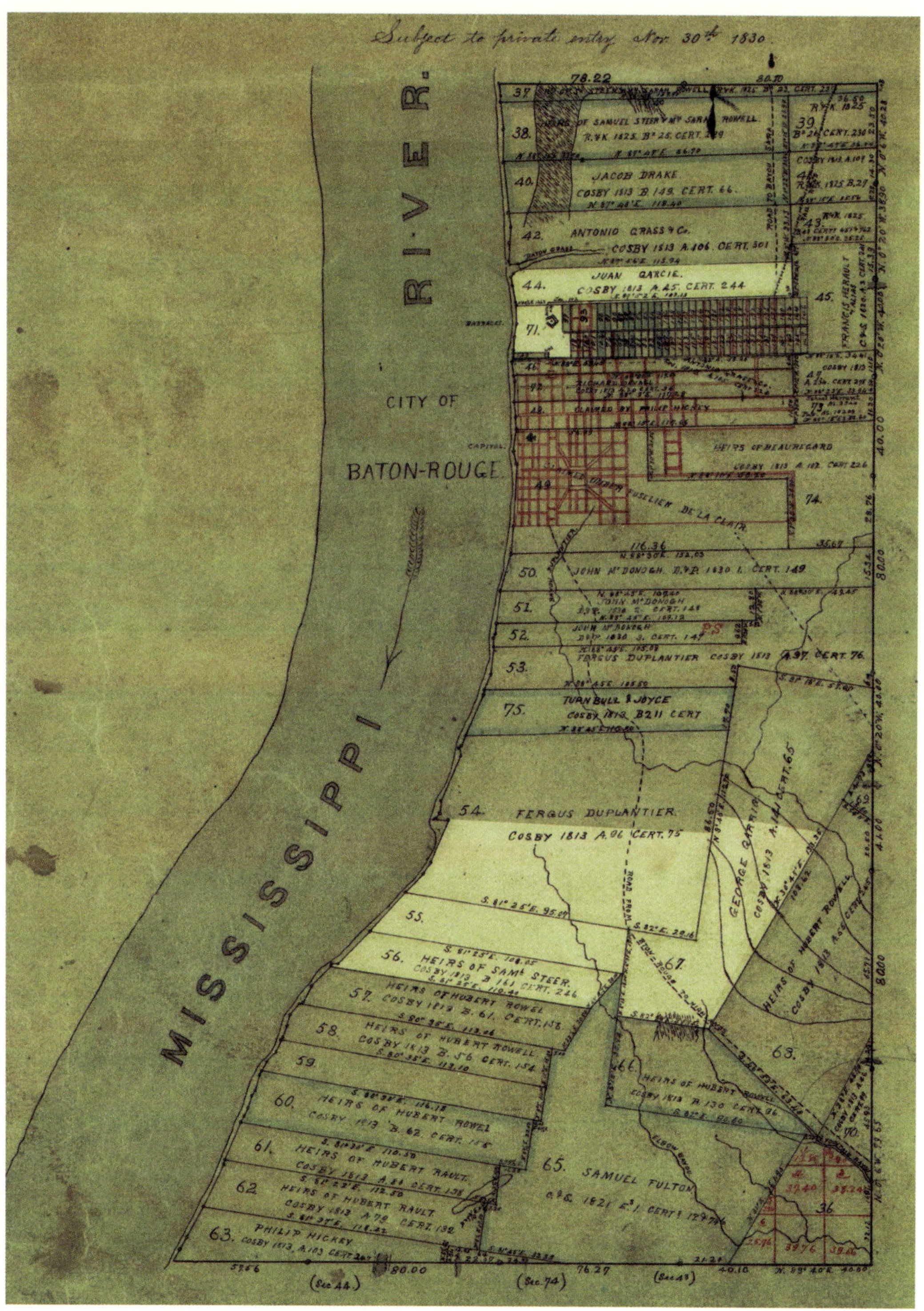

CLOCKWISE:

FIG. 1.8. Old President's, or Commandant's, House, at the center of the downtown campus. LSU Photograph Collection, RG #A5000, Louisiana State University Archives, LSU Libraries, Baton Rouge, LA.

FIG. 1.9. The spacious grounds of the downtown campus in the early years. LSU Photograph Collection, RG #A5000, Louisiana State University Archives, LSU Libraries, Baton Rouge, LA.

FIG. 1.10. The Infirmary and early Mess Hall on the downtown campus. LSU Photograph Collection, RG #A5000, Louisiana State University Archives, LSU Libraries, Baton Rouge, LA.

FIG. 1.11. The Chemistry Laboratory on the downtown campus. LSU Photograph Collection, RG #A5000, Louisiana State University Archives, LSU Libraries, Baton Rouge, LA.

FIG. 1.12. (*facing page*) Map of the downtown campus in 1895. General Catalog, Courtesy of Special Collections, LSU Libraries, Baton Rouge, LA.

to have been much intentionality in the use of a coordinated architectural style in these structures, various plans from the period indicate a strategy of organizing the buildings into two rows, one to the north and one to the south of the President's House. Of these new buildings, Foster Hall, completed in 1901, was the most prominent. It set a standard for the more substantial buildings that came later (figs. 1.8–1.11; fig. 1.12).

These early, unstructured groups of buildings were augmented in the first decades of the twentieth century by a more consciously planned arrangement to the south, starting with Garig Hall and eventually featuring two lines of

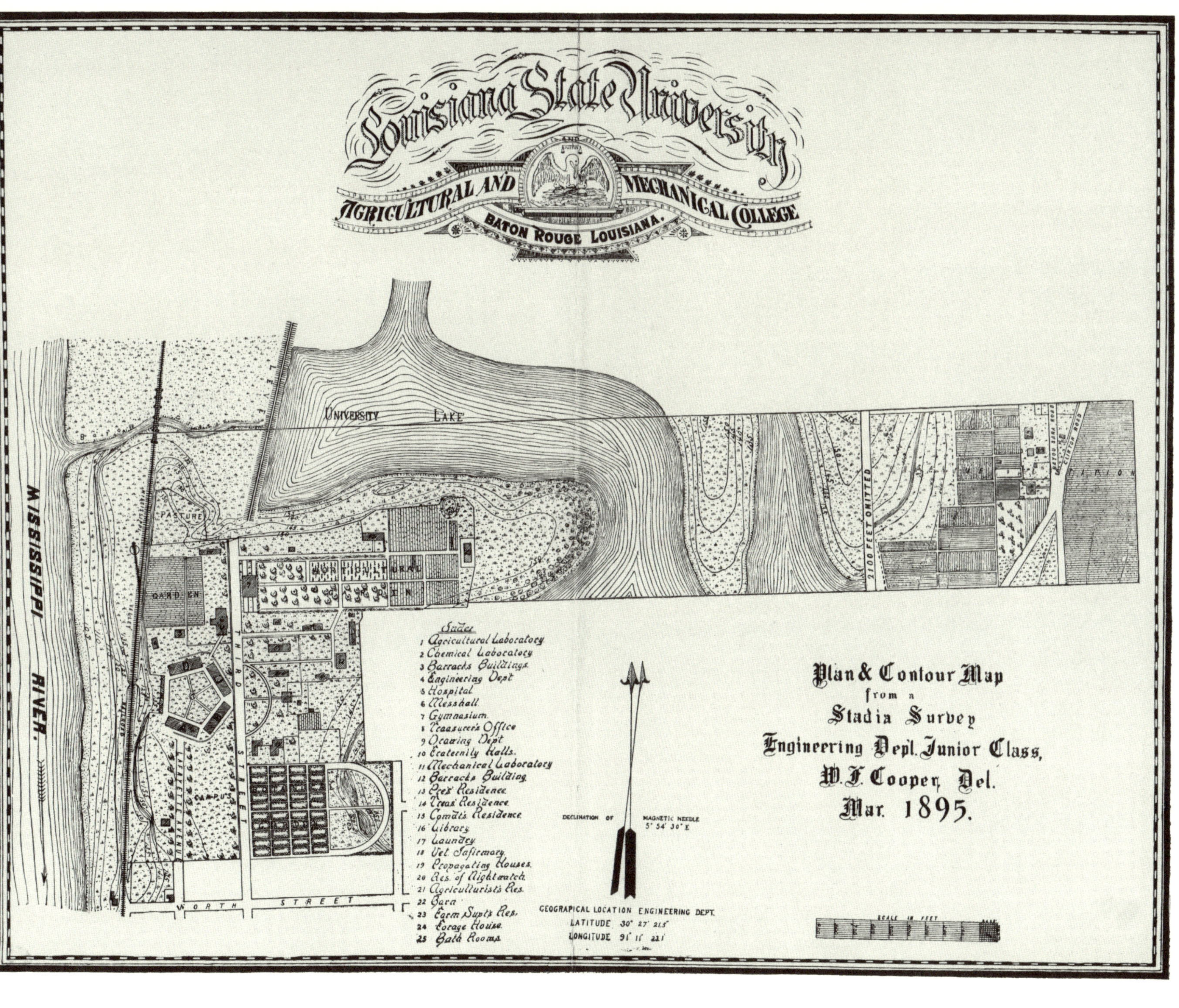
Louisiana State University
and
Agricultural and Mechanical College
Baton Rouge Louisiana.
University Lake
Pasture
Garden
Campus
Mississippi River
Third Street
North Street
2100 Feet Omitted
Index
1 Agricultural Laboratory
2 Chemical Laboratory
3 Barracks Buildings.
4 Engineering Dept
5 Hospital
6 Messhall
7 Gymnasium.
8 Treasurer's Office
9 Drawing Dept
10 Fraternity Halls.
11 Mechanical Laboratory
12 Barracks Building
13 Pres' Residence
14 Treas' Residence
15 Comdt's Residence
16 Library
17 Laundry
18 Vet. Infirmary
19 Propagating Houses.
20 Res. of Nightwatch.
21 Agriculturist's Res.
22 Barn
23 Farm Supt's Res.
24 Forage House
25 Bath Rooms
Declination of Magnetic Needle
5° 54' 30" E
Geograpical Location Engineering Dept.
Latitude 30° 27' 21.5"
Longitude 91° 11' 22.1'
Plan & Contour Map
from a
Stadia Survey
Engineering Dept. Junior Class,
W. F. Cooper, Del.
Mar. 1895.
Scale in Feet

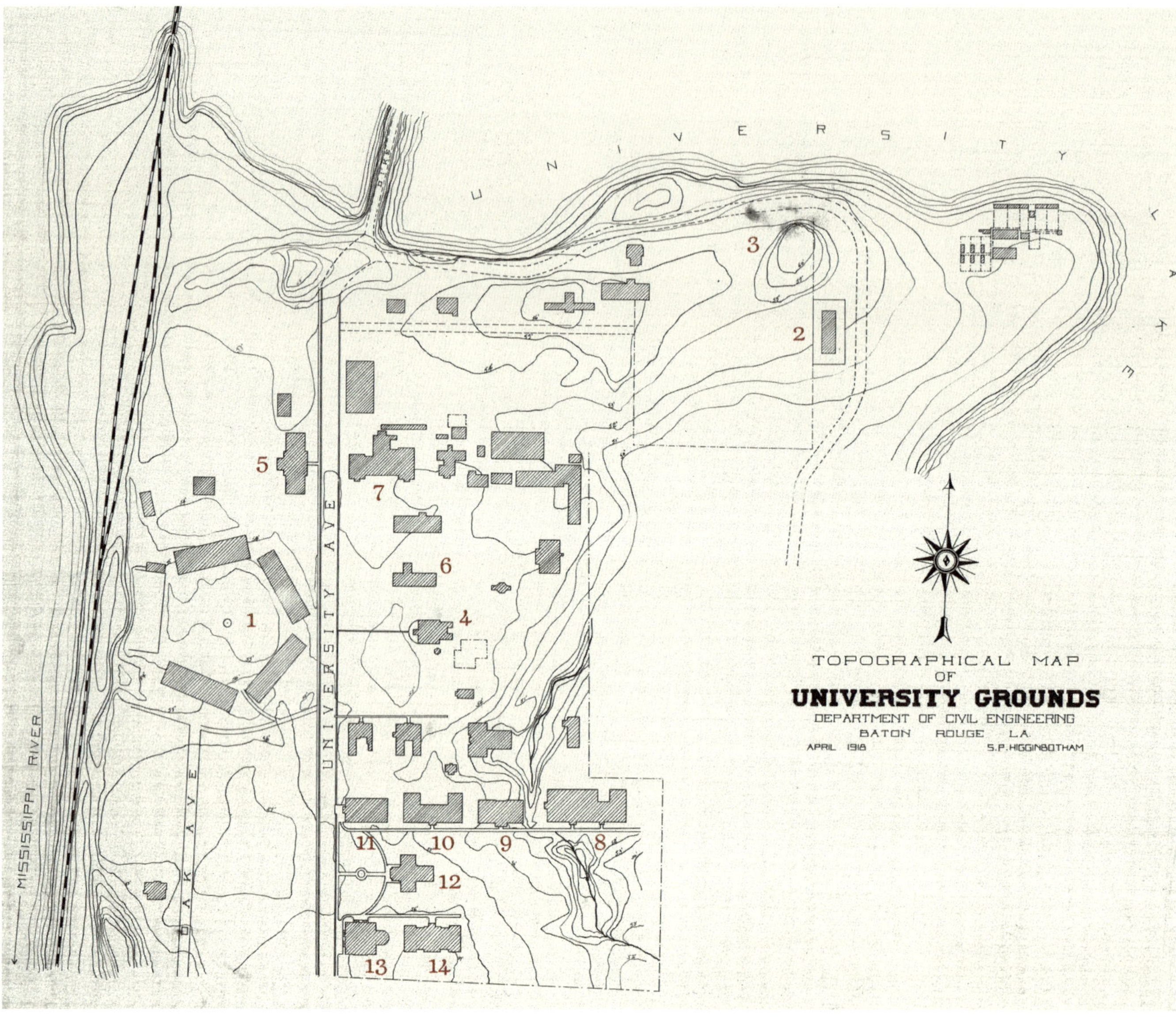

FIG. 1.13. Topographical map of the downtown campus in 1918, showing the old Army, or Pentagon, Barracks facing the Mississippi River, with the President's House on axis, the loosely structured buildings around that, the structures devoted to agricultural uses on the northern side near the University Lake, and the array of newly constructed buildings flanking Hill Memorial Library on the southern side of campus. Courtesy of the National Park Service, Frederick Law Olmsted Historic Site.

1. Pentagon Barracks on site of old fortifications
2. Arsenal
3. Remaining Native American mound
4. Commandant's, or President's, House
5. Infirmary
6. Chemistry Building
7. Foster Hall
8. Robertson Hall
9. Heard Hall
10. Irion Hall
11. Garig Hall
12. Hill Memorial Library
13. Alumni Hall (relocated to current campus)
14. Peabody Hall

more substantial classroom buildings and an alumni hall on the southern edge of campus centered on a new library. Both Hill Memorial Library (1902) and the administration building, Alumni Memorial Hall (1904), were substantial brick masonry structures in a neoclassical style that used lighter-colored cut-stone details for columns and moldings, consistent with the "White City" images then sweeping the nation.[1] Although Garig Hall was built in a romantic German style, Irion, Heard, Robertson, and Peabody Halls were also bilaterally symmetrical with stone details inspired by this neoclassical style (fig. 1.13; figs. 1.14–1.20).

While the arrangement of the various buildings occupying this downtown location may not have been convincing as a completely planned campus, this last group of seven exhibited an increasing sense of architectonic order. These two partial rows of classroom buildings eventually faced each other across a wide, open green space punctuated by the symmetrical domed form of the new Library. This composition put the Library in a central position on what might be seen as an implicit axis, facing the open space of the Parade Ground on one side and the more enclosed space of the inner-campus quadrangle on the other. This grouping of intentionally placed buildings, anchored by a Library, perhaps reflecting Thomas Jefferson's influential plan for the University of Virginia, became increasingly common on American campuses designed after 1900. At the University of Virginia, the library, as a half-scale version of the Pantheon, expressed an interest in Rome as a model and in the idea of the university as a repository of knowledge. This organizational pattern of flanking rows with a signature building at the head would reappear in LSU's new campus plans in the early 1920s.

The Library, on University Avenue, was prominently positioned just inside the main entrance to the campus. The positioning of two lines of classroom buildings at 90 degrees to this entrance avenue suggests a further intentionality. Having the ones along the north face south toward the open space defined by the Library further reinforces this perception. Although the Library was built before the southernmost line of buildings was begun, it became a focal point in the evolving campus design. Peabody Hall, the last of the buildings in this group constructed, was oriented northward, facing the row of existing classroom buildings across the implicit east-west axis established by the Library.[2]

This arrangement of new buildings begun after 1900 indicates some degree of coordination of location and building conception, if not a clear overall master plan. The variety of architectural treatments in the buildings of this group also suggests a loose conception of the unity of the overall architectural expression. The coordination of the design and placement of a variety of different buildings, all built for slightly different uses toward an overall expression, does not occur by happenstance. The extension of a sense of order such as that expressed in the Institution for the Deaf and Dumb and the Blind or at the University of Virginia requires a level of imagination and commitment not yet evident at LSU, in the city of Baton Rouge, or in the state's government buildings.

The general sense of the downtown campus was defined by the impressive live oaks near the President's, or Commandant's, House, creating a landscape not unlike those at numerous plantations throughout the southern part of the

FIG. 1.14. Aerial view of the downtown campus, ca. 1916. The Pentagon Barracks are clearly visible at the left. LSU Photograph Collection, RG #A5000, Louisiana State University Archives, LSU Libraries, Baton Rouge, LA.

FIG. 1.15. Robertson Hall, one of the new buildings on the southern side of the downtown campus. LSU Photograph Collection, RG #A5000, Louisiana State University Archives, LSU Libraries, Baton Rouge, LA.

CLOCKWISE:

FIG. 1.16. Foster Hall, the first substantial new building on the downtown campus. Alleman Estate—Hathaway Gibbens Collection, Earl K. Long Library, University of New Orleans.

FIG. 1.17. Heard Hall, on the southern side of the downtown campus. Alleman Estate—Hathaway Gibbens Collection, Earl K. Long Library, University of New Orleans.

FIG. 1.18. Garig Hall, on the southern side of the downtown campus. LSU Photograph Collection, RG #A5000, Louisiana State University Archives, LSU Libraries, Baton Rouge, LA.

FIG. 1.19. Alumni Memorial Hall, ca. 1910, which anchored the southern corner of the new group of buildings on the southern side of the downtown campus. This building was disassembled and rebuilt on the current LSU campus, where it serves as the Journalism Building today. LSU Photograph Collection, RG #A5000, Louisiana State University Archives, LSU Libraries, Baton Rouge, LA.

FIG. 1.20. Hill Memorial Library on the downtown campus, 1903. LSU Photograph Collection, RG #A5000, Louisiana State University Archives, LSU Libraries, Baton Rouge, LA.

state. Along University Avenue, tall, closely spaced elms and water oaks established a formal axislike entry to the campus that was eventually marked by brick and stone gates (fig. 1.21).[3] The Parade Ground, in the space of the developing new campus east of the Library, was largely devoid of trees or a landscape strategy of any kind. On the northern side of campus, the landscape was defined by the various agricultural and horticultural plots and by the loose collection of accompanying structures (fig. 1.22). In short, there was no overall concept of campus order to coordinate buildings with one another and with the landscape. This site, while large enough to accommodate the traditional academic mission of the time, was constrained in ways that would

FIG. 1.21. Entrance gates to the downtown campus on University Avenue, the northward extension of Third Street. Courtesy of State Library of Louisiana.

FIG. 1.22. View of the agricultural lands along University Lake, on the northern side of the downtown campus, 1899. LSU Photograph Collection, RG #A5000, Louisiana State University Archives, LSU Libraries, Baton Rouge, LA.

limit its use for the new agricultural functions of the Louisiana Agricultural & Mechanical College. By the 1920s it had become clear that the university was hemmed in, preventing any significant growth.

THE TOWN OF BATON ROUGE

Although the region had been inhabited by Native American tribes and a few European farmers before the eighteenth century, the urban history of Baton Rouge begins with the building of the dirt-and-timber Fort New Richmond on the present-day site of the Pentagon Barracks by the British in 1779. This site was acquired soon thereafter by Spain and rebuilt by the Spanish governor of New Orleans. The city developed first under Spanish rule, with a single roadway leading eastward from the site of the new Fort San Carlos. The first "subdivision" in Baton Rouge was made up of deep, narrow house lots laid out along what is now Lakeland Drive. The street just to the south of this is known as Spanish Town Road today. Earlier maps labeled it Boyd Avenue, after the LSU president Thomas Boyd, but the name did not stick (fig. 1.23).

The urban pattern of Baton Rouge developed as haphazardly in those early years as it has since. Permanent settlement had begun just east of the Spanish fort in the area of "Spanish Town." Commercial activity blossomed along the working riverfront, at first around the ferry crossing at the foot of what would become Main Street. A gridded central area some five blocks wide grew up between the military grounds and the projected 1805 Beauregard Town development to the south. This central area accommodated a growing commercial and retail area, with north-south-

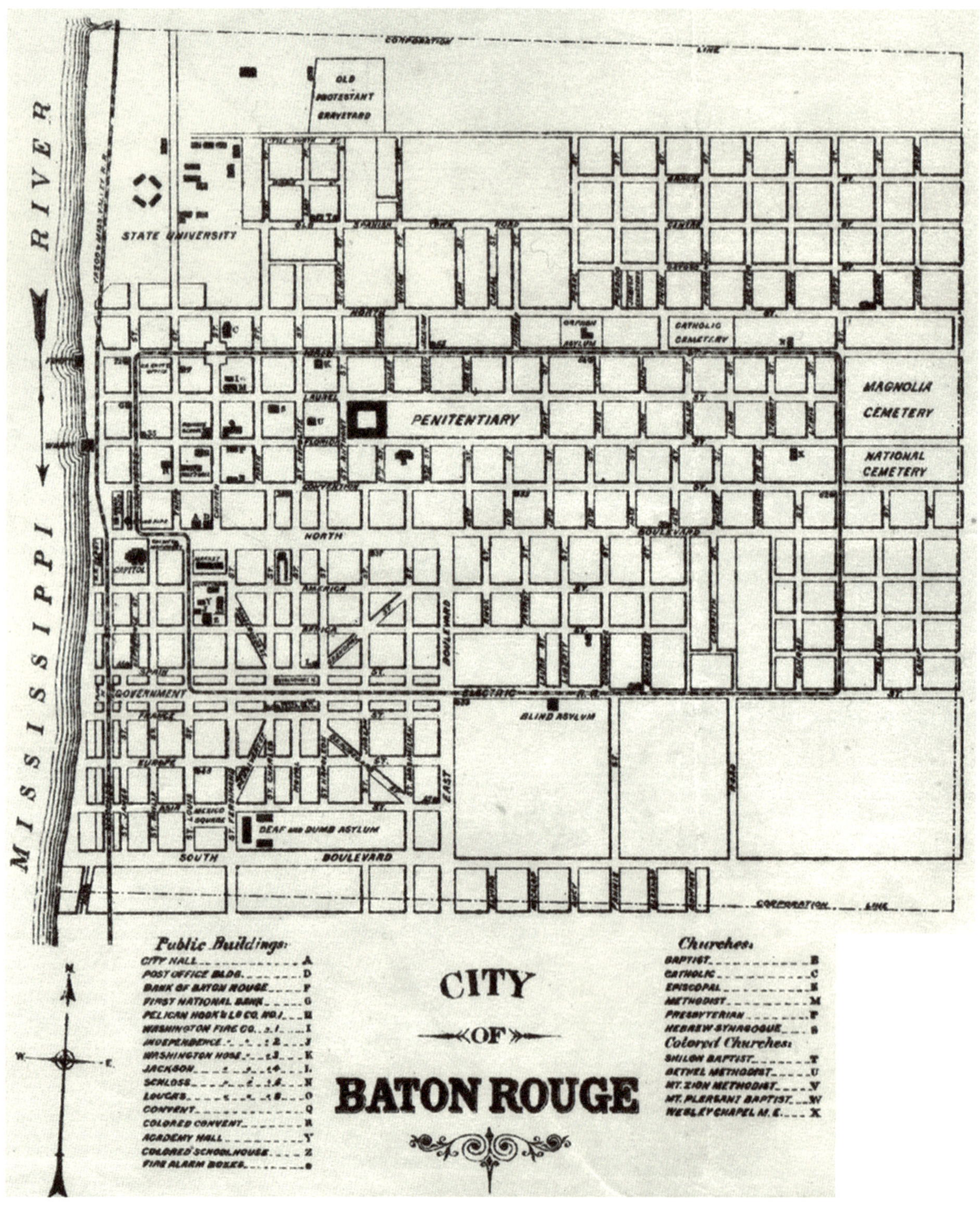

FIG. 1.23. Detail of the 1895 Kaiser and Swensson map of East Baton Rouge Parish, showing the downtown, with the LSU campus grounds at the northern end of the city. Along with the Pentagon Barracks, significant structures include the Old State Capitol, the Penitentiary, and the Institution for the Deaf and Dumb and the Blind on the southern edge of town. Courtesy of Baton Rouge Room, East Baton Rouge Parish Library.

running Third Street eventually replacing Main Street as the commercial core. Third Street, the entry to the campus from the town, became the most highly developed commercial street in Baton Rouge. It had been electrified during the first years of the new century, and by the 1920s it was home to a conglomeration of densely packed buildings and uses. Today's Fourth Street, then known as Church Street because it was lined with religious structures of various denominations, served as a kind of boundary between the business district and growing residential areas to the east. Photographs from the period show a town enveloped by a rich canopy of trees dotted with the occasional spire. St. Joseph's Cathedral and St. James Episcopal Church are the only churches that have survived in this area.

Several prominent institutions were inserted into this evolving urban mixture. Dakin's State Capitol occupied a dramatic site on the river, at the junction of the downtown and Beauregard Town. From this point the double-sided, tree-lined North Boulevard provided a formal break in the otherwise repetitive urban pattern. With the Post Office and City Hall, North Boulevard became the center of civic representation in the growing town. The Institution for the Deaf and Dumb and the Blind had been built on South Boulevard utilizing open land along the southern edge of the growing city. Bounded on the remaining side by East Boulevard, Beauregard Town was initially planned to have at its heart an open square tied to the surrounding residential districts by four diagonal roadways. The Louisiana State Penitentiary was located just a few blocks away, between Seventh and Tenth Streets, until it was moved to Angola in the early twentieth century.

In the years after the university moved to its present site south of the city, much of the old campus was demolished to provide room for the new Louisiana State Capitol building, designed in the 1930s for then-governor Huey Long by the New Orleans architectural firm Weiss, Dreyfous & Seiferth (figs. 1.24 and 1.25). The old President's House, originally built on axis with the Pentagon Barracks, was removed

FIG. 1.24. Aerial view of the new Louisiana State Capitol (*top of photo*), 1930s, with the center of the new capitol garden approximately on the site of the old Commandant's, or President's, House and the remaining LSU building group along the southern edge of the downtown campus. LSU Photograph Collection, RG #A5000, Louisiana State University Archives, LSU Libraries, Baton Rouge, LA.

to make way for the formal gardens built in front of the new Capitol. This axis is still marked, or rather remarked, by a secondary sidewalk through the center of the gardens. Eventually a statue of Governor Long was placed at the intersection of this and the primary north-south axis of the Capitol itself, almost in the exact location of the President's House.

Today one ancient Native American mound stands just west of the Old Arsenal; a second one nearby was destroyed sometime before the Civil War. Like the mounds on the present LSU campus, these two indicated that the region was prized before the coming of Europeans. It appears that the native peoples chose this high ground along the Baton Rouge Reach, on the eastern side of the Mississippi River, for the locations of their most ceremonial structures. There were several such sites in the general area: the one here, the one on the present LSU campus, and the one to the north at or near the site occupied by Southern University.

FIG. 1.25. View south over the newly planted gardens of the Louisiana State Capitol across the remaining LSU campus buildings to downtown Baton Rouge in the distance, 1930s. Courtesy of E. A. McIlhenny Enterprises, Inc., Avery Island, LA.

Although there were no mounds there, the height of the bluff and the view upriver were significant, and there is some indication that a large Native American village was once located in this area. The state university's move in 1926 from one of these sites to another appears to have been coincidental, but it is interesting that all three have been home to state universities. The other local consequential site of Native American construction is located several miles to the southeast, above the point where Bayou Fountain meets Bayou Manchac, also on elevated ground, and contains no less than five prehistoric mounds, giving it a unique significance as well.

2

Frederick Law Olmsted Jr. and the Greater University

Louisiana has a great opportunity and a great obligation to her citizens in the special matter of the right education of real farmers, who are now and probably will always be the foundation of her economic prosperity, who secure today far less prosperity and happiness for themselves and for the state than they might win if their education better fitted them to cope with their problems as farmers and as citizens. And, toward that gradual better fitting of the farmers of Louisiana for their life work the "College farm" of the State University can be a wonderful tool, if to it be added the men and the buildings and equipment necessary to make it a great center of agricultural instruction and stimulus.

—F. L. OLMSTED JR., "Report to Newspapers"

BATON ROUGE, LSU, AND THE COLLEGE FARM

The first decades of the twentieth century saw the city of Baton Rouge begin to grow rapidly. The introduction of a rail line along the river substantially increased the city's capacity for regional trade. The construction of the Standard Oil refinery north of the downtown area in 1909 marked a significant new phase in this process. This refinery, still Exxon's largest domestic oil refinery, was strategically located in relation to trade and high ground. Protected from the Mississippi River's annual floods, the bluffs along the Baton Rouge Reach are the site of the last firm ground adjacent to the river. Oceangoing tankers and freighter traffic could only navigate a short distance north from here. Furthermore, the construction of the Mississippi River bridge just above this refinery in the 1930s guaranteed that Baton Rouge would become the northernmost limit of oceangoing navigation on the river. The refinery dominated the high ground along the river to the north of the downtown, as had earlier light industry, acting as a barrier to any northward expansion of the campus. The land between the refinery and the downtown campus was occupied by University Lake, which prevented the expansion of the city or the campus beyond this point. These features, together with the surrounding city, complicated any future growth of the university. Moreover, these factors prevented the growth and extension of agricultural research and activities necessary for the university's status as an agricultural and mechanical college.

FIG. 2.1. Frederick "Rick" Law Olmsted Jr. in 1925, a few years after his work for LSU. Courtesy of the National Park Service, Frederick Law Olmsted National Historic Site.

The Olmsted Brothers landscape-architecture firm was invited to Baton Rouge in the late spring of 1921 to study the potential relationships between the existing campus and the extensive agricultural tract the university had acquired several miles to the south of the city. Some years after the World's Industrial and Cotton Centennial Exposition, held in New Orleans in 1884, the firm had overseen the development of that parcel into what is now Audubon Park. The Olmsteds had maintained a relationship with the businessman J. K. Newman since that time. Newman's father, Isidore, was a New Orleans banker with a long record of involvement with both the state and the university. The younger Newman brought the Olmsteds in to discuss the beginning of a planning process for LSU. The services of the Olmsted Brothers were arranged and paid for by Newman.[1] His donations of time and energy made possible the involvement of this internationally known firm. When the state was required to pick up the tab for continuation of the process, the situation changed considerably.

By the time they began work in Baton Rouge, the Olmsted Brothers had an established history. The firm's founder, Frederick Law Olmsted (1822–1903), began his career assisting Calvert Vaux in the design of what was to become New York's Central Park in the late 1850s. After the Civil War he renewed his partnership with Vaux, and together they created defining American environments such as Prospect Park in Brooklyn; the first significant picturesque suburb, Riverside, Illinois, outside Chicago; and the extensive park system in Buffalo, New York, to name just a few of the better-known examples. The partnership dissolved in 1872, but Olmsted went on to design a number of significant American parks, not least among them the 1893 World's Columbian Exhibition in Chicago and the famous Emerald Necklace in Boston.

Although Olmsted retired from active practice in 1895, his firm continued as the preeminent designer of American parks and college campuses for the next fifty years. After the founder's retirement, the firm was managed by Olmsted's son, Frederick Law Olmsted Jr., more commonly referred to as Rick (fig. 2.1), and his nephew John Charles Olmsted, whom the elder Olmsted had raised. Together these two men and many collaborators built the largest landscape-architecture firm in the world and created a dazzling array of designs.[2]

One of Rick Olmsted Jr.'s first independent successes was the redesign of the National Mall in Washington, DC, just after the turn of the century. In this he collaborated with noted American figures such as Daniel Burnham, Charles McKim, and Augustus Saint-Gaudens under the auspices of the McMillan Commission. He was deeply involved in the design and establishment of the National Park System, and he produced influential planning reports for many American cities. He was responsible for a number of groundbreaking designs for new towns, such as Forest Hills Gardens on Long Island. Olmsted's firm developed into the world authority on landscape planning. In inviting this firm to Baton Rouge, Louisiana, Newman selected the best of the best. Rick Olmsted was impressed with what he saw in Baton Rouge and on the LSU campus. In the weeks following the visit, he summarized these impressions in a "Report to Newspapers":

> The visit was intensely interesting to me from several distinct points of view. In the first place, just as a matter of sightseeing I greatly enjoyed the old campus, with its fine trees and its quaint solid old buildings inherited from the Army Post days. The curious five-sided court, open to the River and enclosed on the other four sides by the dignified two-story colonnades of the thick-walled, small-windowed former barracks . . . is architecturally unique and has a great deal of pictorial interest and character. The other old buildings too, both in themselves in their relation to open spaces of the grounds and to the planting—there is one really wonderful old oak tree of enormous spread of branches—produce a distinct and very delightful old-time atmosphere which cannot but impress any casual visitor and which must be warmly treasured by the Alumni long after they have forgotten the inconvenience of conducting a modern university in the barracks and storehouses of an old army post.[3]

In spite of such favorable impressions of the spatial character of the downtown site, he observed that "the Campus is completely hemmed in" and that "the conditions which the Louisiana State University will inevitably face in a few years are not peculiar to it or unprecedented. Again and again a growing university in a city has faced them." According to Olmsted, colleges and universities had adopted two distinct ways out of the developing land crisis. On the one hand, schools such as Harvard and Yale, which had decided to remain on their central-city sites, had been forced to purchase nearby properties at high rates and to demolish existing buildings to make room for their growth and expansion. Others, such as Columbia and Johns Hopkins, had moved to larger, more remote sites to guarantee access to sufficient land for expansion over time. He recommended the latter course for LSU, especially given the university's agricultural mission:

> The present investment in buildings is very limited compared with the market price of the surrounding private real estate even today, and to add new buildings on this site to care for the expansion of the University for a few years would only postpone the evil day and increase the investment which would ultimately have to be abandoned. It seems to me clearly the part of wisdom to recognize this coming crisis long before the conditions become insupportable, and deliberately, without haste or waste, plan for meeting present needs in a way that will provide economically and conveniently for the ultimate transfer of the University's expansion to a really adequate site. . . .
>
> . . . the facilities at the State University for the education of farmers, directly and indirectly, are inadequate as compared with those which are offered in the institutions of many other states. The condition is reflected in the relatively small number of students pursuing agricultural studies. It is apparent in the fact that the farming lands of the institution are scattered and are separated from the Shut-in-Campus. It is strikingly apparent in the fact that in a State whose agricultural problems include those of a vast area of fertile lowlands suitable for cane and rice, and where the entire gamut of properly diversified agriculture must be carried on upon bottom-lands a hundred miles from the nearest hill, all the farming done for purposes of research demonstration and instruction has been carried on upon the rather poor hill country to the north and east of Baton Rouge.
>
> . . . the State confronts the practical certainty that in

> a very short time . . . the University will utterly outgrow its present Campus, hemmed in by the River and the City and then the State must, whether it likes it or not, confront the alternative of buying up and tearing down large areas of city property, at great economic waste, and even then having but a cramped patchwork of ill assorted buildings remote from its demonstration farms.

Rick Olmsted also appreciated the variety and prospect of this newly acquired land south of the city:

> The most interesting thing I saw at Baton Rouge was the new "College Farm" so called, about two miles south-of-the State House. It is a tract of 2000 acres in one body, extending from the levee across rich river lowlands to and including some 500 or 600 acres of gently rolling upland above bluff about a mile from the river. So far as I am able to judge it is as nearly ideal as could possibly be found for demonstration farming for the State of Louisiana, embracing as it does the problems of the "hill-farmers" of the northern part of the state and those of the bottomland farmers of the southern part.

He noted that while the valuable lowlands stretching from the bluff to the river offered agricultural-research potential, the lands overlooking these fields displayed a fine collection of existing trees, especially magnolias:

> On the northerly part of the upland portion, nearest the city is a site for college buildings which can hardly be surpassed. Smooth enough to be economical of development; rolling enough to avoid the monotony of an absolute level; high enough to be well drained healthful; commanding a fine outlook from the irregular and picturesque edge of the bluff; and adorned with a goodly number of splendid great old trees, including the finest collection of evergreen magnolias which it has ever been my good fortune to see in all my wanderings in pursuit of landscape beauty.

The "College Farm" to which Olmsted refers was a 1,200-acre tract two miles south of the downtown. The Williams Plantation tract, also known as Gartness, encompassed a swath of land almost a mile wide that extended back from the river for a mile and a half, according to the old French arpent system of land measurement (figs. 2.2 and 2.3).[4] The university had had its eye on this land since its absorption of the Louisiana Agricultural & Mechanical College in 1877. After several overtures to the owners of the land, in 1918 at the request of President Thomas Boyd, Dean T. W. Atkinson purchased an option on the property, which was secured by nine other private Louisiana citizens later referred to as "Friends of the University" in the press. In 1920 Governor John M. Parker pushed the matter through the state legislature, and the property, along with the adjoining Nestle Down Plantation, was secured.

The combined acquisition was more than 2,000 acres. It appears that President Boyd did not initially intend to move the entire university from its downtown location out to this more remote site. Instead, he saw the land as providing for the agricultural college's necessary activities, hence the references to the "College Farm."[5]

The 1895 Kaiser and Swensson map of East Baton Rouge Parish clearly illustrates these tracts in relation to the downtown, the arpent system, and the variety of land-survey techniques used in developing Louisiana (see fig. 2.2). An arpent was a little less than 200 feet. Early French land grants were typically 2 to 4 arpents wide and extended 30 to 40 arpents back, or until dry ground gave way. The Williams Plantation was a product of these long, narrow units. The Highland Road bluff, above Bayou Fountain, is also particularly evident on the map. This natural feature was used to establish another run of arpent property divisions off to the southeast along the bluff. The LSU lands negotiate the difference in orientation between the arpents aligned with the Mississippi River and those aligned with the Highland Road bluff. Thus, the current northern gates of the campus, on Highland Road, are effectively parallel

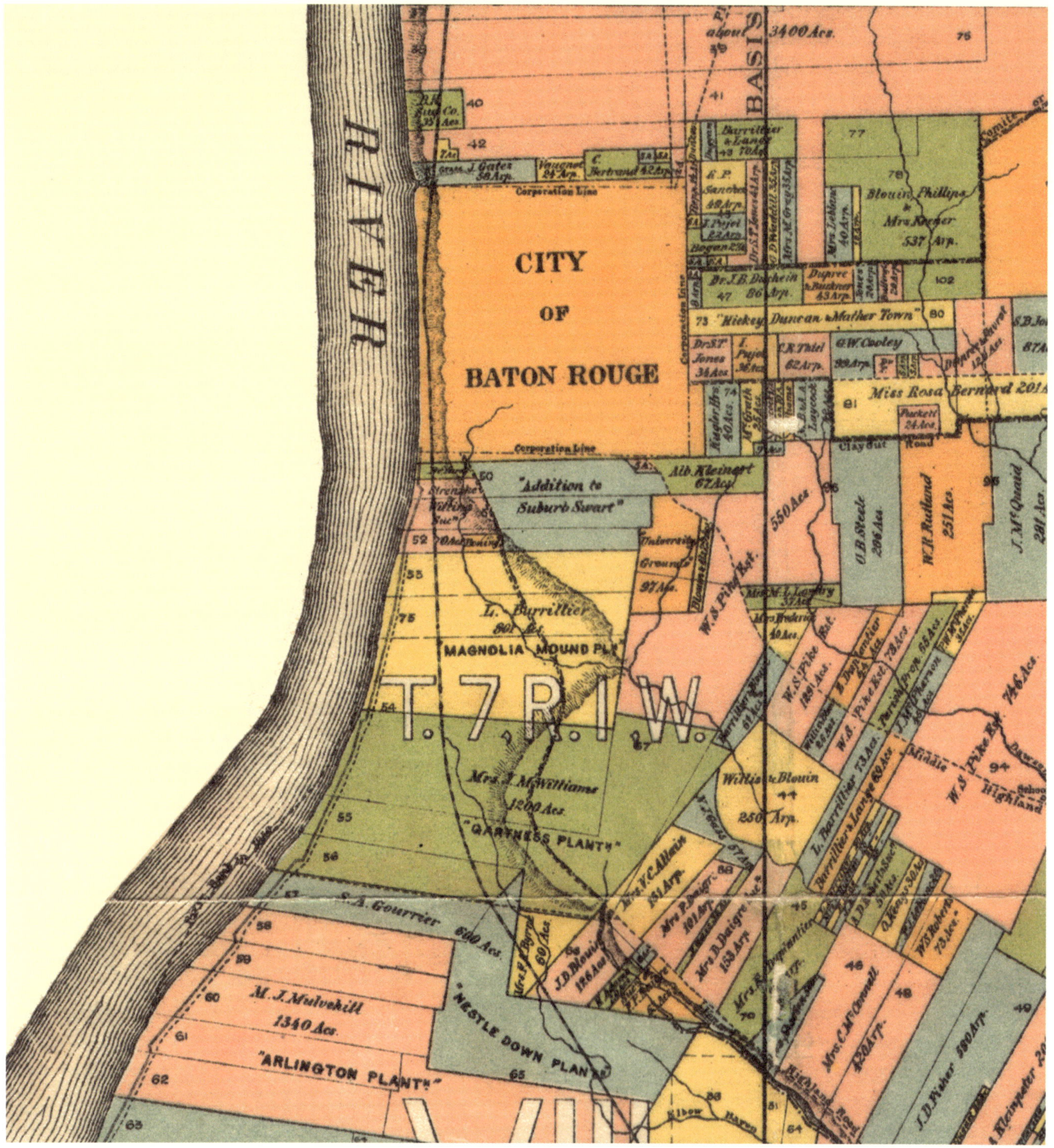

FIG. 2.2. Detail of the 1895 Kaiser and Swensson map of East Baton Rouge, showing the location of the initial land purchase for the current LSU campus in relation to the City of Baton Rouge, the Mississippi River, the Highland Road bluff, the Gartness and Nestle Down Plantations, and the historic French-derived land divisions. Courtesy of Baton Rouge Room, East Baton Rouge Parish Library.

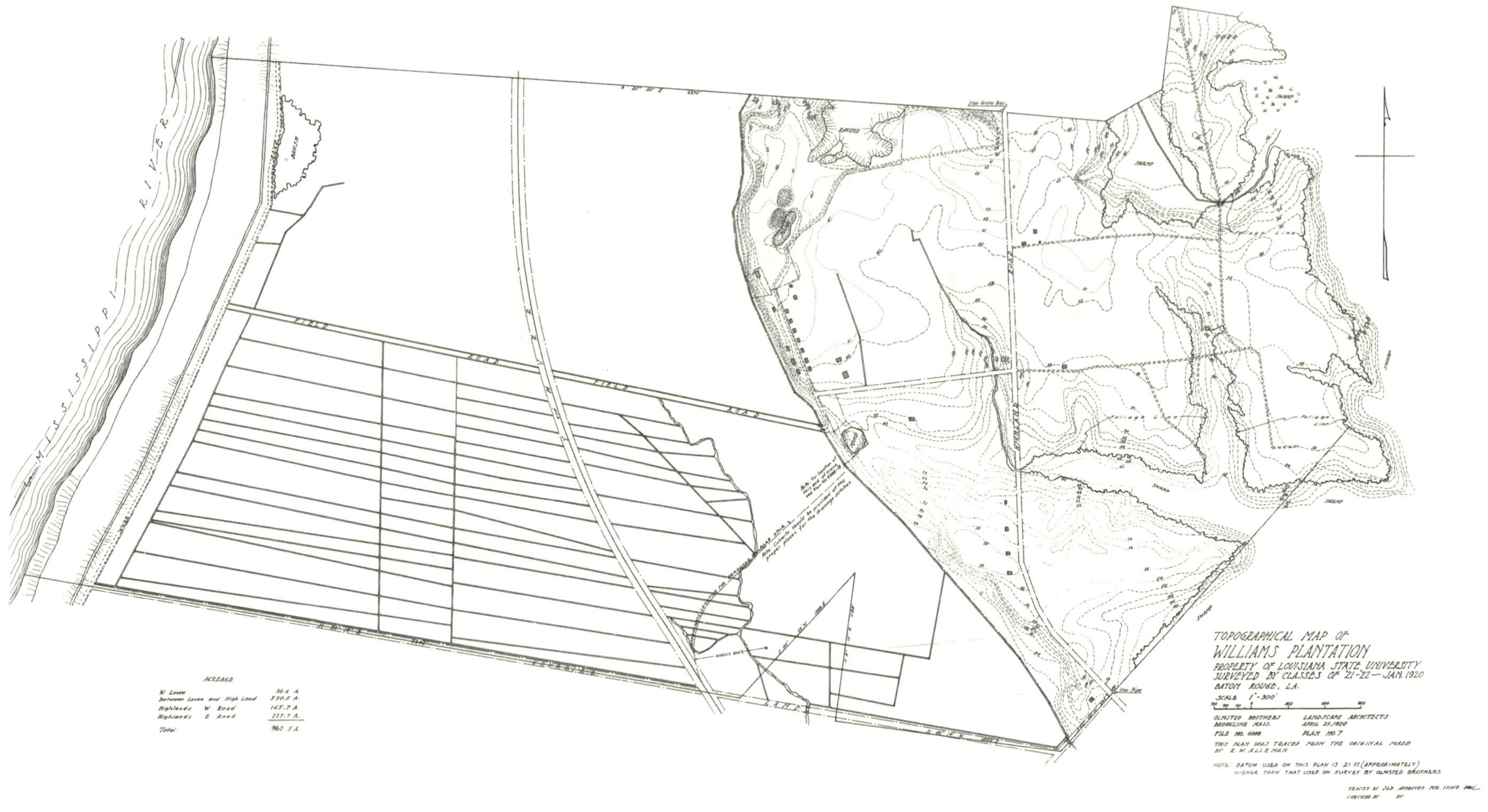

FIG. 2.3. Survey of the Williams Plantation, purchased for the current LSU campus site in 1920. Olmsted Archives, 6888-7. Courtesy of the National Park Service, Frederick Law Olmsted National Historic Site.

to the arpents determined by the river, while the southern Highland gates are parallel to the arpents determined by the bayou. The Williams tract was the largest single assembly of land to the south of the developing urban area at the time. One can see clearly on this and similar old maps how the division of property follows the contours of the river, extending back from it along roughly parallel lines. In other parts of the parish, one can see the more regular geometric grid of property measurement established by the U.S. Land Ordinance of 1785 as it makes it way into southern Louisiana, with its familiar section lines, after the Louisiana Purchase and the coming of the Americans.

These tracts of land purchased for the new university occupy a particularly significant position in the geography of the continent as well, given their relationship to the shifting course of the Mississippi River, which drains more than 40 percent of the continental United States. Together with the Missouri and Ohio Rivers, the Mississippi forms one of the largest river tributary systems in the world. For most of its length, the Mississippi flows within a large alluvial valley that reaches from the middle of North America to the Gulf of Mexico. Major settlements occur at all the points where the river meets the bluffs that define the eastern edge of the valley. Among these are Cairo, Illinois; Memphis, Tennessee; Vicksburg and Natchez, Mississippi; and Baton Rouge. Baton Rouge is the southernmost of these sites, the last one before the great river leaves contact with high ground in its march to the ocean.

The bluff occupied by the Williams Plantation is the southernmost point on the continent where one can see the river from high ground. Perhaps this explains the location of the two prehistoric Native American mounds on this site. Carbon-dating has determined them to be more than six thousand years old, making them older than the Pyramids in Egypt and placing them among the oldest man-made structures in North America. We do not know the purpose of these mounds; they do not appear to contain burial materials, and they are too small to have supported large wooden structures. Their age and their location, however, can be taken to signify that the region's ancient inhabitants considered the site important. The mounds that originally existed on the downtown LSU site and the two on this new tract are far from the only ones in the area. As many as two dozen line the Amite River and other waterways in the Florida Parishes. Not all of these mounds date from the same ancient period. The LSU mounds are evidence that from that ancient period through the location of the Standard Oil refinery in this area, residents have valued this high ground near the river. Both Louisiana Capitol buildings—the mid-nineteenth-century neo-Gothic structure designed by James Dakin and the art deco building designed by Weiss, Dreyfous & Seiferth in the early 1930s—also take advantage of this regional geographical prominence. The history of such monuments in Baton Rouge marks the progressive occupation of this prominent site beginning in ancient times.

DEVELOPMENT OF THE OLMSTED PLAN

The process of designing the new campus is recorded only in the drawings remaining in the Olmsted Archives in Brookline, Massachusetts. Other sources provide very little insight into the process. The drawings, however, have a story to tell. The main characters in the story of LSU's development under the Olmsteds' guidance are the "irregular and picturesque" bluffs overlooking the lowlands, the ancient mounds and their surrounding grove of trees, and the large open area between those trees and the road leading back to town. In January 1920 the LSU engineering class of 1921–22 conducted a comprehensive survey of the new property. This survey remains in the Olmsted Archives (see fig. 2.3).[6] Olmsted Brothers utilized this document, copied it, and commissioned another, professional survey of the property (fig. 2.4). The professionally commissioned survey, dated May 21, 1921, suggests that progress moved quickly following Rick Olmsted's April visit. The initial views of the land record a 20-foot contour difference between the lowland, the bluff, and the upland plateau. The bases of the Native American mounds lie at about 41 feet above mean sea level, and their peaks are another 17 to 18 feet above that (figs. 2.5–2.12).[7]

As is common to the high grounds along the Mississippi River throughout the rest of East Baton Rouge Parish, the land slopes gently to the east, away from the river. Here the land also slopes to the south. The low ground areas to the east labeled "swamp" eventually became today's University Lakes.[8] A distinct eastern boundary created by a "foliage line" is marked on the map in fig. 2.3. The property contained several westward-facing structures along the bluff. These included a corral, a few sheds, a line of various cabins, and a superintendent's cottage. There were also various small cottages scattered around the property and three small ponds, one of which was located in the depression now occupied by the Greek Theater. To the north and northeast of the mounds there was a grove of trees of various sizes. The area had not been used for farming and thus had never been cleared. It was this grove that Olmsted described as "the finest collection of evergreen magnolias which it has ever been my good fortune to see in all my wanderings in pursuit of landscape beauty."

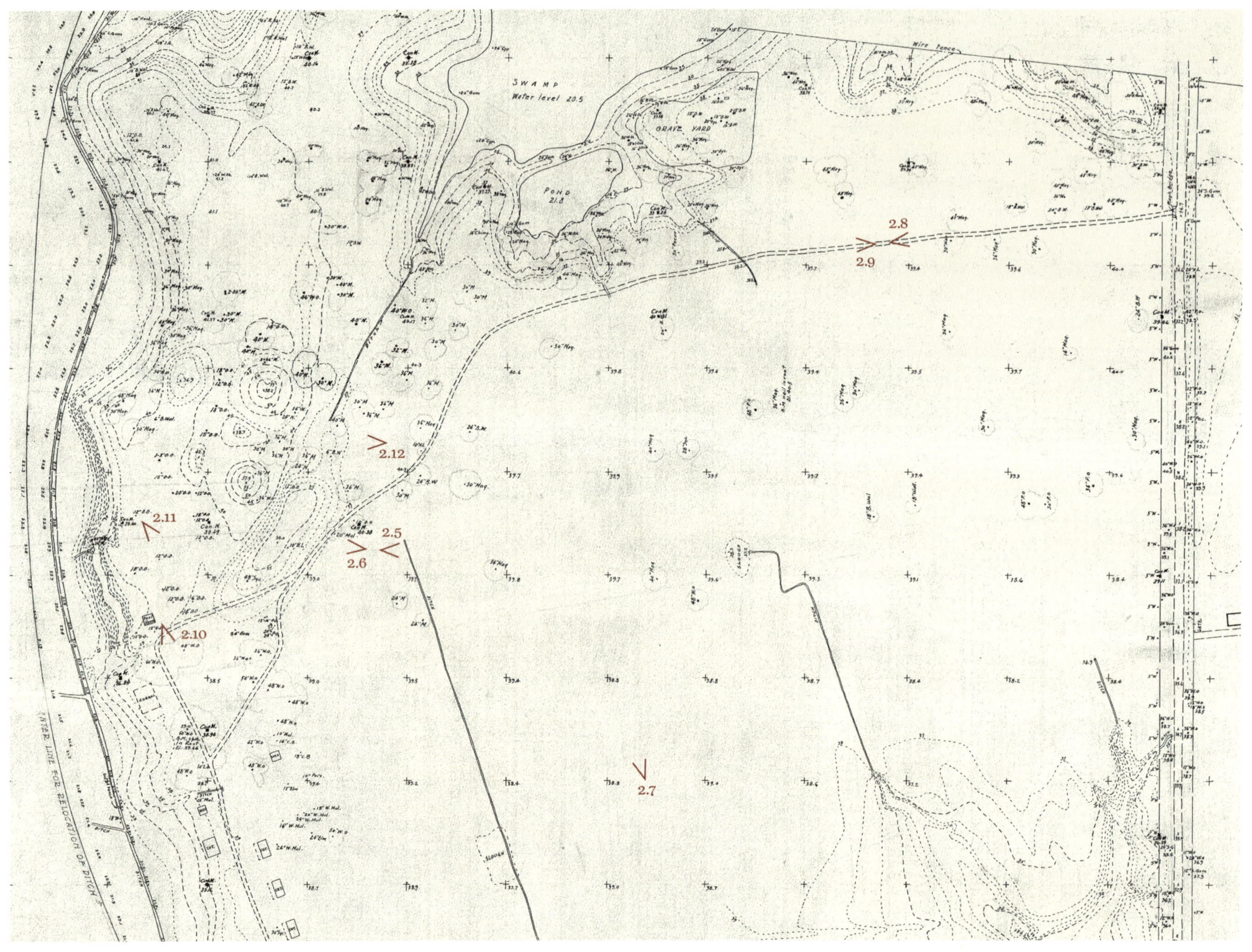

FIG. 2.4. Detailed survey of the upland areas west of Highland Road, indicating locations shown in Olmsted's 1920 photographs of the site. Olmsted Archives, 6888-11. Courtesy of the National Park Service, Frederick Law Olmsted National Historic Site.

FIG. 2.5. *Looking east on proposed axis.* Olmsted photograph album 6888-1. Courtesy of the National Park Service, Frederick Law Olmsted National Historic Site.

FIG. 2.6. *Looking west on proposed axis.* Olmsted photograph album 6888-2. Courtesy of the National Park Service, Frederick Law Olmsted National Historic Site.

FIG. 2.7. *N and NE from near point of proposed administration building,* Olmsted photograph album 6888-3. Courtesy of the National Park Service, Frederick Law Olmsted National Historic Site.

FIG. 2.8. *Near W 800 S 18.5 looking NE and E.* Olmsted photograph album 6888-4. Courtesy of the National Park Service, Frederick Law Olmsted National Historic Site.

FIG. 2.9. *Looking West and Southwest to Magnolia Grove.* Olmsted photograph album 6888-5. Courtesy of the National Park Service, Frederick Law Olmsted National Historic Site.

FIG. 2.10. *Magnolia Grove west side of Indian mounds.* Olmsted photograph album 6888-6. Courtesy of the National Park Service, Frederick Law Olmsted National Historic Site.

FIG. 2.11. *Magnolia Grove west of mounds.* Olmsted photograph album 6888-8. Courtesy of the National Park Service, Frederick Law Olmsted National Historic Site.

FIG. 2.12. *Magnolia Grove west of mounds.* Olmsted's label is incorrect. These magnificent trees were in fact largely along the eastern and northern sides of the mounds, as the surveys show. Olmsted photograph album 6888-11. Courtesy of the National Park Service, Frederick Law Olmsted National Historic Site.

FIG. 2.13. *(facing page)* Initial Olmsted LSU planning study, showing Highland Road, the genesis of the main axis, and consideration of existing tree groups. Olmsted Archives, 6888-13. Courtesy of the National Park Service, Frederick Law Olmsted National Historic Site.

One interesting possible earlier mention of this site in the historical record is suggested by the Civil War historian Shelby Foote in his book on Grant's efforts to capture Vicksburg, *The Beleaguered City.* Foote notes that in early May 1863 Colonel Benjamin Grierson, of the Union army, arrived in Baton Rouge, which was already in Union hands, after a grueling three-week horseback raid from Memphis through Mississippi to break Vicksburg's rail supply lines. Upon arriving in Baton Rouge at the end of this sojourn, Grierson's cavalry "wound slowly around the public square, then south of town to a grove of magnolias two miles south, where they dismounted, unsaddled, and fell so soundly asleep that they could not be roused to accept hot coffee."[9] The grove of magnolias of which Olmsted speaks was the only significant one two miles south of the city at that time, occupying a pastoral spot near the ancient Native American mounds that overlooked the Mississippi River in the distance.

The survey lists a range of other types of trees in this part of the site, including black walnut, water oak, China ball, honey locust, hackberry, sweet gum, and sycamore. These all appear on the final version of Olmsted's Preliminary Plan as groupings near the mounds, around which the new buildings were to be located. Apart from a few scattered trees between this grove and the roadway to the east, the site was mostly devoid of trees of any significant size, as can be seen in period photographs and on the survey (see fig. 2.4).

There is some discrepancy between the surveys regarding the size of the water body and swamp along the northwestern edge of the property. The student survey describes a "ravine" where the Greek Theater is located today. The commissioned survey, however, depicts a water-bearing swamp and a small pond in this location. The commissioned survey also shows a small graveyard on the eastern side of this depression.[10] Although the graveyard survives in the earliest planning study we have of the campus, there is no record of it after that. The surveyors Olmsted commissioned laid out a typical surveyors' square grid of points 200 feet apart aligned with corresponding compass points (see fig. 2.4). The campus plan that developed through the work of Olmsted Brothers, and later Theodore C. Link, does not coordinate with this survey grid, suggesting that aspects of the site itself were utilized when Rick Olmsted

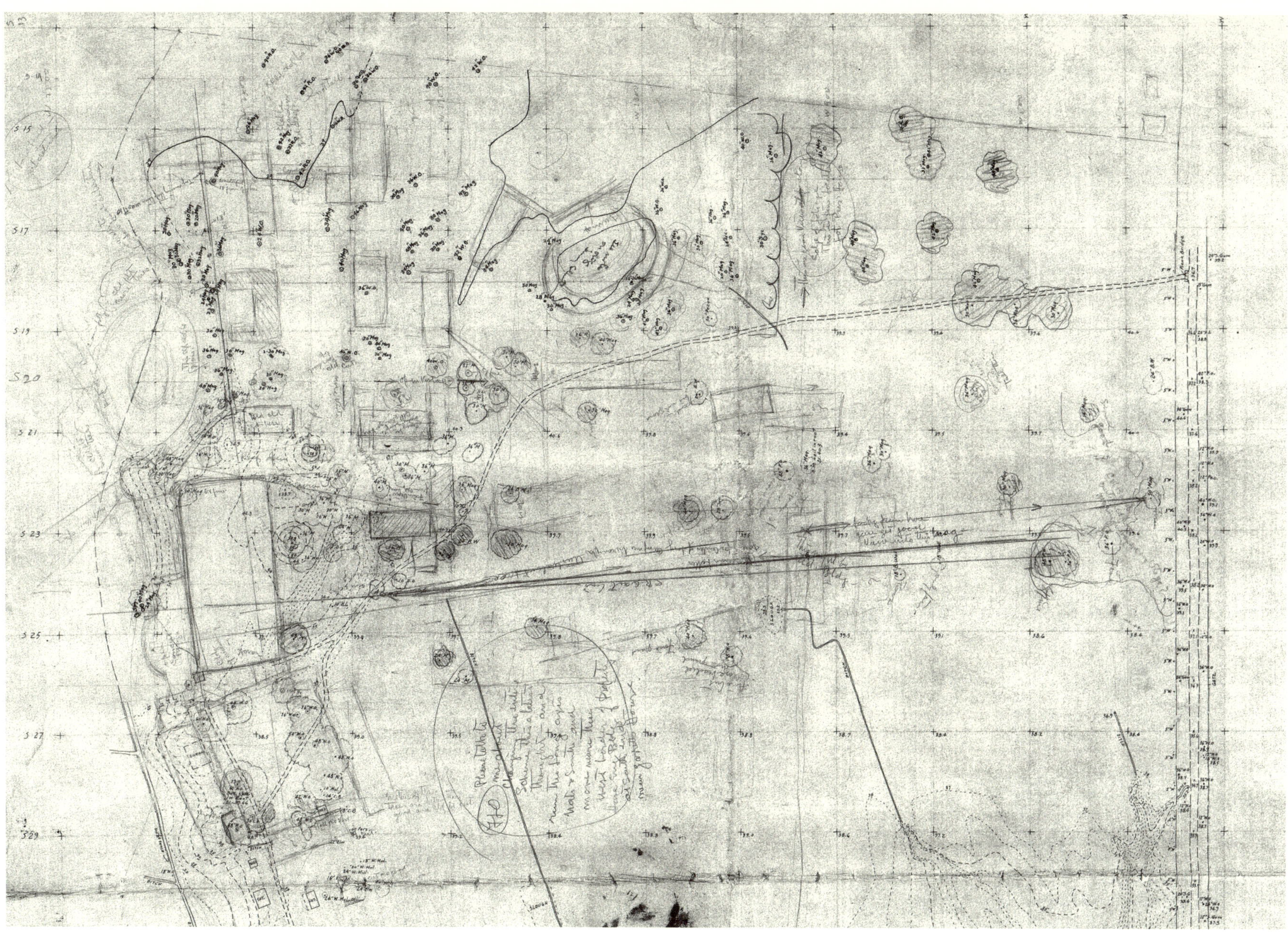

was designing the plan layout. One way to gauge the areas of most interest to the designers is to note the kinds of studies existing in the archival record. There is an enlarged topographic study of the contours and tree groups for the area surrounding the mounds, with its grove of magnolia trees, dated June 21, 1921 (fig. 2.13). This drawing clearly indicates that Olmsted was interested in these tree groupings and their relationship to the mounds. The topography of the bluff itself is shown in more detail here than in earlier drawings.

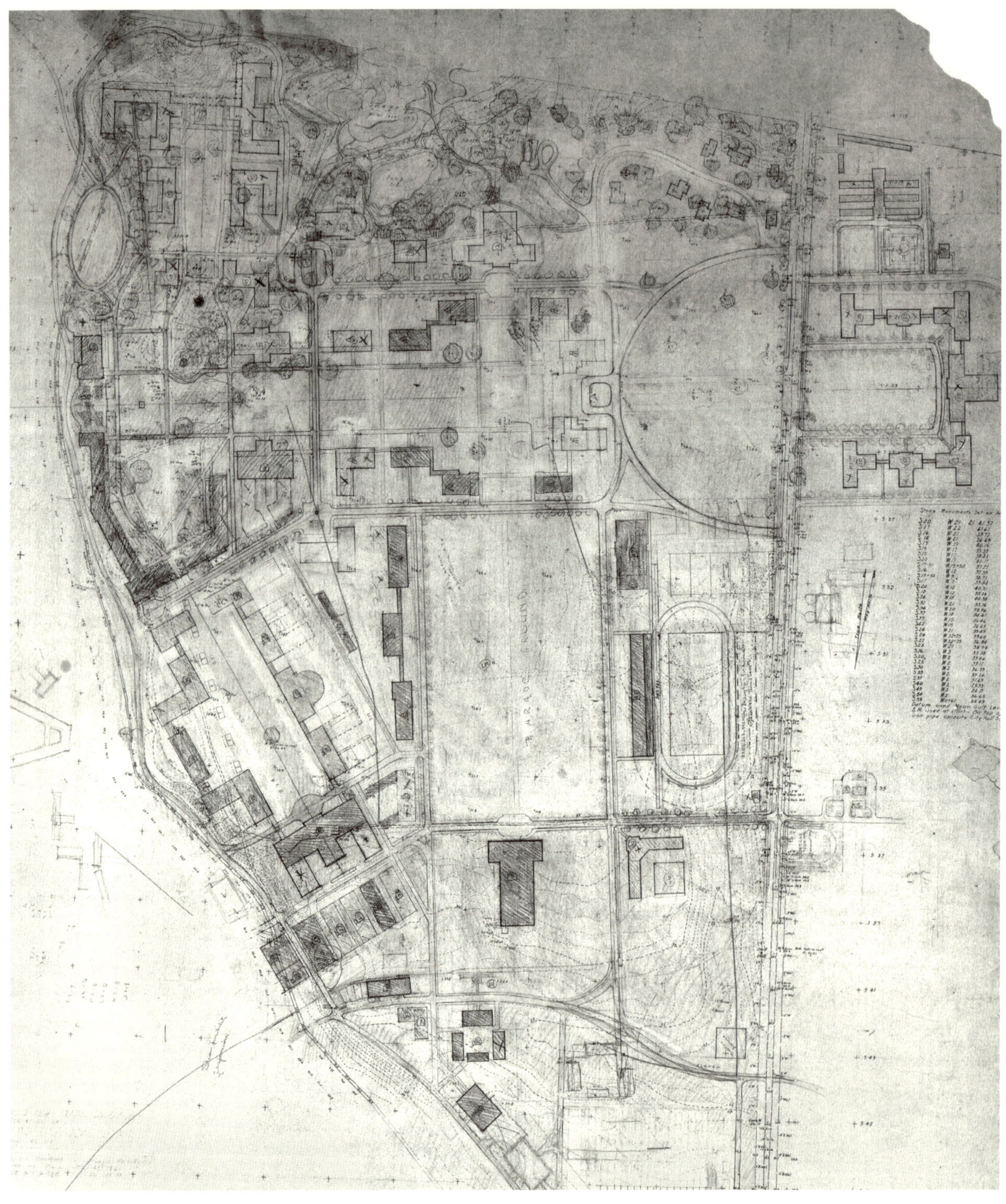

FIG. 2.14. First Olmsted Preliminary Plan, showing development of the open planning axis from the ceremonial entry facing Highland Road to the western bluff overlook. Olmsted Archives, 6888z4. Courtesy of the National Park Service, Frederick Law Olmsted National Historic Site.

The drawing that is most indicative of Olmsted's early concerns and interests is the earliest planning-study overlay existing in the Olmsted Archives, dated May 21, 1921 (fig. 2.14). This drawing reveals Olmsted's initial planning interests and moves. It becomes clear that the designer was responding carefully and creatively to the existing conditions. The drawing is filled with notes articulating his concerns. The most salient concerns of the planning approach evident here are (1) the careful integration of building groups into existing tree groups and mounds; (2) identification of a major axis of entry and design focus leading west across the site from what would become Highland Road through an existing opening in the trees to the most dramatic crest of the bluff; and (3) making use of existing open spaces for courtyards or quadrangles to coordinate building groupings.

This May planning study for LSU shows a group of buildings beyond the trees and to the north of the mounds assembled around what would become the men's dormitory quadrangle. As the sketch indicates, Olmsted concentrated on the southern end of this group, shifting the building locations to create a focus on the northernmost mound and its adjacent trees. Despite the various plan studies of this grouping of buildings that he developed over time, they remained essentially the same. In general, the layout of this group was coordinated by a north-south axis that established a small quadrangle that became more regularized and eastwardly shifting. Although the southernmost end of this planned grouping was not closed off by a building, the open space would have been effectively closed off by the mounds and the magnolia grove. This would have been a pleasant and protected enclave for the male student body at the extreme northwestern corner of the upland area of the property, in the location today occupied by Broussard, and the pentagon created by Lejeune, Beauregard, Z. Taylor, and Jackson Halls.

With the low and swampy areas along the northern site boundary and the tree groupings adjacent to the mounds, the first opening from the fields along Highland Road to a western vista toward the river occurred just south of the southernmost mound. It was here that Olmsted oriented what we might call an axis of entry into the new site from Highland Road and the city beyond. The earliest surveys show that this axis reached across a small existing pond that was eventually filled.[11] The tree groupings, along with this somewhat constricted opening, suggested a sequence of spaces that moved along the bluff. Olmsted sought to build upon this sequence, which he used along with the axis as a starting point for his planning. The 1,700-foot distance across the fields from Highland Road to this grove would lead to a much smaller open place between the trees and the bluff that became the focus of the initial design.

This first planning study shows a rectangular court, or quadrangle, sketched out in plan. As this plan developed, the rectangular area gave way to a formal, plazalike overlook at the terminus of the implied east-west axes of entry, with various annotations describing the vistas to be had at different spots to the west on the existing site. To the immediate south of this area a few trees again created a more enclosed sense of space before opening out along the bluff to the row of cabins and eventually the superintendent's cottage. This appears to have been the origin of the series of three enclosed quadrangles strung along the bluff and reached by the axial approach Olmsted saw from Highland Road to the east. These quadrangles were to be occupied by men's dormitories on the north, laboratories to the south, and engineering shops beyond the laboratories. As early site photographs indicate, the southernmost laboratory quadrangle was laid out parallel to the bluff, which was the orientation of the line of existing cabins and their gravel roadway, as well as the existing field-plowing pattern.[12]

The ceremonial quadrangle was defined by a men's dormitory that snaked along the bluff, the formal overlook plaza, a men's union, the magnolia grove, one of the mounds, and the open vista to Highland Road to the east. The men's dormitory at the southern edge of this quadrangle resembles the Harvard University "river houses," such as Elliot

FIG. 2.15. Olmsted Brothers "in-house" aerial campus perspectival study, showing initial images of a Spanish-style campus architecture aligned along open planning axes to an overlook at the bluffs facing the Mississippi River. Olmsted Archives, 6888-27-sh1. Courtesy of the National Park Service, Frederick Law Olmsted National Historic Site.

House and Lowell House, built in the 1930s, in both scale and the character of the space defined. All of these building ensembles followed loosely the examples of the universities in Oxford and Cambridge, England.

This planning study also shows the first indication of an oval-shaped formal garden located down the slope, below a prominent overlook point adjacent to the men's union. In later drawings, and in the final Olmsted Preliminary Plan, this would become a "sunken garden." All of this is to say that this planning study appears to lay out the origins of a strategy for interacting with and occupying the bluff and existing natural features. It is a design approach the younger Olmsted inherited from his father:

> In dealing with existing real landscapes, I have been guided by an injunction impressed on me by my distinguished father: namely, that when one becomes responsible for what is to happen to such a landscape his prime duty is to protect and perpetuate whatever of beauty and inspirational value, inherent in that landscape, is due to nature and to circumstances not of one's own contriving, and to humbly subordinate to that purpose any impulse to exercise upon it one's own skill as a creative designer.[13]

DESCRIPTION OF THE OLMSTED PLAN

By September 1921 the initial planning ideas had congealed into a diagram that would hold through Olmsted's final Preliminary Plan, of October (see fig. 2.16). This intermediate planning study displayed the series of three quadranglelike open spaces along the bluff that were complemented by a fourth laid out along the axis of entry. This fourth quadrangle for arts and sciences was tied to Highland Road by a sweeping curved drive that defined the main entry to the university. This diagram of quadrangles converging at a central open space facing west and containing the existing magnolia grove and ancient mounds is the basis of the Olmsteds' plan (figs. 2.15–2.17).

Another feature of the final Preliminary Plan is a rather formal, enclosing dormitory complex for women along the entry axis on the other side of Highland Road. There is a lesser north-south planning axis juxtaposing a theater with a Gym Armory across a Parade Ground at 90 degrees to the main east-west entry axis, as well as a picturesque arrangement of faculty houses along the northern edge of the property culminating in a President's Residence, which backed up to the location of the existing graveyard above the swampy ravine and a Campus Chapel. A miscellaneous collection of other, farm-related buildings is laid out along the southern reaches of the campus bluff to the point where it ran along Highland Road, and there was a spot for a football field between Highland and the Parade Ground. The

FIG. 2.16. LSU Preliminary Plan, by Rick Olmsted, showing a series of quadrangles surrounding a central library facing the bluff overlook. North is to the left on this plan. Olmsted Archives, 6888-28-pt4. Courtesy of the National Park Service, Frederick Law Olmsted National Historic Site.

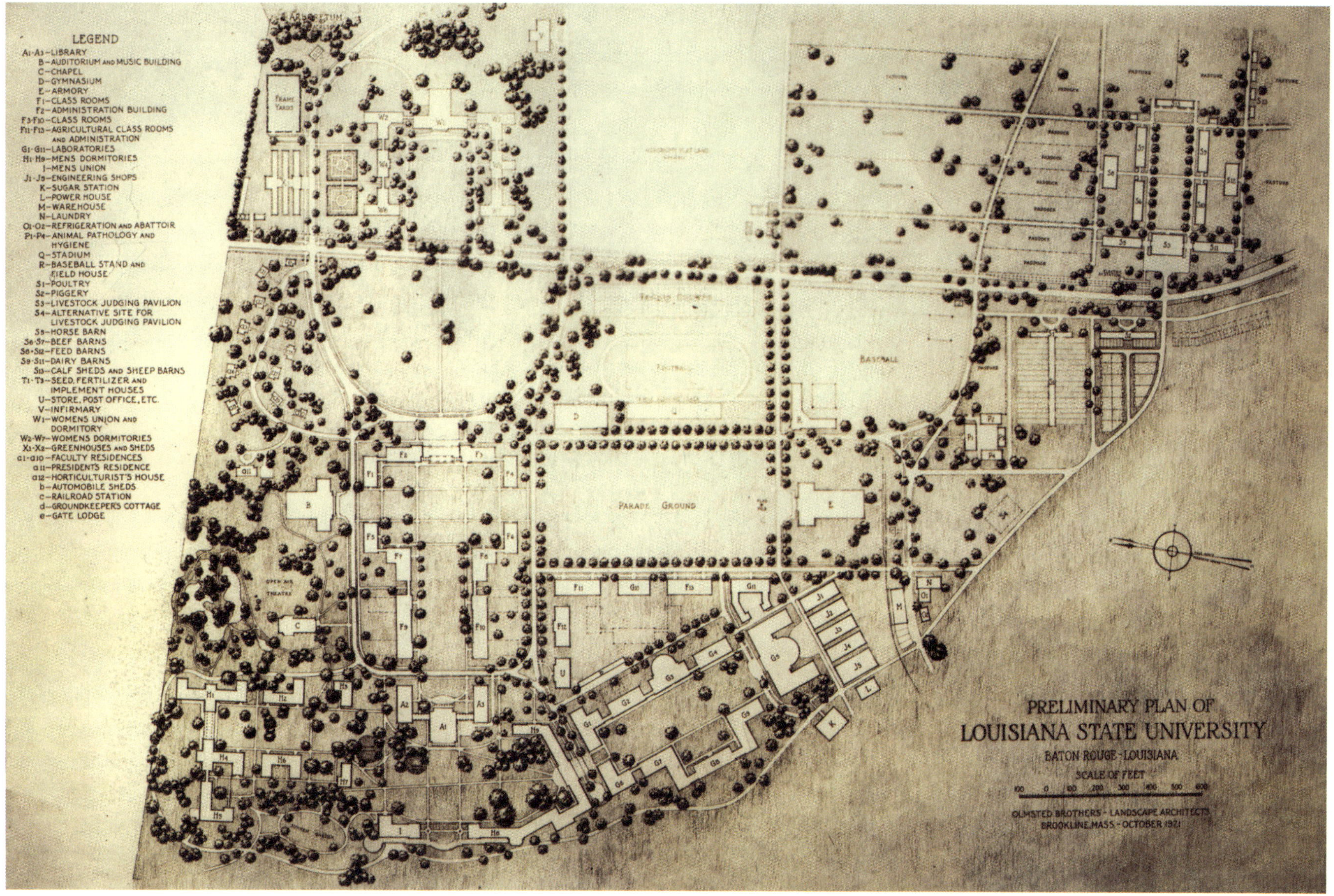

FIG. 2.17. Professionally drawn official perspectival view of the LSU campus that was circulated around the state in 1921. Olmsted Archives, 6888-18. Courtesy of the National Park Service, Frederick Law Olmsted National Historic Site.

inclusion of a parade ground and a gym armory in these plans reflects both the university's military heritage and the influence of the 1862 Morrill Act.

The area around the "ravine" on the northern edge of the property was developed in a picturesque manner that contrasted with the more formal geometries of Olmsted's academic quadrangles. In both the detailed plan and the preliminary studies, this area has a campus chapel. The main campus theater, an existing graveyard, and the house for the university president were arranged around the upper edges of a low swampy area with a distinct pond (figs. 2.18 and 2.19).[14] The pond was an existing feature that designers explored in great detail. It was located in the spot occupied by the Greek Theater today. Although there is no record of the development of this feature in the correspondence, a number of beautiful studies for an outdoor theater in this area exist in the Olmsted Archives. In these schemes Olmsted considered using the slopes around the pond as a grassy amphitheater, defined by the branches of overhanging trees and the views over the water to a low stage for theatrical performances. This scheme was more elegant and informal than the hard-edged and uncomfortable seating that was eventually built by others in this location. The informality of this arrangement would have contrasted with the more formal "sunken garden" proposed to the west along the bluff. The arrangement of faculty houses would have provided a kind of buffer zone between the formality of the academic buildings and any surrounding development, which was not likely to be as institutional in character. There are awkward places in the plan, such as the triangular area between the laboratories and the Parade Ground. The triangular effect would not have been apparent to the daily user at ground level, however.

All in all, it is a richly textured plan with specific features that carefully adapt to the existing site and present a fine unity of composition—a real masterpiece.[15] This is essentially the plan that appeared as the final Preliminary Plan, with minor modifications, in October 1921. That October plan was also illustrated by an aerial rendering contracted by the firm (see fig. 2.17).[16]

FIG. 2.18. One of numerous sketch studies for the Greek Theater area on the northern side of Olmsted's campus design. Olmsted Archives, 6888-43-sh5. Courtesy of the National Park Service, Frederick Law Olmsted National Historic Site.

FIG. 2.19. Study of the Greek Theater area, showing a sloped-lawn configuration leading down to a pond with a performing area beyond. Olmsted Archives, 6888-43-sh1. Courtesy of the National Park Service, Frederick Law Olmsted National Historic Site.

There are several differences between the September study and the final one from October. In both versions of this developing campus scheme, there is judicious use of regular tree planting along long, straight streets. The final Preliminary Plan, of October, shows this kind of arrangement primarily surrounding the Parade Ground occupying the north-south axis and along adjacent streets. The earlier internal office rendering also sketchily indicates this kind of treatment along Highland Road and defines a tree-lined entryway leading up to the memorial, or entry, arcade, although this appears to have been erased from the earliest study plan (see fig. 2.14). Significantly, the regularized street-tree arrangement is replaced in both the final Preliminary Plan and the General Plan in favor of a more irregular scheme. The final commissioned rendering seems to show a continuous, if not rigidly spaced, canopy along Highland Road. Otherwise, the original open space is shown loosely planted, with no clear indication of tree type desired. But the most notable difference is the continuous open axis of entry. In the final plan a large university library building is located at the intersection of the entry and the ceremonial quadrangles. This library, with its adjacent wings, blocked the east-west flow of open space first perceived on the site, indicated in the earliest planning studies and still evident in the in-house aerial pencil rendering (see figs. 2.14 and 2.15). This library is situated at the center of the campus quadrangle areas, one façade facing the entry into the campus to the east, through the fine and liberal arts quadrangle, and the other facing west, into the ceremonial quadrangle, with its mounds and magnificent westward vista.

Ever since Thomas Jefferson added a library as a focal point in his University of Virginia plan, this building type has figured strongly in American campus design. In using a half-scale version of the Pantheon, which was originally built as a unique temple to all of the Roman gods and to the concept of empire, Jefferson adapted the reference to universality to a liberal and secular context that fit well with his conception of the role of the university in modern life. In plans such as those for Columbia, Emory, and the University of California at Berkeley, the large, dominant library buildings act either as a central focus around which the campus is organized or as the termination of the primary axis, as in Jefferson's final plan. In Olmsted's final Preliminary Plan for LSU, the library building sits in the midst of the major organizational axis as it moves westward over the bluff toward the river and the horizon beyond, effecting a merging of associations and placing the university and its collections of knowledge in the broader context of the natural world, a less humanistic and more romantic focus. The library, and the collections it would hold, acts as a kind of mediating element, negotiating the transition from state institution to the broader vista beyond.

BUILDINGS AND EXECUTION

When the question of architectural style came up in the design period, Rick Olmsted suggested that while something harking back to Louisiana's French or Spanish roots might be appropriate, his firm's focus was landscape architecture. The university would have to hire an architect to develop the form and substance of the buildings, and questions of style were better left to that phase of development. The firm did, however, produce internal studies, probably at the hand of Alexander Scholtes, a consultant and part-time employee who did renderings.[17] Several of these study drawings are included in the Olmsted Archives collection of LSU-related items. They depict a campus architecture redolent of the Spanish colonial governments in Mexico. Some of the drawings show a formal, symmetrical arrangement of buildings not unlike that created by the Spanish Cabildo and Presbytere on Jackson Square in New Orleans. Others seem to explore an adobelike language of intersecting forms with continuous covered galleries. The final contracted rendering the firm provided to the university shows a similar kind of imagery, but with very little defining detail. In both the sketches and the final rendering, the buildings are shown light in color, and not brick (figs. 2.20–2.24).

The Olmsted Brothers' LSU plan was developed through a thorough study of the facilities utilized for modern education at a number of the nation's most prestigious universities. Their work involved determining the square footage of classroom and accessory spaces needed for each academic discipline. The firm was initially asked to plan for a student population of three thousand, some

FIG. 2.20. Detail of an "in-house" Olmsted Brothers design study of a Spanish-style campus architecture for LSU, showing the integration of various buildings in symmetrical groupings with arcades and small corner-tower accents. Olmsted Archives, 6888-27-sh2. Courtesy of the National Park Service, Frederick Law Olmsted National Historic Site.

FIG. 2.21. Detail of the Olmsted Brothers design study, showing a typical entry for a dormitory grouping. Olmsted Archives, 6888-27-sh2. Courtesy of the National Park Service, Frederick Law Olmsted National Historic Site.

FIG. 2.22. Detail of the Olmsted Brothers design study, showing the Armory and other buildings with integral covered arcades. Olmsted Archives, 6888-27-sh2. Courtesy of the National Park Service, Frederick Law Olmsted National Historic Site.

FIG. 2.23. Detail of the Olmsted Brothers design study, showing the Administration Buildings on either side of a ceremonial entry arcade with the Armory in the distance. Olmsted Archives, 6888-27-sh2. Courtesy of the National Park Service, Frederick Law Olmsted National Historic Site.

FIG. 2.24. Another detail of the Olmsted Brothers design study. Olmsted Archives, 6888-27-sh2. Courtesy of the National Park Service, Frederick Law Olmsted National Historic Site.

three times greater than the student population at the time.

Olmsted Brothers' General Plan for Louisiana State University, like the final Preliminary Plan also dated October 1921, shows the full extent of the two tracts of land the state had acquired, comprising approximately 2,000 acres (fig. 2.25). Their suggested development of the tracts is consistent with Rick Olmsted's first observations; that is, more space was needed for the university's agricultural-research mission. The majority of the property acquired as lowland in the flood plain was designated as pasture and as experimental fields for rice and sugar production. The college buildings ride the bluff, overlooking these extensive fields to the Mississippi River in the distance.

On the other side of the academic buildings and across Highland Road are a women's dormitory complex on axis with the main entry, a formal arrangement of livestock buildings and related pastures, large open, flat fields for agronomy, a network of greenhouses, an area for fruit cultivation, and a large arboretum. The arboretum, to be approximately 30 acres in size, was to be located in the area presently occupied by the University Lab School, fraternity houses, and the LSU System Building. This portion of the site backed up to the then-swampy area surrounding the eastern edge of the university's property, the area eventually made into the network of lakes defining the eastern edge of the campus. The General Plan shows the arboretum in this area as a picturesque network of walks and paths fanning out behind the women's dormitories replete with various specimens of trees and shrubs, perhaps like the Arnold Arboretum, which had been developed by Frederick Law Olmsted as part of his Emerald Necklace, the chain of parklands encircling Boston. LSU's arboretum would have complemented and extended the university's agronomy research for years to come.[18]

Following the submittal of the Preliminary Plan in October 1921, Olmsted Brothers negotiated with LSU to further develop the work into a fully detailed campus master plan. While the firm was not hired to develop the Preliminary Plan further, it was contracted over the next year to design a rearrangement of farm buildings for the southern

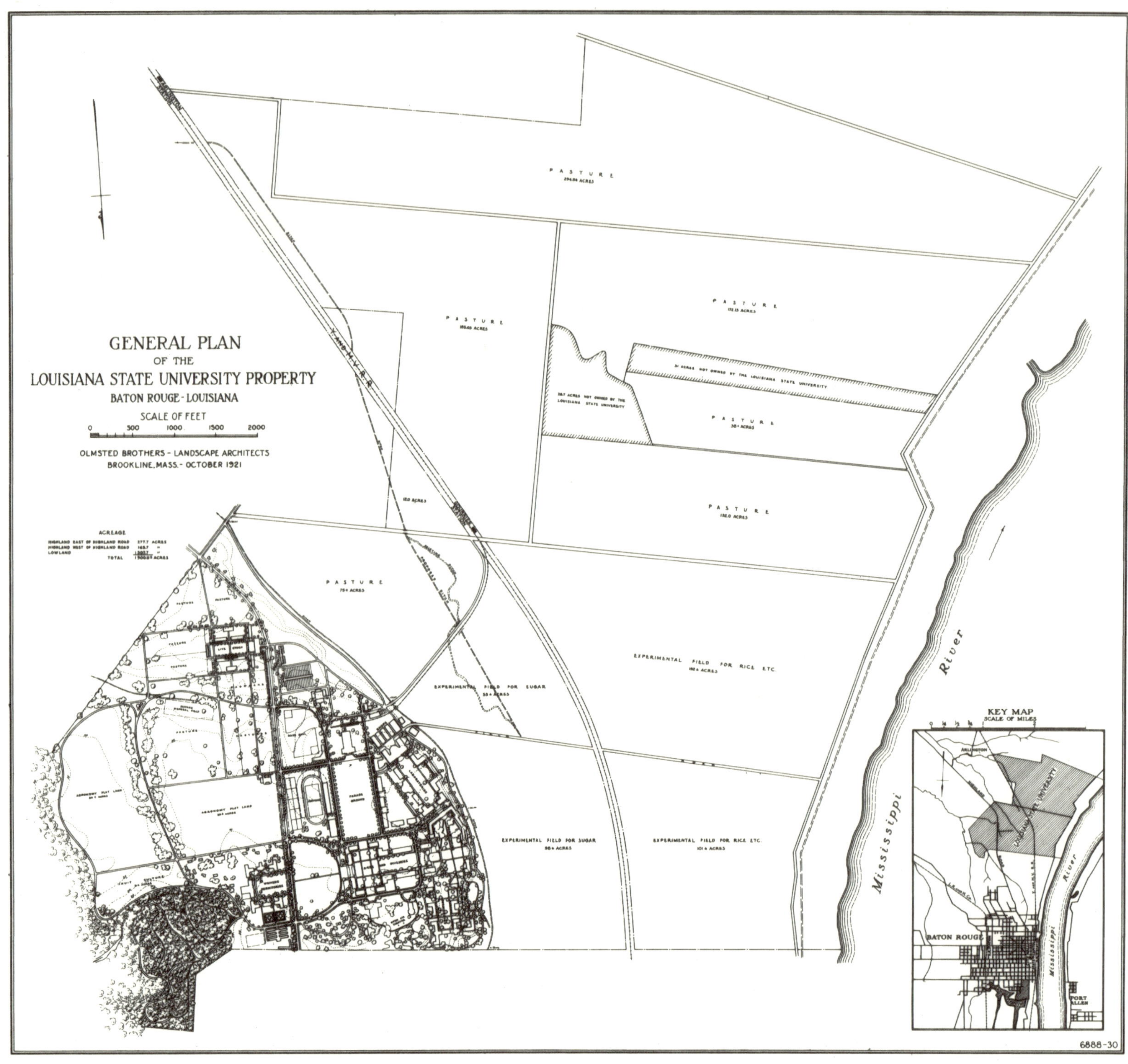

GENERAL PLAN
OF THE
LOUISIANA STATE UNIVERSITY PROPERTY
BATON ROUGE - LOUISIANA
SCALE OF FEET
0 500 1000 1500 2000
OLMSTED BROTHERS - LANDSCAPE ARCHITECTS
BROOKLINE, MASS. - OCTOBER 1921
ACREAGE
HIGHLAND EAST OF HIGHLAND ROAD 277.7 ACRES
HIGHLAND WEST OF HIGHLAND ROAD 165.7
LOWLAND
TOTAL 1500.0± ACRES
PASTURE
PASTURE
PASTURE
PASTURE
PASTURE
PASTURE
EXPERIMENTAL FIELD FOR SUGAR
EXPERIMENTAL FIELD FOR RICE ETC.
EXPERIMENTAL FIELD FOR SUGAR
EXPERIMENTAL FIELD FOR RICE ETC.
Mississippi River
KEY MAP
SCALE OF MILES
0 ¼ ½ ¾ 1 2
ARLINGTON
LOUISIANA STATE UNIVERSITY
BATON ROUGE
Mississippi River
PORT ALLEN
6888-30

FIG. 2.25. (*facing page*) LSU General Plan, by Olmsted Brothers, showing the campus plan along with the full extent of state-owned property in 1921, including the Gartness and Nestle Down Plantations, in relation to the existing rail line and downtown Baton Rouge. North is downward on this map. Olmsted Archives, 6888-30. Courtesy of the National Park Service, Frederick Law Olmsted National Historic Site.

FIG. 2.26. The designs of the "Swine Palace" and associated barns were provided by the Louden Machinery Company of Fairfield, Iowa, through a contract with Olmsted Brothers. The reconfiguration of this group of structures was Olmsted Brothers' last involvement with LSU. Jasper Ewing & Sons Photograph Files, Mss. 3141, Louisiana and Lower Mississippi Valley Collections, LSU Libraries, Baton Rouge, LA.

edge of campus, along the bluff. Governor Parker was anxious to show progress in the development of the site and its agricultural mission. The arrangement that was eventually followed was not the one first proposed in the Preliminary Plan. In the initial plan, Rick Olmsted located a formal quadrangle of livestock-related buildings centered on a judging pavilion and surrounded by paddocks and pastures on the eastern side of Highland Road. This grouping was opposite facilities for poultry and a piggery that would have backed up to the bluff, but these facilities were relocated between Highland Road and the bluff. In this position, the central judging pavilion could be seen from the New Orleans railroad and the extensive network of lowland fields stretching out to the river in the southwest, providing visual evidence to New Orleans–bound riders that the construction of the state university had begun (fig. 2.26).[19]

3

Theodore C. Link, Architect

I wish to state that the work in charge of your Committee appeals to me intensely, particularly for the reason that it might give me a fitting opportunity to conclude a long and useful career with a monumental achievement in which my name might be linked with yours as the creators of the foremost seat of learning in the South.

—THEODORE LINK TO GOVERNOR JOHN PARKER, MARCH 25, 1922

Throughout the preliminary design of the new campus, the Olmsted Brothers firm resisted efforts to provide images of the architecture of the new campus, noting that since the university would be required to hire an architect, or architects, to design the buildings, it would be inappropriate for the firm to do so. As we have seen, there were internal sketches exploring the use of a Spanish mission style for the development of buildings for the new campus. There is no evidence that anyone in Louisiana ever saw these studies. The firm did contract the services of E. M. Parsons & Company for a colored architectural rendering to present, along with their Preliminary and General Plans, to the Building Committee in Baton Rouge in December 1921. This rendering does not show much architectural detail, however; it shows very little that could be seen as stylistic, and it was certainly not meant to indicate such detail. Over the previous summer, Thomas Boyd and the Building Committee had begun to receive expressions of interest from local architects eager to take on this significant commission.

It was during this time that the project attracted the attention of the St. Louis–based architect Theodore Clarence Link (1850–1923), who was then working in Jackson, Mississippi. Link was a German-born engineer. He trained at Heidelberg and later studied at the École Centrale in Paris, both first-rate educational institutions.[1] He arrived in the United States in 1870 and worked in Texas as an assistant railroad engineer for several years. In 1874 Link began work on the design of Forest Park in St. Louis. Two years later, he became the city's superintendent of public parks. Although he opened his own architectural office in 1886, Link does not seem to have ever had any formal architectural training, and no details of his informal instruction have been uncovered. This was a period before most states issued architectural licenses and when architectural training in the United States generally involved apprenticeship (fig. 3.1).

By the time he began to work on the LSU commission, Link had an accomplished architectural practice in St.

Louis, with such regionally noted buildings as that city's Union Station to his credit (fig. 3.2). Link won the Union Station commission in a national competition in 1891. His design for the well-known edifice was an eclectic and rambling mix of Richardsonian Romanesque features, opulent and expressive if not completely integrated or harmoniously composed. During the decades preceding his move to Baton Rouge, Link was largely engaged with the growing state college and university system in Mississippi. Link's work in Mississippi began with his design of the new State Capitol in Jackson from 1900 to 1903. The building's imposing, elaborate neoclassical design in white stone was inspired by the U.S. Capitol in Washington, DC. The design of the Mississippi Capitol is more disciplined than is typical of buildings in this style and was appropriate for its monumental function (fig. 3.3).

While Link was in the state, he worked on several buildings at the University of Mississippi and Mississippi State College. In 1916 he returned to Mississippi to renovate the original State Capitol in Jackson (1839). Following this renovation, he took over a massive statewide building campaign that included many state colleges and hospitals from

CLOCKWISE:

FIG. 3.1. Theodore C. Link. Courtesy of Mississippi Department of Archives and History.

FIG. 3.2. Link's competition-winning design for Union Station in St. Louis. Postcard in author's personal collection.

FIG. 3.3. Mississippi State Capitol Building, Jackson, designed by Link in 1900. Courtesy of Mississippi Department of Archives and History.

FIG. 3.4. Sketch by Link for an unbuilt ceremonial entry to the Mississippi State Normal School in Hattiesburg, showing his familiarity with Italian Renaissance design before his work at LSU. This design is an adaptation of Filippo Brunelleschi's early-fifteenth-century Ospedale degli Innocenti in Florence. Courtesy of Mississippi Department of Archives and History.

1918 to 1921.[2] His work on an array of projects as director of works for the Mississippi State Bond Improvement Commission clearly demonstrated his talent as an architectural designer and practical professional capable of carrying out complex projects. This experience in neighboring Mississippi not only put Link in a good position from which to solicit the work in Baton Rouge but made him uniquely suited to taking on the scope of the LSU project (fig. 3.4).[3]

Link met with the Building Committee in early February 1922 and made his formal application for consideration on February 11.[4] During this meeting and in later correspondence, he argued persuasively against what he characterized as the "absent treatment" the project would receive if an out-of-town firm (i.e., Olmsted Brothers) were hired to coordinate the overall design. He offered to move himself and select members of his staff from Jackson to Baton Rouge for the duration of the project if he were selected.[5] In a letter to Governor Parker of March 25, 1921, he wrote about avoiding the pitfalls of "divided responsibility" that a long-distance arrangement would inevitably produce:

> The idea of divided responsibility had a thorough test during the recent war period. It proved unsatisfactory in every respect. It was found impossible to harmonize the various interests, resulted in constant bickering among the associated professions creating much confusion and duplication; it was the direct cause of the many slips and irregularities which were the subject of subsequent congressional investigations. And, worst of all, it proved a bottomless pit when they counted the cost. My experience in Mississippi, where, in one instance, I gave way to the expediency of political procedure and appointed with me another architect has only strengthened my attitude against this method of procedure. In this connection I might also mention that dealing with one responsible party will relieve your Committee of much of the irksome details and friction incident to the

> employment of several professionals of equal importance and particularly from the importunities of an army of job seekers and their numerous friends.

Along with a careful list of the potential difficulties he could help the committee avoid, this letter also reveals a thoughtful consideration of the problems facing LSU based on his work in Mississippi.

> I feel that somebody ought to profit by the accumulated experience so unique that it comes but rarely and only to few architects in a lifetime. I fully believe that it could be considered a most regrettable economic waste if this accumulation of valuable experiences were allowed to pass with me. . . . The problems which had to be solved here were not simply the creation of new buildings of good design and construction, but they involved the correction of conditions caused by the ignorance and mismanagement of several generations. It required a patient and persistent digging to the very roots of each institution in order to get . . . [illegible] results for the rehabilitation to educational and economic efficiency. Every subject had to be dissected and diagnosed before a remedy could be applied. It broadened and amplified the intimate knowledge already possessed of the needs and requirements of collegiate work, and developed certain convictions which I am anxious to see carried out.

In addition to arguing against hiring an out-of-state firm to supervise and control the work, Link also disputed the idea that any special talent was required to do the "landscape work":

> The landscape work, which has of late developed into a profession of much mystery and importance, is to me the easiest part of the scheme, I have practiced it at one time as a profession. . . . Anyone with a full appreciation of beauty as expressed in nature can compose groups of trees and shrubs in an ideal . . . [illegible] landscape just like Raphael and Corot composed them on canvas. I can make a landscape architect of you after six months study of the same books which made the elder Olmsted famous. Much of the landscape work will be done in conjunction with the road building, grading and shaping. For the rest I would employ an horticulturist of the garden variety to the planting. In this department alone I can give enough money for an additional building.

In view of the careful attention Rick Olmsted and his office demonstrated in the development of their plan for the campus, this almost contemptuous write-off of the landscape and planning effort provided by that firm must be seen either as a calculated attempt to secure the entire commission or as an unfortunate misunderstanding of the subtlety and richness of the ways in which the earlier scheme had been fit into the existing landforms. Link continued:

> I believe you can feel what I mean by going through any of the latest examples of modern college groups. They lack warmth, they lack the intangible touch of loving care, the intimate human element. The melting of landscape and buildings into one cannot be done by long distance or specifications only. . . . The classrooms and laboratory have been reasonably well perfected, but the modern college dormitory with its over-emphasized bachelor idea and its deliberate attempt of weaning the student from Home and Mother is entitled to a psychological correction. Stately aloofness in not conducive to studious habits. Spectacular architectural effects transposed . . . [illegible] the student into strange and unfamiliar surroundings and he will seek elsewhere what he does not find on the campus. . . . I believe most of this is due to the foresaid "absent treatment" for the reason I have offered to divorce myself from every other distracting element and devote myself to your work exclusively, living on the spot and communing daily with those magnificent magnolias until they and I have become sworn friends. . . .

> Referring specifically to the architectural development of the scheme it stands to reason that if it has to be done quickly I would have to draw upon other offices for help. The best process, in this case, would be to make the studies of all plans and elevation in my office and from these the working drawings could be developed by others, preferably by Louisiana architects of my selection. It is the only way to get a harmonious "ensemble" free from jarring discords. . . . If time is given for more deliberate proper all architectural work would be done in my own office.

Theodore Link was hired by the Building Committee on August 1, 1922, "over the protest of a committee of the Louisiana Chapter of the American Institute of Architects, which was present, and contended that such a state building project should be undertaken by an architect from the state."[6]

Accompanied by his son Clarence, who had worked with him for several years as an assistant, Link settled in downtown Baton Rouge while working on the campus design. The size of his Baton Rouge office staff remains unknown, but there is evidence to suggest that he utilized space on the second floor of the State Capitol, on North Boulevard, for some of this time. It is clear, however, that the work of reviewing the master plan, designing the various necessary buildings, and developing the working drawings for these and other technical aspects of the overall plan, such as utility tunnels and a storm-drainage system, proceeded quickly. But after a short illness, the elder architect passed away suddenly on November 12, 1923. Along with the General Plan (fig. 3.5), the designs for fourteen of the nineteen buildings constituting the core of the campus had been completed by the time of his death. Contracts had been released for the Power House, the Engineering Laboratory and Shops, the Main Engineering Building, the Agricultural Group, the North and South Administration Buildings, David Boyd Hall, the original Law Building (now Thomas Boyd Hall), Peabody Hall, Hill Memorial Library, and the sanitary and storm-sewer systems, among others (see the appendix). Link had also just completed his design for Memorial Tower, which he considered to be among his best efforts. All in all, Link's work was a remarkable achievement for just over a year's time.

FIG. 3.5. *(facing page)* Digital scan of the only known copy of Link's General Plan. The original is a blueprint, and the colors have been reversed here for clarity. Office of the Chancellor Records, RG #A0001, Louisiana State University Archives, LSU Libraries, Baton Rouge, LA.

Clarence Link continued to supervise the Baton Rouge staff. With the death of Theodore Link, however, local architects increasingly called for the selection of a local firm to supervise the work. Eventually, Clarence was replaced by the New Orleans firm of Wogan & Bernard, which had been engaged with the project previously as an assistant firm.[7] The firm's primary role from this point forward appears to have been to complete the unfinished Link designs. The design work the firm did followed the plan ensemble and the model buildings Link had developed. Wogan & Bernard, however, revised some of the outlying buildings on the overall General Plan and added a few of their own conception during the late 1920s. Eventually Wogan & Bernard was replaced by another New Orleans firm, Weiss, Dreyfous & Seiferth (WDS), which became a favorite of Huey Long's. Long became governor of the state in 1928, almost two years after the formal dedication of the partially complete new university on April 30, 1926. WDS was responsible for several of the buildings on the main quadrangles. The designs of Allen, Audubon, Nicholson, and Himes Halls are generally compatible with Link's original designs, but show somewhat less attention to details. WDS also designed and executed a number of other significant buildings on campus, including the Huey Long Field House, the new Law School, and a series of new dormitories (see the appendix).

ADAPTATION OF THE OLMSTEDS' PRELIMINARY PLAN

No direct evidence indicates why, or by what process, Link altered the design logic and configuration of Olmsted Brothers' Preliminary Plan. Apparently, the university was concerned about the size and scope of the earlier plan; it wanted to reduce the size of the building project

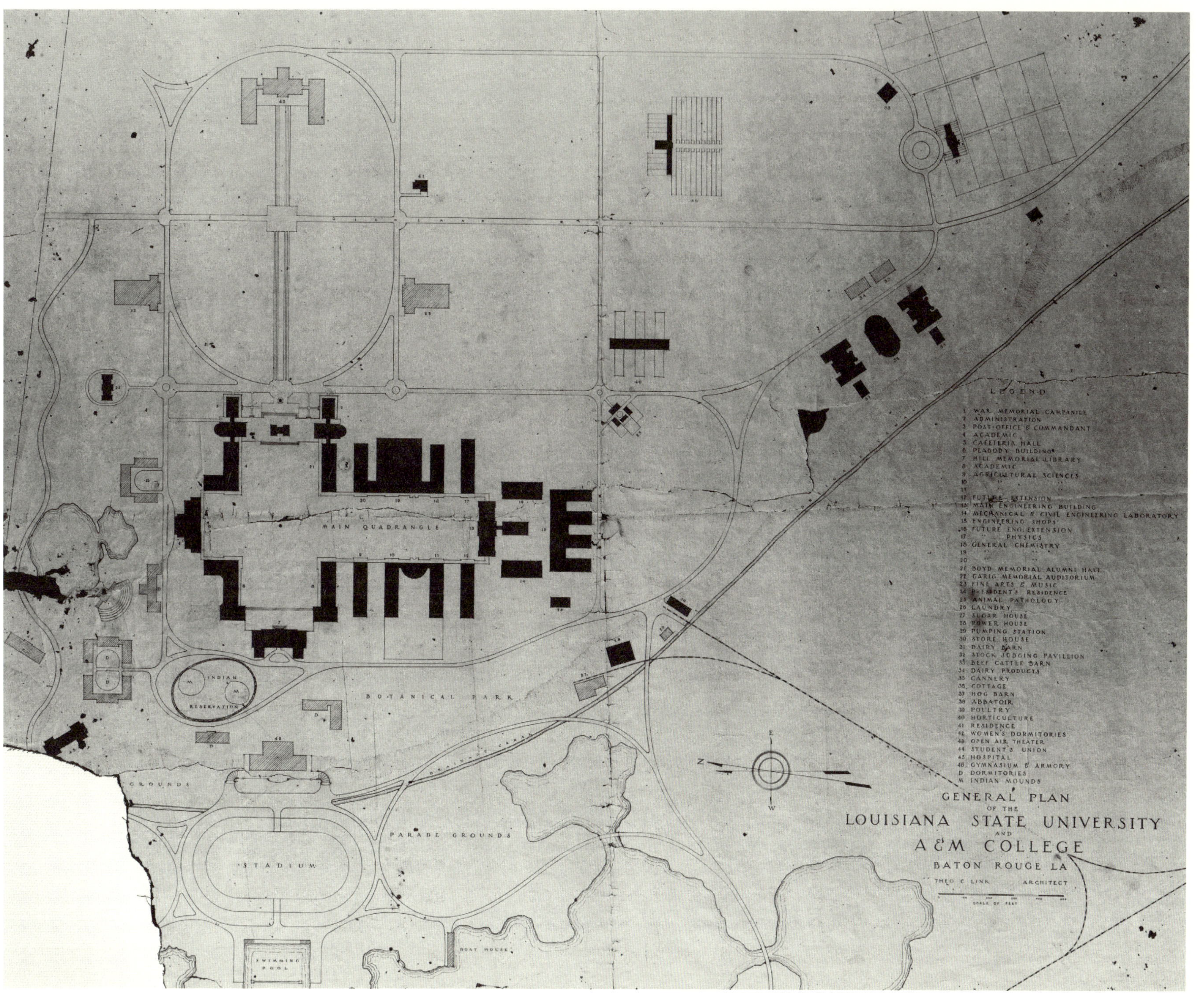
MAIN QUADRANGLE
INDIAN RESERVATION
BOTANICAL PARK
GROUNDS
PARADE GROUNDS
STADIUM
SWIMMING POOL
BOAT HOUSE
LEGEND
1 WAR MEMORIAL CAMPANILE
2 ADMINISTRATION
3 POST-OFFICE & COMMANDANT
4 ACADEMIC
5 CAFETERIA HALL
6 PEABODY BUILDING
7 HILL MEMORIAL LIBRARY
8 ACADEMIC
9 AGRICULTURAL SCIENCES
10 " "
11 " "
12 FUTURE EXTENSION
13 MAIN ENGINEERING BUILDING
14 MECHANICAL & CIVIL ENGINEERING LABORATORY
15 ENGINEERING SHOPS
16 FUTURE ENG. EXTENSION
17 " PHYSICS
18 GENERAL CHEMISTRY
19 " "
20 " "
21 BOYD MEMORIAL ALUMNI HALL
22 GARIG MEMORIAL AUDITORIUM
23 FINE ARTS & MUSIC
24 PRESIDENT'S RESIDENCE
25 ANIMAL PATHOLOGY
26 LAUNDRY
27 SUGAR HOUSE
28 POWER HOUSE
29 PUMPING STATION
30 STORE HOUSE
31 DAIRY BARN
32 STOCK JUDGING PAVILLION
33 BEEF CATTLE BARN
34 DAIRY PRODUCTS
35 CANNERY
36 COTTAGE
37 HOG BARN
38 ABBATOIR
39 POULTRY
40 HORTICULTURE
41 RESIDENCE
42 WOMEN'S DORMITORIES
43 OPEN AIR THEATER
44 STUDENT'S UNION
45 HOSPITAL
46 GYMNASIUM & ARMORY
D DORMITORIES
M INDIAN MOUNDS
GENERAL PLAN
OF THE
LOUISIANA STATE UNIVERSITY
AND
A&M COLLEGE
BATON ROUGE LA
THEO C LINK ARCHITECT
SCALE OF FEET

to accommodate only fifteen hundred students as one way of reducing costs. There were also specific concerns about the location and configuration of the agricultural and livestock barns at the southern end of the property. Olmsted Brothers, however, was altering that portion of the plan and provided designs for some of these buildings through the Louden Machinery Company of Fairfield, Iowa, contracted for this purpose.

The plan that Theodore Link developed for LSU was an adaptation of Olmsted Brothers' Preliminary and General Plans of the previous year. The architect began with certain fundamentals of the Preliminary Plan, such as the use of quadrangles as a way of organizing groups of buildings and the main east-west axis of entry with a memorial structure centered on a circular entry drive.

At one time LSU possessed an original print of Olmsted Brothers' Preliminary Plan, which may have provided a starting point for Link's work. A digital scan of that print, which is all that remains, shows evidence that it was used as a basis for the study for adapting the plan into something more like the one eventually prepared by Link. Indentions that can be seen on the scan of the print suggest that it was drawn over with tracing paper. This was a widely used method of design study throughout the century. It is difficult to know the sequence of the overlay studies, but even with no direct evidence it is possible to reconstruct some version of the plan studies created in this way. The studies for new buildings indicated on Link's General Plan follow a slightly different axis of orientation than that used in the Olmsted plan. Link rotated the entire plan, so that the east-west axis of entry was exactly perpendicular to Highland Road, abandoning Rick Olmsted's focus on an existing opening to the bluff in the grove of trees surrounding the Native American mounds.

Whereas the Olmsted plan countered the east-west, or main, axis with an irregular north-south line used to orient the courtyards, or quadrangles, that followed the changing line of the bluff, Link's study explores a strict, 90-degree contrast and establishes a strong north-south axis (figs. 3.6 and 3.7). This orientation follows the relationship between the Parade Ground and the Armory shown on the Olmsted plan. In fact, that plan utilized a secondary north-south axis to coordinate these two secondary features with the overall plan, marking its presence by the slightly widened dimension of the Fine and Liberal Arts Quadrangle, centered on the theater, opposite the Armory in the distance.

In simple terms, it appears that Link, or the study's author, shifted the Engineering Quadrangle, the laboratory buildings, and the shops of the Olmsted plan to the east and changed their orientation so that they followed the secondary axis of the Olmsted plan. The individual buildings in this cluster turned 90 degrees from their earlier position, putting their short sides along the quadrangle, so that their arrangement resembles that popularized by Jefferson at the University of Virginia. Turning the short ends of these buildings to the quadrangle before extending backward allowed more square footage of classroom and related space to be brought into close contact with the central axis.

Link's study is also interesting because of the double lines of trees indicated along each side of the two new axes, one from Highland Road to the terminal Library building, the other running from north to south down the center of what would become the South Quadrangle of Link's plan. Although we have no way of knowing whether Link or anyone associated with LSU ever saw the in-house aerial design studies produced by the Olmsteds, at least one of those shows a similar flanking of the main east-west axis by rows of closely spaced trees leading from Highland Road up to the university entryway. This feature did not show up in the professional rendering Olmsted Brothers sent to Baton Rouge. As can be seen in figure 3.5, Link or his associates explored a similar approach, extending such an allée all the way from the Tower to the Library and along the secondary north-south axis as well, leading southward to the culmination of this Engineering Quadrangle in a large building with an auditorium.

LINK'S PLAN

Theodore Link's "General Plan of the Louisiana State University and A&M College" was completed and apparently published or made publicly available by April 21, 1923.[8] In some ways, it represents a simplified version of Olmsted Brothers' Preliminary Plan; in other ways, however, it is fundamentally different. Olmsted Brothers' network of four or more quadranglelike spaces was replaced by a single cruciform-shaped space developed along two architectural axes, one running east-west and the other north-west. Olmsted Brothers' primary axis of entry, running east-west from Highland Road, was essentially maintained, utilizing a similar semicircular forecourt. The idea was to treat this side of the university plan as a public face; the entryway into the greater university and all it held was kept. The two flanking towers and the central colonnade of the earlier plan were replaced by what may be Link's most accomplished single building design, the almost 180-foot-high Soldiers and Sailors Memorial Tower. This evocative design, although diminutive in plan size, sets the stage for the architectural and spatial richness to follow (see fig. 4.1). It was originally meant to function as a military sally port similar to the entry into Rice University designed by Cass Gilbert several years earlier.

The main axis of entry on the Link plan positions Memorial Tower more than 750 feet back from Highland Road and continues beyond it almost as far as the front of the new Hill Memorial Library. The façade of the Library, at the culmination of this axis, was given a strong and simple horizontal emphasis, as though it were meant to contrast with the vertical rise of Memorial Tower. The axis centers on an east-west-oriented northern quadrangle measuring approximately 290 feet by 630 feet, a broad and receptive space flanked at its entry by the ornate forms of the university's original Administration Building group on the southern side and the Post Office and the Commandant's Building on the north (David Boyd and Thomas Boyd Halls today). This symmetrical entry composition became the most elaborate ensemble in the otherwise relatively calm architectural manner of the campus buildings. The compositional and ornamental richness of this outward-facing group contrasts with the much more sedate façade of Hill Memorial. By 1924 the drawings articulate Thomas Boyd Hall as an Administration Building and the one behind it as an Academic & Law Building.

Just beyond this first ensemble, the east-west axis of entry on Link's General Plan provides the setting for an Academic Building and Boyd Memorial Alumni Hall (Thomas Boyd Annex and Himes Halls today). Whereas in one of the Olmsted plan drawings this grouping is labeled the "Fine Arts Quad," the Link General Plan does not include such a specific designation. Link identifies only "academic" functions here. Peabody Hall is the only one of these flanking academic buildings entirely designed and detailed by Link. His floor plans list an assembly room, a chemistry lab, a room for biological sciences, a kindergarten, an agricultural lab, an agricultural classroom, a room for physics, a sewing room, a cooking room, and several other classrooms on the first floor. A lecture room, a psychology lab, faculty offices along an open porch, and the dean's office in the corner tower are located on the second floor. This diversity of room assignments, coupled with a lack of other useful documentary evidence, makes it difficult to establish any strong sense of clustered disciplines in these four buildings as had been suggested in the Olmsted plan.[9] The grouping of buildings coordinated by this axis eventually was given the name North Quadrangle. The relocated engineering group from the Olmsted plan was oriented according to the new north-south axis, becoming the South or Main Quadrangle, and a final Engineering Quadrangle was identified behind the Main Engineering Building at the plan's southern end.

In Link's General Plan, the east-west axis continued beyond the library, or rather picked up again beyond it, to establish the location of a Gymnasium & Armory, the Football Stadium, and a campus Swimming Pool. This would

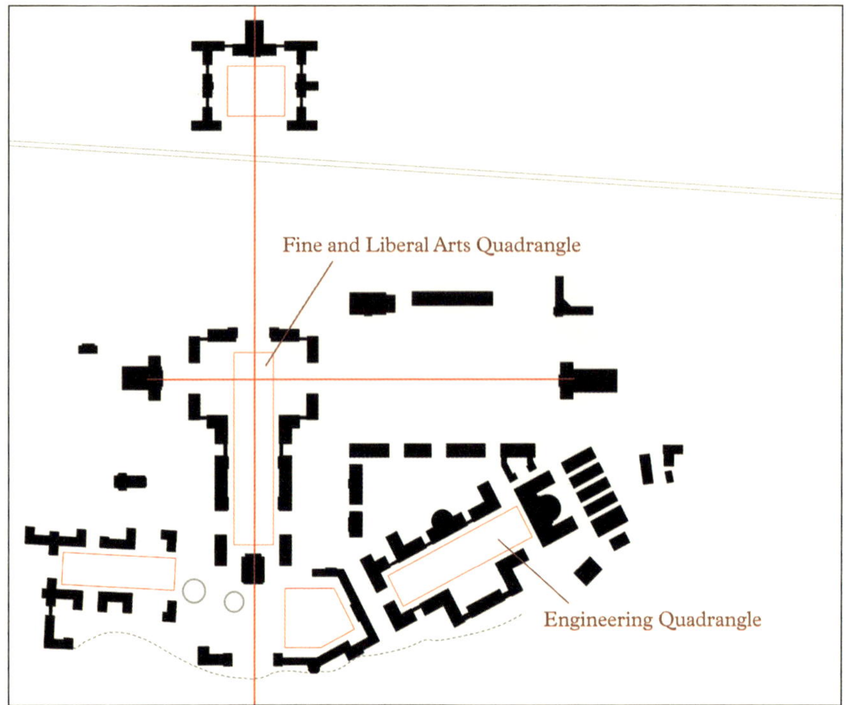

FIG. 3.6. Rick Olmsted's Preliminary Plan of the campus, showing the primary and secondary axes in relation to the Indian Mounds and the bluff with various quadrangular building groups. Drawing by author.

FIG. 3.7. Link's General Plan, showing rotation of axes in relation to Highland Road and consolidation of the two main quadrangles into a singular cruciform-shaped open space. Drawing by author.

have been a thoughtful arrangement of athletic-related structures utilizing the topographical change of the bluff to great effect. The Gymnasium & Armory was to sit on top of the bluff facing east, with a large terrace along its western façade leading to sets of dramatic stairways going down the hill to the stadium. As with the Los Angeles Memorial Coliseum, also begun in 1921, as a memorial to veterans of the First World War, this location would have made possible a relationship between the height of the bluff and the playing field on the lower level of the agricultural lands beyond. The possibilities for architectural and ritual drama inherent in such an arrangement would surely have been attractive to the planners. The LSU stadium was eventually moved to a location slightly further away from the bluff and other campus buildings, giving it more room to grow in size over the years.

The east-west axis of entry sets the stage for a secondary or internal north-south axis that provides the setting for the majority of buildings in the heart of the plan. This internal axis runs from the front of the university's original Cafeteria Hall (Foster Hall today) to the north to the flagship Main Engineering Building (Atkinson Hall) a thousand feet away to the south. Cafeteria Hall was more than likely conceived and designed by Link, although the drawings were completed by Wogan & Bernard after his death.

The classroom buildings along the western side of this Main Quadrangle were dedicated to agricultural sciences.[10] The southernmost building on this side, what is today Audubon Hall, is designated "Future Extension." Along the opposite, eastern side are three interconnected pavilions that define a large building dedicated to general chemistry and a fourth "Future Physics Building." The only known copy of Link's General Plan shows a small feature at the location of the fountain that was put on the west side of the southern quadrangle and another one directly across the quadrangle, breaking up this stretch with four building façades on each side. Many smaller, less complete diagrams of Link's plan serve as key plans or locational diagrams within the working drawings of the various buildings, showing many slight variations.

The mass of the Main Engineering Building (Atkinson) terminates this southern quadrangle. In the Link General Plan, this building is shown as having a central projecting pavilion and two smaller flanking pavilions. The building footprint also shows a secondary unidentified structure connected to the rear, or southern, side. Three other buildings form a smaller Engineering Quadrangle on this side of the Main Engineering Building. The westernmost of these was drawn by Link and built as an Engineering Building (the Art Building today). The southernmost, the Engineering Shops complex, also was built as indicated here. The easternmost building defining this small quadrangle was not built in the initial phase. When it eventually was built as Howe-Russell, its size and role in the campus plan were greatly altered.

The General Plan indicates connecting walkways along the front of most of the inner campus buildings. These reach from Thomas Boyd Hall around Peabody Hall to stop short of Hill Memorial Library, picking up again at Allen and continuing to David Boyd Hall. The Main Engineering Building, however, is shown and was built as a break in this almost continuous network of covered passageways.

There is also ample evidence that Link intended for there to be an extensive network of sidewalks crossing the quadrangles. An official "aeroplane" rendering produced in 1923 and labeled "accepted and authorized by the building committee" is the most descriptive document we have of Link's overall intentions (see fig. 5.5).[11] This drawing illustrates an internal sidewalk scheme, as does a working drawing sheet dated March 7, 1924. Although it was produced after Link's untimely death, he is listed as the architect. In effect, the network can be divided into two parts, the primary arrangement identifying and surrounding the crossing of the two quadrangles and the treatment of the South Quadrangle beyond that (fig. 3.8).

The crossing is defined by a rectangle marked by four small towers, one each on Peabody Hall and what would become Allen and Himes Halls and the Thomas Boyd Annex. A circle at the center of the northern quadrangle connected to each small tower location by a diagonal concrete sidewalk establishes a design motif. This circle and its flagpole mark the crossing of the two main axes of the plan with the campus's two primary architectural symbols—the circle and the vertical line. From the four small towers, other diagonal sidewalks lead to entry plazas in front of the west façade of Memorial Tower, the Cafeteria, and Hill Memorial Library. These small plazas were to be further defined by pairs of symmetrical, flanking reflecting pools. The plaza in front of the Cafeteria is shown with a small lawn at its center, the other two as paved. On the southern side of the central rectangle these diagonal sidewalks continue to describe another full rectangle by crossing each other and eventually meeting at the front of the second building along either side of the South Quadrangle, today's Stubbs Hall and the first pavilion of Coates Hall. This motif continues all the way down to the Main Engineering Building, where again there is a pair of reflecting pools flanking a small plaza. Like the one shown at the opposite, or northern, end of the quadrangles, this plaza has a small lawn at its center. The design indicates sidewalks running fully around both the North and the South Quadrangles just against the building façades. This entire network is also indicated on the 1923 aerial rendering. The sidewalk plan shows a uniform treatment of orthogonal crossing sidewalks in the four rear courtyards located between the buildings along the western side of the South Quadrangle. These were to be of gravel, not concrete, however.

Many other outlying buildings are shown on Link's General Plan, the most distinctive being the cattle complex formed by the Dairy Barn, the Beef Cattle Barn, and the Stock Judging Pavilion. This complex was relocated from the Olmsted plan site on the other side of Highland Road. These buildings were among the first structures the univer-

FIG. 3.8. Link's plan for the sidewalks inside the LSU quadrangles. Office of the Chancellor Records, RG #A0001, Louisiana State University Archives, LSU Libraries, Baton Rouge, LA.

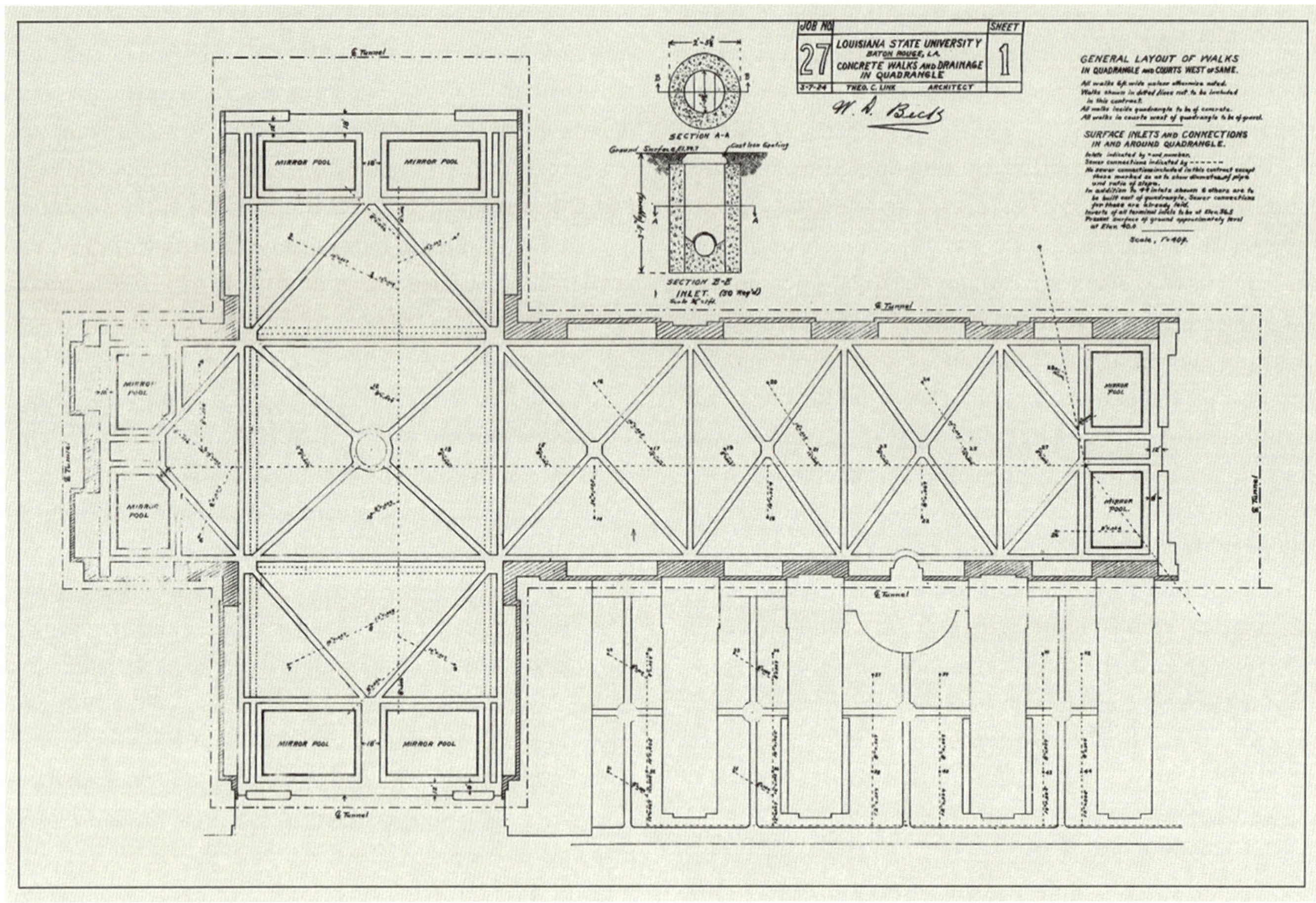

sity built on the new site and are shown here in the configuration eventually provided by the Olmsteds. Visible from both Highland Road and the New Orleans–Baton Rouge rail line just to the west, they confirm the agricultural dimension of the new university. The Stock Judging Pavilion stands fully visible from this location.

The General Plan suggests an unexpected variety of men's dormitories in the area between the core campus and the bluff. Six of these are shown, with little apparent reasoning to their placement or configuration. In fact, this is perhaps the most loosely conceived group of structures indicated on this drawing. A Student's Union shown in the extreme northwestern corner of the site also seems rather randomly placed. It is perhaps oriented only to look out over the low ground beyond the Open Air Theater. Olmsted Brothers' studies of such a theater were among the most beautiful drawings in their collection of LSU work. Their theater, however, occupied an existing depression originally filled with a shallow pond to the east of the site shown here. The present Greek Theater was eventually detailed by Wogan & Bernard in the location originally suggested by the Olmsted plan, but with the pond drained and built-up seating, as was shown on Link's General Plan for the first time. This location of the theater is also shown in the 1923 aerial rendering. A President's Residence is shown at the northern end of what is today Tower Drive, near its location on the Olmsted plan. In that plan this building related to the open low area around the ponds, but here it is tied more formally into the main structure of the campus plan.

The unidentified open space with the generous circular entry drive is flanked by two large buildings, the Garig Memorial Auditorium to the north and a building for fine arts and music to the south. These two buildings seem dedicated to the public face of the university and are not otherwise tied to the formal structure of the campus but reflect a similar placement in the Olmsted plan. In fact neither of these was built. The location of the auditorium was taken in the early years by Smith (now Pleasant) Hall; the location of the other eventually became the site of the LSU Union in the 1960s.

On Link's plan, an ensemble of Women's Dormitories is shown across Highland Road in roughly the same location as on the Olmsted plan, along with various other structures for horticulture, animal pathology, poultry, and hogs in the fields along Highland Road to the south. There is also a residence intended for the dean of agriculture in the location where the President's House stood during the early years.

The only other group of structures on this plan are those indicated below the bluff: the Power House, the Sugar House, the Pumping Station, the Store House, a Laundry, an Abbatoir (slaughterhouse), a Cannery, and a Dairy Products Building. Of these, the Sugar House was built as shown. In the outlying areas below the bluff this plan contains a Botanical Park, a Parade Grounds, and a large grouping of man-made lakes sporting a Boat House. Other isolated buildings include a Cottage to the extreme south along Highland Road. There is also a curious curving roadway shown at the northern edge of the plan, reminiscent of the picturesque area of the earlier Olmsted plan. Significantly, the chapel has disappeared as well.

By July 20, 1923, the Football Stadium had been relocated in Link's drawings from its initial position along the main east-west axis. The new location was a couple hundred feet to the south and rotated to parallel the bluff at that point. This was the third and final location for the proposed stadium. Also by this date, the design of the inner core had almost reached Link's final version. The footprint of Memorial Tower, however, does not yet match its final design. Link's designs for the Tower did not fully mature until mid-October of 1923. The footprint of the Cafeteria Building does not yet exhibit its corner or entry wings.

The four buildings located at the crossing of these two axes today each contain small towerlike corner pavilions that mark their unique role in the plan's symmetries. These do not appear in the General Plan.[12] Rather, the eastern and western ends of the four corner buildings are shown to protrude, as do the other classroom buildings along the Main Quadrangle to the south. Peabody Hall and the proposed Academic Building east of it are the only ones on Link's plan that turn the corners, with sides facing both the east-west and the north-south axis. Peabody, the only one of the classroom buildings that Link completed personally, has two very interesting second-floor porches.[13] The four corner towers mentioned above show up on the plan for the storm-sewer system dated July 20, 1923, but they are not on the general plan for the tunnel system dated December 22, 1922. They appear to have been a refinement to the overall plan developed over the spring and summer of 1923, eventually appearing as they do in Link's design for Peabody Hall. Following Link's untimely illness and death in November 1923, some aspects of his work continued to be influential, especially his vision for the inner-campus buildings, their arcades and architectural features. The outlying buildings, however, for which the plan did not provide firm guidance, developed somewhat more randomly.

At least two more versions of Link's General Plan were drawn over the next decade or so. We do have one digital scan of a print of a follow-up study (fig. 4.7). This drawing depicts the inner-campus area only and is oriented in the opposite direction to that shown in Link's General Plan. His initial drawing and those produced by Olmsted Brothers were oriented with the east upward, as was the sidewalks plan; this follow-up study and all of the subsequent key plans among the working drawings are oriented with the west upward. This change in orientation seems to indicate a further step away from Rick Olmsted's vision. This study maintains all of the buildings in Link's General Plan, makes a few additions, and alters the layout of the first outer layer of buildings. We see here a proposed extension to the northwestern corner of Peabody Hall and similar extensions to what would become Nicholson and Audubon Halls. The group of Chemistry buildings along the eastern side of the South Quadrangle also exhibit extensions to the east. The two outermost buildings of this chemistry group are shown here for the first time as possible additions as well.

Interestingly, the open spaces between the buildings that line both sides of the South Quadrangle are shown with sidewalks that depict formal arrangements. An additional formal garden-type area with groups of surrounding structures was added to the western edge of the group of buildings devoted to Agricultural Science. While these garden-type spaces are not shown in any of the drawings in the Link collection, they were eventually developed as planted corridors and courtyards. Otherwise, the main features of the inner-core plan and the Engineering Quadrangle remain unchanged.

The arrangements of outlying buildings are what vary most significantly from Link's General Plan. The dormitories making up the Pentagon group appear in a replica of the barracks on the downtown campus, which make reference to the presence of military cadets on campus. A large courtyard building nearby appears to be a relocated version of a similar one shown in the location of this Pentagon group on Link's General Plan. Across the entry circle is an expanded auditorium building. The Open Air Theater has returned to its original location. A number of smaller structures line the northward extension of what is today Infirmary Drive. There is also a building shown immediately adjacent to the Native American mounds. All in all, these outlying structures indicate the lack of a significant ordering concept beyond the organization of the central campus quadrangles and their axes. While such minimal organization of these outlying buildings was seen in Link's General Plan, it is even more pronounced here, foreshadowing the haphazard growth of the campus in the following decades.

The other additional plan, from 1938, was by WDS. This drawing provides the most detailed illustration of the locations and footprints of the buildings defining the quadrangles on Link's original plan. Meant primarily to illustrate the location of an underground feeder system for the new Commerce Building (Himes), it does not show many of the outlying buildings. It does, however, indicate no real concept of overall or sympathetic order in the placement of these outer buildings, a problem that has continued since that time (see fig. 4.8).

In spite of the tightly coordinated groupings of the many various buildings shown in both the Link and Olmsted plans, there is no direct evidence that underlying planning grids were used as regulating devices. The layout of several aspects of the Link General Plan does, however, seem to correspond to the use of a proportioning system based on a "root-2" rectangle. The scale of the planning module here appears to be 212 feet by 300 feet, a rectangle with the proportions of 1:1.414. This proportional system, used frequently in the Western architectural traditions, derived from the use of the side and the diagonal of a square to construct a rectangle (fig. 3.9). This proportional relationship also seems to appear in the organization of the individual façades of many of Link's buildings at LSU.

The appearance of this rectangle in Link's General Plan is seen in the rectangular shape made by the four roadways surrounding the part of the plan that is known as the Parade Ground today. These outline a root-2 rectangle of some 636 feet by 900 feet. Dividing these overall dimensions by 3 gives what appears to be a general large-scale planning module of 212 feet by 300 feet. This module appears to be, if not a basis of the design, then at least a clear expression of an overall geometric ordering system. One such module describes the open space of the terrace and

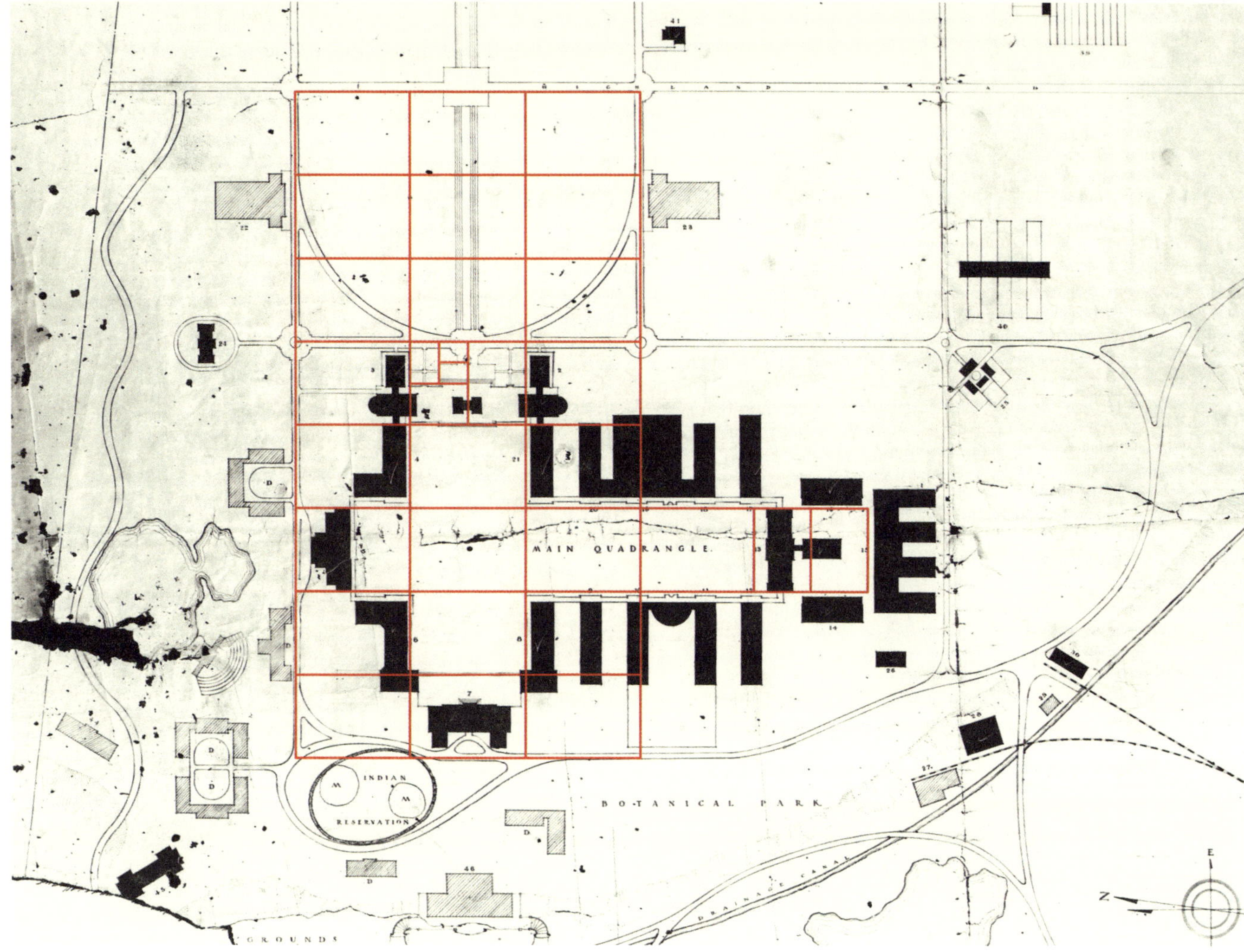

FIG. 3.9. Detail of Link's General Plan with a layout study by the author showing the probability of an underlying proportional root-2 organizational scheme. Overlay by author.

entry court fronting Memorial Tower. Three of these describe the North Quadrangle, between this terrace and the one at Hill Memorial. The centerline of this quadrangle lies on the centerline of these three modules. Four and a half mark the extent of the longer north-south quadrangle, with the bodies of Foster and Atkinson each fitting within one such module. If the distance from Highland Road to what became Tower Drive is marked by three of these modules, then the distance from there to the roadway indicated just behind Hill on Link's plan is described by five modules. This may not be conclusive proof that such a planning module was used, but the coincidence is striking. However, the way in which the diagonal sidewalks cut off the corners of the pools in front of the Cafeteria indicates that the overall campus diagram may not have been constructed using a rigorous proportional system. This is also suggested by the fact that the four sets of reflecting pools define slightly different rectangles. There is no evidence that a similar planning grid was utilized by the Olmsted Brothers firm in the layout of its Preliminary Plan.

Virtually the only indication of a campus landscaping strategy associated with Link's General Plan is that shown on the aerial rendering of 1923, and that indication is slight. The focus of the drawing is on today's Parade Ground, placed center front. This space is primarily an open one, with just two groups of live oak–like trees on either side of the main axis of entry and a few smaller groups in the corners. The tree-lined streets that exist today, that were contemplated by both Link and the Olmsteds and that existed on the downtown campus, are nowhere to be found. The only other distinctive landscaping features are slight groups of tall, thin Italian cedars, three along Highland Road on each side of the axis of entry, and a ring marking the edge of a new pond indicated in the low area just north of the Open Air Theater. Olmsted's group of existing magnolia trees is also indicated surrounding the Native American mounds.

The plan for the Women's Dormitory, which Link's earlier General Plan positioned as the terminus of the eastern end of the main axis, is not in evidence on this aerial rendering, nor is the returning circular drive. In its place are the first signs of a different concept of the role of Highland Road in the overall composition. The scale of buildings along its eastern side is residential, and tennis courts are shown directly opposite the open space of today's Parade Ground. Other than to anchor the Women's Dormitory group, no clear role had been indicated for Highland Road on Olmsted's Preliminary Plan or Link's General Plan.

The 1928 Wogan & Bernard plan altered the concept shown in the aerial rendering by locating the tennis courts behind a series of four Student Center Churches along Highland Road. By that time a residence for the dean of agriculture had been built on the corner of Highland and Raphael Semmes Roads, later known as the Old President's House because it was briefly used by the university president. The present Faculty Club, which sits across the street, is first shown here at the corner of Highland and Dalrymple Roads, leaving the entire block for the churches.

The Women's Dormitory complex is identified on this 1928 plan in a new location, where Smith (today Pleasant) Hall was eventually built. The large, unidentified courtyard building shown at this location on Link's aerial rendering conforms with this. Otherwise, a series of Fraternity Houses appear along Highland and Dalrymple.

This Wogan & Bernard plan does suggest a uniform setback for the buildings along Highland Road. This was the case with the residential-scale buildings shown on the aerial rendering but is more striking and perhaps intentional here, given the variety of buildings projected. While the variety of outlying buildings shown on the early plans changes for no apparent reason from this point in time, the concept of organizing the buildings along Highland Road does seem to emerge by 1928.

DIFFERENCES BETWEEN THE TWO PLANS

It is impossible without further evidence to determine whether Link's arguments against hiring Olmsted Brothers were based solely on his stated convictions or on his desire to influence the outcome of the selection process in his favor. Whatever the case, his comments certainly seem to indicate a disregard, if not a lack of understanding, of both Olmsted Brothers' accomplishments and the senior Olmsted's legacy. The Olmsted plan was broad in scope yet attentive to detail. Skillfully and persuasively integrating the various features of the university into the existing landscape, it was as visionary as that of any American university then in existence.

The choice of Olmsted Brothers in the first place was brilliant. Not hiring that firm to continue full services was a tragic loss, given the kinds of environments it carried through to fulfillment. The choice of Link also proved significant, as the architecture he developed displays an intertextual richness not typically found in American university campus design. With few exceptions, LSU has not generally been able to live up to the standards set by these earliest planning efforts.

While Link's General Plan continues some of the building forms and plan orientations of the Olmsted Preliminary Plan, it also makes a significant break. Rick Olmsted's vision for the campus layout clearly derived from his appreciation of the overall landscape. He utilized the axial view from Highland Road toward the western bluff as an organizing feature while integrating the plan's buildings and open spaces carefully into the pattern of trees and views available from that vantage point. Theodore Link's plan dropped much of this strategy. It maintained the east-west entry axis of the earlier plan and the relationship of this to Highland Road with a slight shift in orientation. The essential idea and scale of the quadrangle as a spatial device for organizing academic buildings remained strong. The Link plan built the minor secondary axis of the Olmsted plan into a major organizing feature. It also continued the grouping of academic buildings in discipline-related quadrangles. In the Link plan, the relationship to the bluff is much more incidental to the architectural and experiential order. In the Olmsted plan, the order was tied to the Highland Road corridor, while its main features were determined by the line of quadrangles along the bluff. The carefully studied, if casual, effects of the Native American mounds and the grove of existing magnolias on the Olmsted plan are only the most obvious aspects of this strategy. In the final version of the Olmsted plan, the presence of the main university library acted as a negotiator between these two complementary concepts of order. One might say that it tied the more formal architectonic order of the fine-arts quadrangle and the axis of entry to the less formal array of open spaces along the bluff.

Link's plan is more insular and self-referential. His academic groups ignored the better parts of the site—the mounds, the magnolias, and the vista to the river. The plan was very difficult to expand, a problem typical of such closed-end plans. While this would have been the case with Olmsted's plan as well, the larger size of the campus it depicted would have postponed the need for expansion, and perhaps its examples of loosely connected quadrangles would have developed as a way of coordinating expansion. In abandoning a tie to the naturalistic order of the site, Link greatly reduced the richness of his composition. In the absence of such a tie, the more formal architectonic order of primary, secondary, and tertiary axes defined by building mass gained in significance. As a less complex ordering system, it is perhaps more obvious and more easily understood. Link's plan was one in which the role of the buildings as carriers of meaning was strengthened, even displacing the perception of patterns in the landscape.

4

Architecture of the Campus

In the Eighth Ward of this parish is being laid the foundations of a great university that will be the means of educating every country boy and girl in agriculture and science. It will prove in years to come as the greatest investment of the state and its dividends will be men and women learned, intelligent and industrious in the art and practice of agriculture. When all the oil, gas, salt and sulphur are gone, their place will be taken as wealth producers by the intelligent development of the rich farming lands of the state and these will last to the end of all time. . . . This is a common interest in which every citizen should share and in which every citizen will prosper in this parish and in all other parishes of the state.

—*Baton Rouge Morning News,* September 12, 1923

THE IMAGE OF THE CAMPUS

Theodore Link had a long and prolific career as an architect. From the mid-1880s until his death in Baton Rouge in 1923, he was responsible for the design of significant works in several parts of the country. Over his career, he demonstrated a large repertoire of historical architectural styles. Perhaps his first significant commission, the competition-winning design for Union Station in St. Louis in 1891, was in the heavy Richardsonian Romanesque style popular in the Midwest at the time (see fig. 3.2). His designs for the Mississippi State Capitol in 1900 were in a thickly layered neoclassical style then common for capitol buildings across the nation (inspired by the U.S. Capitol in Washington, DC) and similar in appearance to the Minnesota State Capitol designed a few years earlier by Cass Gilbert (see fig. 3.3). The architectural languages used by Link for these two powerful buildings bracket the range of popular styles being used across the country in the first decades of the new century. For Mississippi State College in Starkville, he produced a design for a dramatic, Gothic-style Mess Hall (now Perry Hall). For the University of Mississippi he designed red-brick Georgian-style blocks, and for the Mississippi State Normal College he proposed an unbuilt Tuscan entry colonnade similar to what he would later design for LSU (see fig. 3.4). This portfolio of work demonstrates his mastery of the range of eclectic historically based architectural-design languages popular in the United States at that time.

At the Mississippi State College for Women in Columbus, Link used the need to add three new buildings to an

FIG. 4.1. Lovett Hall at Rice University in Houston, designed by Ralph Adams Cram in 1911, with a military-style sally port as the main pedestrian entry into the central quadrangle. Photograph by the author.

FIG. 4.2. The Allen Memorial Art Museum at Oberlin College in Ohio, designed by Cass Gilbert in 1917, utilizing an Italian Renaissance–inspired architectural language. Wikimedia Commons.

existing group as an opportunity to study the development of a coherent campus plan. When he began his work for the Columbus site, there were ten to eleven existing buildings. He produced a master plan showing an additional thirteen structures arranged around a central open academic quadrangle, linked by a network of major and minor planning axes articulated by sidewalks. Although this plan was not followed in subsequent years, it demonstrated an ingenious way to bring cohesion to the otherwise disparate group of existing buildings. It shows that Link was both concerned with, and skillful in, the broader aspects of organizing campus architecture. For the University of Mississippi in Oxford, Link produced the same kind of study, there taking advantage of the need for singular additional structures to suggest overall principles of campus order that could be used as guidelines for future growth toward a coherent whole. In all of these works, Link followed the established trends of his day, adapting various features of historical European architectural styles to the problems at hand. Each project demanded the choice of a particular reference or starting place, be it English, Spanish, French, or some other style.

While Thomas Jefferson's designs for the buildings at the University of Virginia had explored the limits of Georgian English Palladianism to make references to Roman architecture for teaching and ideological purposes, and the design of Stanford University in the 1880s by Frederick Law Olmsted Sr. and the Boston architects Shepley, Rutan & Coolidge (the successor firm to H. H. Richardson) had set a new standard in the relation of architecture and campus planning, the first decades of the twentieth century were a watershed period in the adaptation of architectural style to emerging campus-design patterns in the United States.[1] The Boston architect Ralph Adams Cram was a pioneer in creating a university Gothic style in his master plans and building designs for West Point (1904) and Princeton (1906), while he used the Georgian style effectively at Exeter (1911) and the Tudor style at the University of Richmond (1910). At Rice University (1908), Cram developed a richly textured Byzantine architectural language adapted with neoclassical symmetries to a daring new campus master plan. His design for Lovett Hall at Rice (1911) includes a military-style sally port as the main pedestrian entry into the central quadrangle, a feature that would reappear as a key part of Link's work at LSU (fig. 4.1). The New York architect Cass Gilbert, the designer of the quasi-Gothic high-rise Woolworth Building (1913), explored the use of Renaissance-inspired designs at the University of Minnesota (1909) and Oberlin College (1917) in Ohio (fig. 4.2). The Pittsburgh architect Henry Hornboestel's plans for the Carnegie Technical Schools (now Carnegie-Mellon University) and Emory University in Atlanta (1915) furthered the adaptation of neoclassical and Italian architectural forms to campus design. At Emory in particular, he adapted inspirations from Italian garden and villa design to provide a Renaissance-style architecture executed in marble.[2]

At LSU, the specific motivators behind the choice of an architectural style for the new campus have not become part of any known public record. The downtown campus had been constructed with a wide range of building types and styles. The later building programs there had begun to tend toward a conservative academic neoclassicism. During the preliminary planning process, Olmsted Brothers suggested that the architecture of the new campus reflect the colonial roots of Louisiana culture by using a French or Spanish style. Within their own office, studies were made of a kind of Spanish mission style that looks almost Mexican to modern eyes. The professional artists they contracted were careful not to indicate much more than an ordered collection of buildings working together in the expression of a coherent master plan (see fig. 2.17).

Beyond this, one reliable explanation for the choice of the Italian Renaissance–inspired architectural language of the LSU campus comes from an article published by John Joseph Earley (1881–1945), of Washington, DC. Earley ran a studio he had inherited from his father, the sculptor James F. Earley, which was devoted to the exploration of color and other artistic effects in architectural concrete. The use of concrete as a means of architectural expression was relatively new in the early 1920s. Although it had been used in certain engineering and industrial applications for several decades, it was not generally considered appropriate for architecture's finer expressions. The American architect Frank Lloyd Wright had been one of the first to explore its potential in his design for the Unity Temple (1904) outside Chicago. Concrete would become an important part in the work of Europeans such as Le Corbusier in the later 1920s and 1930s, reaching maturity in such buildings as Wright's Guggenheim Museum, the Dulles Airport by Eero Saarinen, and the contemporary work of the Spanish architect-engineer Santiago Calatrava today.

J. J. Earley explored a different route. While architects like Wright, Le Corbusier, and Saarinen were principally interested in the spatial and sculptural potential of the material, Earley was interested in its ability to re-create the richly colored and textured surfaces of the Italian Renaissance.[3] He was inspired, for example, by the terra-cotta roundels of the Florentine artist Andrea della Robbia that grace such buildings as the Ospedale degli Innocenti by Filippo Brunelleschi in Florence (fig. 4.3).[4] Earley's work in this genre began with Meridian Hill Park in Washington, DC, in 1914 (figs. 4.4–4.6).[5] Meridian Hill Park was designed by the landscape architects George Burnap and Horace Peaslee, and it was the chairman of the Fine Arts Commission, the architect Cass Gilbert, who first suggested the use of colored stone aggregates set in concrete. This work, as well as many other examples in the region, greatly resembles some of the work Earley would later do at LSU.[6] He spent years developing techniques that allowed him to create numerous beautifully colored mural-like applications in the DC area. Earley was enthusiastic about this new material's aesthetic qualities and the inventive ways in which it might be used, writing, "by considering the particles of aggregate as spots of color in juxtaposition, all the knowledge and much of the technique of the Impressionist or the Pointillist school of painting, was immediately applicable to concrete."[7] "Concrete is so wonderfully responsive," he wrote, "that it has wound a spell around me and around the men in my studio. When the work is taken from the molds each morning and the colors are exposed, there is

CLOCKWISE:

FIG. 4.3. The early-fifteenth-century Ospedale degli Innocenti in Florence, by Filippo Brunelleschi, showing the often-copied colonnade and later terra-cotta roundels, or *tondi*, by Andrea della Robbia. Courtesy of Hidden Italy, www.museumsinflorence.com/musei/ospedale_degli_innocenti.html#.

FIG. 4.4. Meridian Hill Park, in Washington, DC, one of the first demonstrations of J. J. Earley's ornamental concrete. Courtesy of Anthony Threatt.

FIG. 4.5. Another view of Meridian Hill Park illustrating the variety of ornamental techniques pioneered by J. J. Earley. Courtesy of Anthony Threatt.

FIG. 4.6. These balustrades by Earley at Meridian Hill Park are similar to the ones he would later provide for the LSU campus. Courtesy of Anthony Threatt.

something so spectacular, so magical about it that our enthusiasm never abates."[8]

Although Earley produced a series of articles over the years for the American Concrete Institute and published at least one short illustrative book on his work, there is no direct indication of how he became involved with LSU. In the early 1920s he had been called to Nashville to provide a protective resurfacing for the full-scale replica of the Parthenon that had been built in plaster as a temporary structure for the 1897 Tennessee Centennial Exposition.[9] Link, then working in Mississippi at the university in Oxford, could easily have been aware of this work. Whatever his involvement, J. J. Earley left an indelible impression on the architecture of the LSU campus, and it is from this enthusiast for the Italian Renaissance that we get the best description of how its forms found their way into Louisiana's history:

> It became immediately apparent that the South could lay claim to a style of its own. In the South that style of building, which is generally spoken of as a "mission" building, is accepted and used for first-class structures. A mission building was originally the expression of someone's memory of buildings of the domestic type in Spain or Italy. Mission buildings have been well suited to the use and climate of the South, therefore, the architects decided that the buildings of the Louisiana State University should be a domestic type of the style of building developed in Italy during the Renaissance.[10]

The architecture of Link's design for the campus is highly coordinated with the overall master plan to provide a unified composition not often seen. As Earley noted,

> It was desired that these buildings should be an intuitive course in architecture for the students, and that they should take home improved standards in architecture to be reflected in the architecture of the state when these young people in turn began to build. That this hope might be well founded, simplicity, permitting intimacy, encouraging emulation and making the buildings a part of the life of the people, was preserved.[11]

MEMORIAL TOWER AND THE ADMINISTRATION GROUP

Link's General Plan, as well as the various slight alterations to it that followed, shows numerous buildings wrapped around and defining several quadrangles. The names of these buildings and the quadrangles themselves have changed over time and were inconsistent in the early years. For purposes of clarity, the 1928 Wogan & Bernard plan is the best to use to accompany a comprehensive description (fig. 4.7). This plan breaks the large, cruciform-shaped quadrangles into North and South Quadrangles, corresponding to the Fine Arts and Science Quadrangles of earlier plans. Labeled on the 1928 plan is the smaller Engineering Quadrangle, to the south of the Main Engineering Building. This plan also shows the arcades and corner towers generally in their present positions and similar to those found on a 1938 plot plan by Weiss, Dreyfous & Seiferth showing the projected further development of the central quadrangles (fig. 4.8).

The building names used on these various early campus plans differ substantially from one plan to the next and from the names most of the buildings carry today. The building names and numbers used on this Wogan & Bernard plan are used here, with the present names, if different, following in parentheses. The Soldiers and Sailors Memorial Tower (1), or Campanile, has had the same name throughout its history. Immediately to its north (to the right on this plan) and connected to it by the elevated terrace are the North Administration Building (2) and the Law Building (3) (together known as Thomas Boyd Hall today). To the south, in positions mirroring those of the North Administration Building and the Law Building, lie the South Administration Building (19) and D. F. Boyd Memorial Hall (18) (jointly known as David Boyd Hall today).

Moving from this entry group of five buildings along the northern side of the North Quadrangle, we come to the Social Sciences Building (4, the only partially unbuilt gap in the original plan, a site imprecisely occupied by Thomas Boyd Hall Annex today), followed by the Cafeteria, or Dining Hall (5, Foster Hall), and the George Peabody Building (6, Peabody Hall). Hill Memorial Library (7) occupies the end of this quadrangle, with the Language Building (8, Allen Hall) defining its southern edge and marking the southwest corner of the crossing. Marking the opposite, or southeast, corner, the Mathematics Building (17, Himes Hall) completes this North Quadrangle. The South Quadrangle is further defined along its western side by the Home Economics Building (9, Stubbs Hall), the Animal Industry Building (10, Prescott Hall), the Agricultural Auditorium (11, Dodson Auditorium), and the Biology Building (12, Audubon Hall), the latter three designed as a group dedicated to agricultural sciences. A Forestry and Horticulture Building (13, known as the Agricultural Administration Building today) completes the side. The eastern side of the quadrangle is defined by the larger Chemistry Laboratory (16, Coates Hall), which presents itself to the southern quadrangle as three distinct buildings, and the Physics Laboratory (15, Nicholson Hall) at the southern end. The Main Engineering Building (14, Atkinson Hall) completes the southern end of this South Quadrangle. Behind the Main Engineering Building to the south, the Steam and Hydraulic Engineering Laboratory (47, Art Building), the

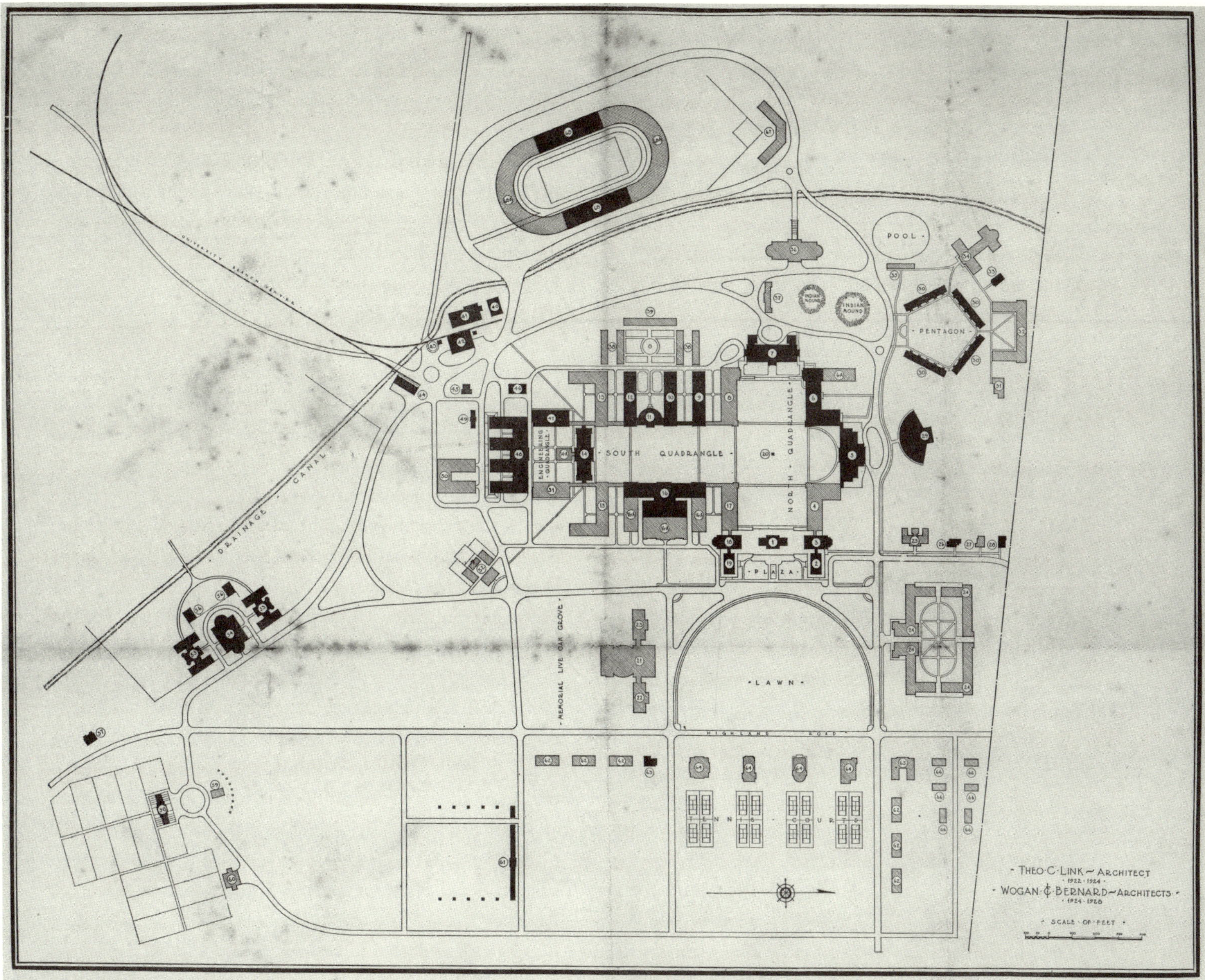

FIG. 4.7. The 1928 Wogan & Bernard plan, showing existing and proposed buildings along the quadrangles and around the perimeter of the campus. Al Alleman Collection, Mss. 2877, Louisiana and Lower Mississippi Valley Collections, LSU Libraries, Baton Rouge, LA.

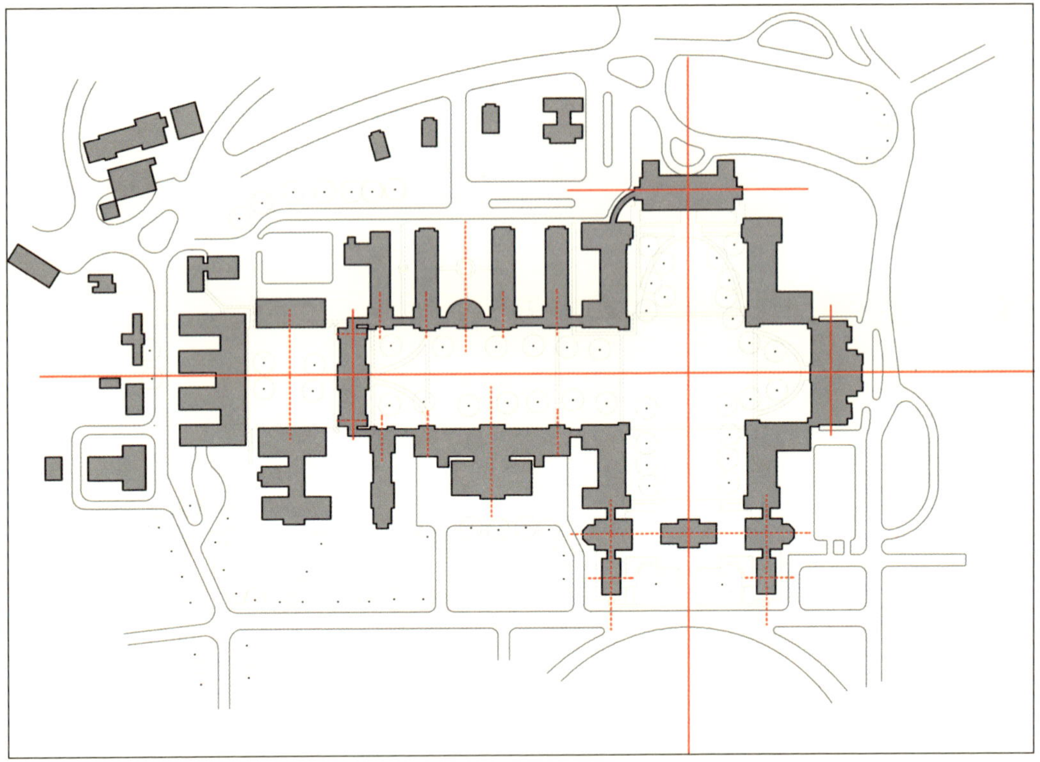

FIG. 4.8. 1938 campus plot plan by Weiss, Dreyfous & Seiferth, showing the projected development of Link's central quadrangles, along with overlay of primary, secondary, and tertiary axes in red. Redrawn by author with axes added.

Engineering Shops (48), and an Electrical Engineering Building (51, Howe-Russell) define a much smaller Engineering Quadrangle.

As noted in the descriptions above, Link's General Plan was organized around two primary axes. The four main buildings at the ends of these axes, each representing a different division of the university, were given unique architectural forms. Further, the two buildings at the ends of each of the two axes form related pairs, with complementary formal attributes. The vertical reach of Memorial Tower contrasts with the horizontal expression of Hill Library. The singular face of the Cafeteria contrasts with the various projecting parts of the Main Engineering Building, and all of these buildings are scaled to be read from a distance. Such formal richness and reciprocity are apparently examples of what Earley was referring to when he described Link's desire to create "an intuitive course in architecture." These relationships are perhaps more clearly discerned in the 1938 plot plan of the central campus produced by WDS (see fig. 4.8).

Beginning with the first of these four main buildings, on the public face of the university as seen from the sweeping circular arc of the Parade Ground, the vertical form of Memorial Tower is bracketed by the outward-reaching arms of its two adjacent building subgroups. These five are the most elaborately designed and ornamented structures in Link's plan. The foremost of these, originally known as the North and South Administration Buildings, were to contain the offices of the president, the registrar, and the dean of women, as well as the post office, the bookstore, and offices for the military department. Standing just behind them are the connected forms of David Boyd Memorial Hall and the Law Building. The first of these contained a faculty room, offices for the treasurer and the purchasing agent, some classrooms, and the Department of Commerce. Taken together, these subgroups and Memorial Tower, with its slightly elevated terrace, provide a formal, symbolic entry to the university. The ideal of a bilaterally symmetrical and hierarchically organized architectural composition is clearly emphasized here as a kind of introduction to the architectural themes of the campus. Not only the entire group of buildings but the subgroups as well are organized using such patterns of order, so that the idea of harmonically repeating geometric order is developed right from the start.

The North and South Administration Buildings are ornamented with four highly colored circular panels, or roundels, representing the different academic disciplines of the university. This architectural detail is a prime example of Earley's research into the expressive potential of architectural concrete. The details were inspired by della Robbia's terra-cotta roundels mentioned above (figs. 4.9 and 4.10). Similar forms had been used several years earlier by Gilbert on his Renaissance-inspired design for the library at the new University of Texas campus in Austin. In Texas they represent the twelve signs of the zodiac. At LSU these four emblems seem to represent chemistry, agriculture, engineering, and education. The group of four is repeated on the northern and southern elevations of both buildings. The two buildings just to the west of these Administration Buildings are connected to them by carefully detailed colonnades and rise into elaborate, vertical, false façades along the minor central axis of the foremost buildings. These are the only places where these kinds of details occur in Link's plan, and they seem aimed at presenting a public face to the university with a level of refinement not seen throughout the campus (figs. 4.11 and 4.12).

As we have seen, Link's General Plan is based on two primary axes defining the quadrangles, an east-west axis and a north-south axis. A secondary set of axes defines the centerline of each of the four terminating buildings, at right angles to the primary one through each of these buildings. A third level in the hierarchy of axes can be seen in the pavilions at the ends of Atkinson Hall and marking the centerlines of the David Boyd and Thomas Boyd Hall groups. Lastly, a minor axis marks the side entryways into the North and South Administration Buildings from a point just in front of the Tower, establishing a fourth level in this hierarchy. This means that there are more compositional axes associated with the entry and administration group of five buildings than there are anywhere else in the plan, just as there is more ornament and architectural detail at these key points.

FIG. 4.9. Terra-cotta roundel by Andrea della Robbia on the Ospedale degli Innocenti in Florence. Photo © Adrian Fletcher, www.paradoxplace.com.

FIG. 4.10. Roundels by J. J. Earley on Thomas Boyd and David Boyd Halls, depicting agriculture, chemistry, engineering, and law. Courtesy of Jim Zietz, LSU University Relations.

FIG. 4.11. Pencil drawing of the David Boyd Hall group as designed by Link in 1923. David F. Boyd Hall Pencil Drawing, Mss. 265, Louisiana and Lower Mississippi Valley Collections, LSU Libraries, Baton Rouge.

FIG. 4.12. Memorial Tower and the Administration entry group designed by Link, as seen from the Parade Ground. By Michael Roper and Anthony Threatt after Theodore Link.

The two buildings in each of these flanking subgroups are connected to each other by means of an arched passageway with Tuscan columns. This traditional design element is referred to as a "Palladian motif" because it was used to such great effect by the Renaissance architect Andrea Palladio. In fact, Palladio appears to have been the source for much of the imagery and forms of the original quadrangle buildings. This particular motif appears again at another critical point, within the university library, at the far end of the entry axis.[12] This architectural form has a long and distinguished history, beginning with its use in the ceremonial gateways of ancient Rome. This can be seen in the entablature broken by an arch in such places as the gateway remaining in the North African Roman town of Timgad or the Arch of Constantine near the Colosseum in Rome, creating a series of rectangular openings flanking a larger central passage (see fig. 4.30).

Palladio, who worked in Venice and the surrounding region during the sixteenth century, is among the most influential architects in history. There are two main reasons for the scope of his influence. Especially in his designs for villas throughout the Veneto, his work codified the experiments of architects across the Italian Renaissance. He often approached the design of the ensemble of structures necessary for the operation of the agricultural estates as one interrelated design. In buildings such as the Villa Badoer and the Villa Emo, to cite two examples, Palladio arranged the various structures hierarchically using strict bilateral symmetry (fig. 4.13). The design of the entire group is guided by the use of a coherent proportional system throughout, with buildings, walls, openings, architectural orders, and other ornamentation rigorously coordinated.

Many of these compositions utilize outlying support buildings in the form of outward-reaching arms, which invite the visitor as they embrace the entry pathway. The use of classically inspired symmetry is based on what can be characterized as an A-B-A rhythm, where the essentially three-part compositional order is articulated by the use of different elements. In a building such as the Villa Saraceno, for example, the front façade is divided into three basic parts, the central arcaded porch (B) and two flanking walls (A), in a basic rhythmic structure of A-B-A (figs. 4.14 and 4.15). But each of these parts can itself be divided into smaller units. The flanking walls are made up of flat closed portions (a) flanking central open windows (b), a-b-a. The central porch has three arched openings (d) bracketed by four piers (c), c-d-c-d-c-d-c. The entire pattern of symmetry in this rather simple façade can be expressed as a-b-a / c-d-c-d-c-d-c / a-b-a, an elaboration of the elementary A-B-A symmetry underlying such complexity.

This kind of order making applies throughout these beautiful buildings, sometimes with an almost musical cadence, always with an open space in the center. In Theodore Link's General Plan for LSU, this kind of symmetry can be found at all levels down to the smallest detail. Thus not only are specific architectural elements inspired by Palladio's villas, but the campus and building designs reflect his classically inspired ordering system as well.

Palladio's influence also has to do with the quality of his work, as illustrated in his *Four Books of Architecture* (1570), one of the seminal works in Western architectural theory and illustration. This was the first important work to provide reliable images of existing Roman buildings. Moreover, Palladio provided guides to the proportional order exhibited in each of the buildings he illustrated. Along with illustrations of Roman buildings, he included illustrations of many of his own works, similarly annotated. This volume gave architects throughout Europe and beyond an essential tool and contributed significantly to Palladio's reputation and influence. The *Four Books of Architecture* was translated into English by the seventeenth century and has since extended Palladio's influence around the world.

As mentioned above, the five buildings forming the entry ensemble at LSU contain the most detail and greatest number of formal elaborations. The buildings are connected by a slightly elevated terrace some six steps up from the ground plane. This terrace is partially contained by a balustrade with four highly ornamented light towers with illuminating globes at their peaks framing the entry steps. These four lights are unique in the campus plan. They surround and seem to gesture to the form of the Campanile, which is topped with a light and a dome. The most highly ornamented features of the entire LSU General Plan as prepared and executed by Link, they bracket the Tower and its memorial function (see fig. 4.22).

FIG. 4.13. The Villa Badoer, near Vicenza, by the Cinquecento Italian architect Andrea Palladio, showing the use of bilateral symmetry, hierarchy, and a variety of architectural elements to coordinate and give status to groupings of buildings on an agricultural estate. Courtesy of Province of Rovigo, Department of Culture, via Ricchieri n. 10-45100 Rovigo, Italy.

One of the basic formal devices encountered in the study of architectural form is that of threshold and enclosure. For all else that a work of architecture may do, it divides the world into an inside and an outside. Unlike simpler buildings, however, a work of architecture seeks to make a comment on or embellish this division in some way. A basic way of doing this is to provide a flourish of detail at the point where the envelope establishing the division is opened, typically the entry. In classical and traditional architecture this is done in a variety of ways and at different scales, such as

FIG. 4.14. An unbuilt eastern façade alternative for the Chemistry Building by Link, showing typical similarities to Palladio's design for the Villa Saraceno. Office of the Chancellor Records, RG#A0001, Louisiana State University Archives, LSU Libraries, Baton Rouge, LA.

FIG. 4.15. The Villa Saraceno, near Vicenza, by Andrea Palladio. Groupings of three are used to order the façade: three basic parts to the massing, three arched openings in the center part, three basic vertical divisions. Wikimedia Commons.

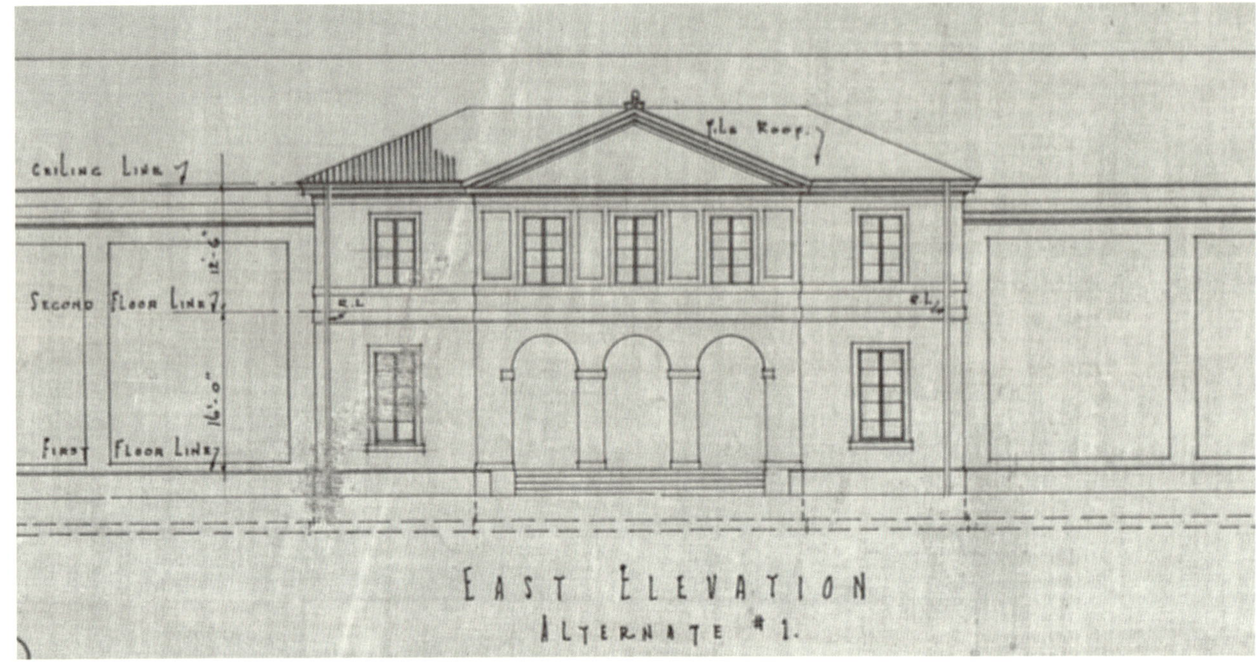

the way in which a piece of decorative molding surrounds a window or a doorway is punched through a wall that is otherwise meant to be read as stable and resolute. The larger the penetration, or the more important the contents of the interior, the larger the ornamental treatment. The detail and compositional richness of these five buildings and their terrace can be thought of as an expression of this fundamental architectural idea.

The Campanile itself presents first a three-part form, with the central section being larger and stepping forward; it is also raised another five steps from the surrounding terrace. On each of its two primary sides this central block is dominated by two pairs of large Roman Tuscan columns more than 20 feet high. The Roman Tuscan order is used throughout Link's campus design (see Conclusion, fig. C.2).

The Roman Tuscan column can be thought of as a Roman equivalent to the earlier Greek Doric column, with influences from the Etruscan culture of central Italy. It differs from the Greek in that the shaft does not have flutes and the column has a base. It is a form used frequently to suggest participation in the ordered world of classical design but without pretense to elegance. It was used in Rome, for example, as the lowest of the three orders on the façade of the Coliseum, with the higher ones each a step up in refinement. It was used also as the basis of the design for St. Paul's Covent Garden (1630), by Inigo Jones, the first church building in England expressive of the Italian Renaissance, seen by Jones and many after him as marking a return to the roots of classical architectural expression. In general, the columns Link designed for the LSU campus are more beautifully scaled and proportionally adjusted and executed than those designed by subsequent campus architects.[13]

The central mass of the Campanile offers an entry on the centerline of the building that takes one into an open space at the heart of the structure. The wings are divided into four bays with windows by the addition of three engaged Tuscan columns, or pilasters, on each side. This arrangement places a column, rather than an opening, in the center of each side. Many such patterns, typical of classical architecture, are repeated in each of the terminal buildings. Not only does each have a central entry, but its sides are articulated with an even number of bays, so that a column line falls in the center of the sides, another of the ways the classically derived system of architectural order expresses hierarchy and interest.

Originally the Tower was designed to contain two large, elegant rooms, the Alumni and Founders Halls, and an open central octagonal space, the Soldiers and Sailors Memorial, with bronze gates to the exterior, directly under the tower (figs. 4.16 and 4.17). The walls of this central room show several different aggregate and concrete color mixes and finishes developed by Earley for use in decorative treatments. In that original form the central, octagonal domed room served as an exterior memorial room, a reference certainly to the military tradition of the sally port.[14] It was designed to have only the bronze gates and no exterior doors. These gates were set deep within thickened exterior walls so that when open they would still seem recessed. The two side doors leading from this central space into the flanking halls were the exterior doors. This octagonal room contains four large bronze plaques listing parish by parish the names of the state's veterans who lost their lives in World War I. The sentiments of the period are enunciated by the following moving passages:

> We are the dead. Short days ago, we lived, felt dawn, saw sunsets glow, loved and were loved, and now we lie in Flanders fields. To you from failing hands we throw the torch; Be yours to hold it high; If you break faith with us who die we shall not sleep.
>
> —McCRAE

> Comrades true, born anew, peace to you; Your souls shall be where the heroes are, and the memory shine like the Morning Star, brave and dear, shield us here.
>
> —JOYCE KILMER

FIG. 4.16. The bronze gates at Memorial Tower. Originally protecting the central memorial space, the gates were slightly relocated when it was closed to the outside in the late 1940s. Courtesy of Jim Zietz, LSU University Relations.

FIG. 4.17. One of the bronze panels commemorating the Louisiana soldiers and sailors who lost their lives in the First World War. Courtesy of Jim Zietz, LSU University Relations.

FIG. 4.18. (*facing page*) Artistic rendering of an early design for Memorial Tower by Hugo Graf for Link, showing a somewhat more romantic, or ornamented, composition than the one finally developed. Memorial Tower Sketch, Mss. 265, Louisiana and Lower Mississippi Valley Collections, LSU Libraries, Baton Rouge.

Link completed the design of this building a few weeks before his death in November 1923. He considered it to be among his most successful and powerful designs. It has impressed many others since. Particularly noteworthy is the similarity between the massing of Memorial Tower and that used by WDS for Huey Long's New State Capitol years later. Memorial Tower is one of a number of architectural monuments built across the country in the wake of the Great War. Only the ensemble known as Liberty Memorial, by the architect H. Van Buren Magonigle, at the site of the National World War I Museum in Kansas City, Missouri, rises to this level, however. The virtues of sacrifice, honor, courage, and patriotism are spelled out there in a symbolic program with an Egyptian-inspired architectural language.

Link's design process and the specific historical references for the LSU design remain largely unknown. One indication of his thought process is provided by an undated rendering by the artist Hugo Graf for Link of what must have been an earlier design (fig. 4.18). Graf was a St. Louis artist and draftsman who had worked for Link previously and had gone on to establish a successful regional architectural practice.[15] This rendering shows a very different architectural style from the Italian one settled on by Link for the LSU buildings. In this drawing, Memorial Tower is shown in an elaborate brick-and-stone design vaguely reminiscent of British Georgian palace architecture, with some Roman elements thrown in. Although the architectural style portrayed is very different from the one eventually used, the overall ensemble pictured is similar to the final design. It is a symmetrical and hierarchical grouping of several related buildings with emphasis on the center. On the flanking buildings are arched windows in cubic masses. They are replete with stone urns and roof balustrades, as in this version of the Tower itself. The central entryway stands out as an oversized arch set in a protruding templelike façade, not unlike the one Link used for the LSU Cafeteria (see fig. 4.23). The Tower appears to be open through its base, suggesting the kind of memorial space shown in Link's final working drawings. There are also covered colonnaded walkways to either side, reminiscent of those added to the Queen's House in Greenwich, England. In the final design for this Administration Group, however, these were moved to the sides and the Tower was left to stand alone (fig. 4.19). The final form of the Tower is more reminiscent of Italian precedents such as San Giorgio del Greci and other Venetian examples (fig. 4.20). It is also similar to a design Ralph Adams Cram used several years later for a First World War memorial carillon in Richmond, Virginia, and to Sather Tower at Berkeley, completed by John Galen Howard in 1914, among many other examples.

While it does not depict the building as it was ultimately built, the Graf rendering is evocative, the Tower standing tall against a tempestuous late afternoon sky, at its top a beacon of light and symbolism held aloft. Link's design of this Soldiers and Sailors Memorial Tower is a tribute to the sacrifice of those Louisiana citizens who lost their lives in the war and to the state's role in providing the opportunity of education to its citizens. Standing as it does at the foot of the large open circle of the Parade Ground, it evokes the military association, but it goes even further in utilizing two of the most ancient architectural devices, the tower and the open circle (fig. 4.21).

The technique of perspectival composition—the use of vistas, the placement and juxtaposition of images and building groups, with associated meanings or references—is also a typical aspect of the planning methodology developed in the Renaissance, as exemplified by the embrace of the façade of St. Peter's at the Vatican by Bernini's arcade, the approach to Michelangelo's Campidoglio in Rome up the stairway to the center of the group, and many other later European classically inspired building groups. Such ensembles are meant to be seen perspectivally, from a central view-

point that locks everything into place. The landscaping materials indicated in the 1923 rendering of Link's plan, with carefully scaled shrubs flanking the terrace entry, larger groups of oaks framing the central vista, and the Italian

FIG. 4.19. Memorial Tower and the Administration entry group in the late 1920s. Courtesy of East Baton Rouge Parish Library.

FIG. 4.20. The sixteenth-century Campanile of San Giorgio del Greci in Venice, showing the kind of Italian inspiration that motivated Link in his design for Memorial Tower. Wikimedia Commons.

FIG. 4.21. Aerial view of Memorial Tower and the Administration entry group, showing the edge of the Parade Ground and the initial landscaping. Fonville Winans Aerial Photographs, Mss. 4605, Louisiana and Lower Mississippi Valley Collections, LSU Libraries, Baton Rouge, LA.

cedars across Highland Road, all work in concert (see fig. 5.5). This building group serves as a "Gateway to Learning" and introduces the student and the visitor to the meaningful integration of architectural plan, form, and detail found throughout the Link plan for the quadrangles area.

THE HILL MEMORIAL LIBRARY GROUP

The second subgroup of buildings in Link's campus plan, Hill Memorial Library and Peabody and Allen Halls, is found at the other end of the east-west entry axis (figs. 4.22 and 4.23). The ensemble formed by these three buildings terminates that axis. The space at this western end of the northern quadrangle is closed by the full width of the library building, raised on its own terrace. On each side, the elevations of Allen and Peabody are broken into three parts each. The first of these buildings to be finished, Peabody Hall was designed and begun by Link. The bulk of the southern façade was made up of an arcade with an open porch on the second floor above. This form is typical of

FIG. 4.22. Hill Memorial Library from the Memorial Tower terrace, with Peabody Hall to the right, in 1927, showing one of J. J. Earley's ornamental concrete lampposts and balustrade. Courtesy of LSU *Gumbo,* 1927.

FIG. 4.23. Building elevations by Link, ca. 1923. Elevation views of the four building groups terminating the internal planning axes in the original LSU campus plan, derived from the original construction drawings, showing the use of bilateral symmetry, hierarchy, and a variety of architectural elements to provide coordinated building groups while giving status to the primary figures: Memorial Tower, Hill Memorial Library, Foster Hall, and Atkinson Hall. By Michael Roper and Anthony Threatt after Theodore Link.

FIG. 4.24. Southern side of Peabody Hall, showing Link's "cloister" arcades and the original second-floor balcony during construction. Al Aleman Collection, Mss. 2877, Louisiana and Lower Mississippi Valley Collections, LSU Libraries, Baton Rouge, LA.

FIG. 4.25. Arcades at the Villa Emo, near Vicenza, by Andrea Palladio. Photograph by Giampolo Bordignon Favero, of the Corpus Palladium, 1972.

many Renaissance cloisters in Italy. In fact, the first-floor arcades were labeled "cloister" on Link's original working drawings for this building.[16] That term would show up for the next decade in reference to the LSU arcades. A strong horizontal line at the sill of the second-floor windows establishes the balustrade height for this porch and continues around the building. This horizontal band is found on many of the buildings making up the quadrangles (fig. 4.24).

The portion of the façade of Peabody that steps out and engages the Library terrace contained an assembly room on the first floor and a lecture room on the second. Both were large open spaces. These wings were not built as originally shown, in that Link's drawings indicate a hipped roof fronted by a pedimented façade stepping out a few feet further. Rather, the entire end was clipped off in an unsatisfactory manner, similar to the treatment of the ends of David Boyd and Thomas Boyd Halls as they face the Tower terrace. The same thing occurs at Allen Hall. The construction drawings for Allen Hall, however, done more than ten years later by WDS, show the condition as built at Peabody and duplicated here. The westernmost part of the southern face of Peabody steps forward to engage the terrace fronting the Library. The terrace opens to the quadrangle by way of a broad set of steps some 125 feet wide, not quite as broad as those at the Tower terrace (153 feet). The mass of Hill Memorial Library sits back almost thirty feet from the ends of the adjacent buildings. This allows the terrace to jut out beyond the open corners of the space, providing a kind of back door into the main space of the quadrangle.

In Link's original plan, the arched arcades reach around most of the quadrangles but not everywhere.[17] These arcades appear very similar in size and character to those used by Palladio in the Villa Emo in the Veneto (see fig. 4.25). They were to begin at the rear of the entry group with the buildings known as David Boyd and Thomas Boyd Halls today. On the northern side of the North Quadrangle, the arcade continued around the corner, across the front of the Cafeteria to Peabody, and on around the corner, to stop just before the terrace at Hill Memorial. On the southern side of the Northern Quadrangle, the arcades ran around the corner of what is Himes Hall today and were integrated into the front of the Chemistry Group, along the South Quadrangle. At the southern end of this quadrangle the arcades end at the central hallway of the Main Engineering Build-

ing. Along the western side of the Main Quadrangle, the arcade repeats its pattern between the façades of the various buildings before turning the corner at Allen Hall and running almost up to the Library terrace.

Thus, the four terminal buildings had different relationships to the arcades. On the Cafeteria the arcades ran (and still run) along the face of the building, while on the Engineering Building they stopped and encouraged one to walk inside the building to continue under cover. At the Library they also stopped short of reaching the terrace, much less the building itself. This arrangement was altered as the buildings were constructed, perhaps with changes made after Link died. Unfortunately, the arcades at Allen and Himes Halls were never included along the northern façades, as was done by Link for the southern face of Peabody Hall. Some WDS campus drawings show the addition of semicircular segments of arcade connecting Allen and Peabody Halls to the ends of Hill, but only one of these was built.

The remaining portion of the southern façade of Peabody Hall is made up of a diminutive tower, one of four intended to mark the corners at the crossing of the larger dual-quadrangle space. These towers are similar in size and character to elements used by Palladio.[18] Taken together with the various elements described, these towers can be seen as playing several roles in the overall compositions. On the one hand, when seen in elevation from the entry to the east, they help to establish the hierarchy of pieces typical of a Palladian bilaterally symmetrical composition. When seen perspectivally from this vantage, they help to form an embrace of the form of the Library in the center of the compositions, as at the Campidoglio in Rome, as noted by Steen Eiler Rasmussen in his excellent short introduction to the role of architecture in building cities, *Towns and Buildings.* On the other hand, when seen from an oblique vantage from elsewhere in the quadrangle, they mark the crossing of the axis and frame the central space at its heart. They also repeat the circles theme (figs. 4.22–24 and 4.27).

At the center of the group forming the western terminus of the entry axis sits the austere, dominant mass of Hill Memorial Library (fig. 4.26). The building's two-story eastern façade shows different expressions on its upper and lower floors. Across the entire façade at the second level run the full arched windows of the two great reading rooms. This is an expression derived most directly from the Boston Pub-

FIG. 4.26. Hill Memorial Library, designed by Link, in its original form, with larger arched windows indicating the great reading room on the upper floor. Office of the Chancellor Records, RG #A0001, Louisiana State University Archives, LSU Libraries, Baton Rouge, LA.

FIG. 4.27. Peabody Hall with its corner tower from across the open central space of the quadrangle as it appeared in the 1940s and 1950s. Courtesy of LSU University Relations, Public Affairs Photos.

FIG. 4.28. The Boston Public Library, by McKim, Mead & White, completed in 1898, showing the use of bilateral symmetry, hierarchy, and various architectural elements to articulate varying functions, such as the three arches for entry, the small windows of the ground-floor utilitarian and office functions, and high arched windows across the second floor indicating the great reading room. From Craven, *Monograph of McKim, Mead & White,* plate 100.

FIG. 4.29. Detail showing the corner of the Bibliothèque Sainte-Geneviève in Paris, by Henri Labrouste, completed in 1850. The great Louisiana-born Boston architect Henry Hobson Richardson worked for Labrouste while studying at the École des Beaux-Arts in Paris in the 1860s, and Charles McKim worked for Richardson in Boston after also attending the École des Beaux-Arts and before beginning his own successful firm in New York. Both American architects were trained in a tradition of mastering the adaptation of historical precedent in the creation of new designs. Wikimedia Commons.

lic Library, designed by Charles McKim and completed twenty-five years before Link's design for Hill (fig. 4.28).[19] In that magnificent building, one great room occupies the entire upper floor facing the public space of Boston's Copley Square. The building revolutionized library design in the United States and brought a high standard of historical eclecticism to American architecture. McKim had been trained at the École des Beaux-Arts in Paris. He was the third American to attend that prestigious institution.

While in Paris, McKim was exposed to the elegant architectural envelope of the Bibliothèque Sainte-Geneviève, designed by Henri Labrouste (fig. 4.29). Both this building and the Boston Public Library adapted the traditional Italian *piano nobile,* or noble living floor, of the villa for use in public buildings. The ground floor is treated as a kind of base supporting an apparently open colonnade on the upper floor containing the primary room of the structure. It is an expression that has a rich history in the architecture of the Italian Renaissance, with origins in the exterior of buildings such as the Tempio Malatestiano (known as San Francesco today) in Rimini, renovated by the architect and theoretician Leon Battista Alberti about 1450. The Boston Public Library is considered the first large urban free public library in the world, a place where anyone, regardless of class affiliation or personal wealth, could request a book to read in the public reading room. By using a building such as this as the model for the LSU Library, the architects could be seen as associating the institution with both the right of public access and the enlightened use of historical models. As we have seen, historical models inspired Link and were precedents for his LSU designs. The right of public access has become a hallmark of the Western liberal democracies formed in the wake of the Enlightenment.

At Memorial Tower the axis of entry draws one into and through the central octagonal, domed gallery. At Hill Memorial this axis terminates as it pulls the visitor directly into a vestibule and stair hall. From this point two large, symmetrical marble stairs invite one to climb up to a central lobby on the main floor, from which there is access to either of the two great general reading rooms, on the northern and southern sides. On the eastern side, above the entry vestibule, was a finely crafted manuscript room, now lost, with a vaulted plaster ceiling, the only one of its kind in Link's plan. Upon entering this room one walked through

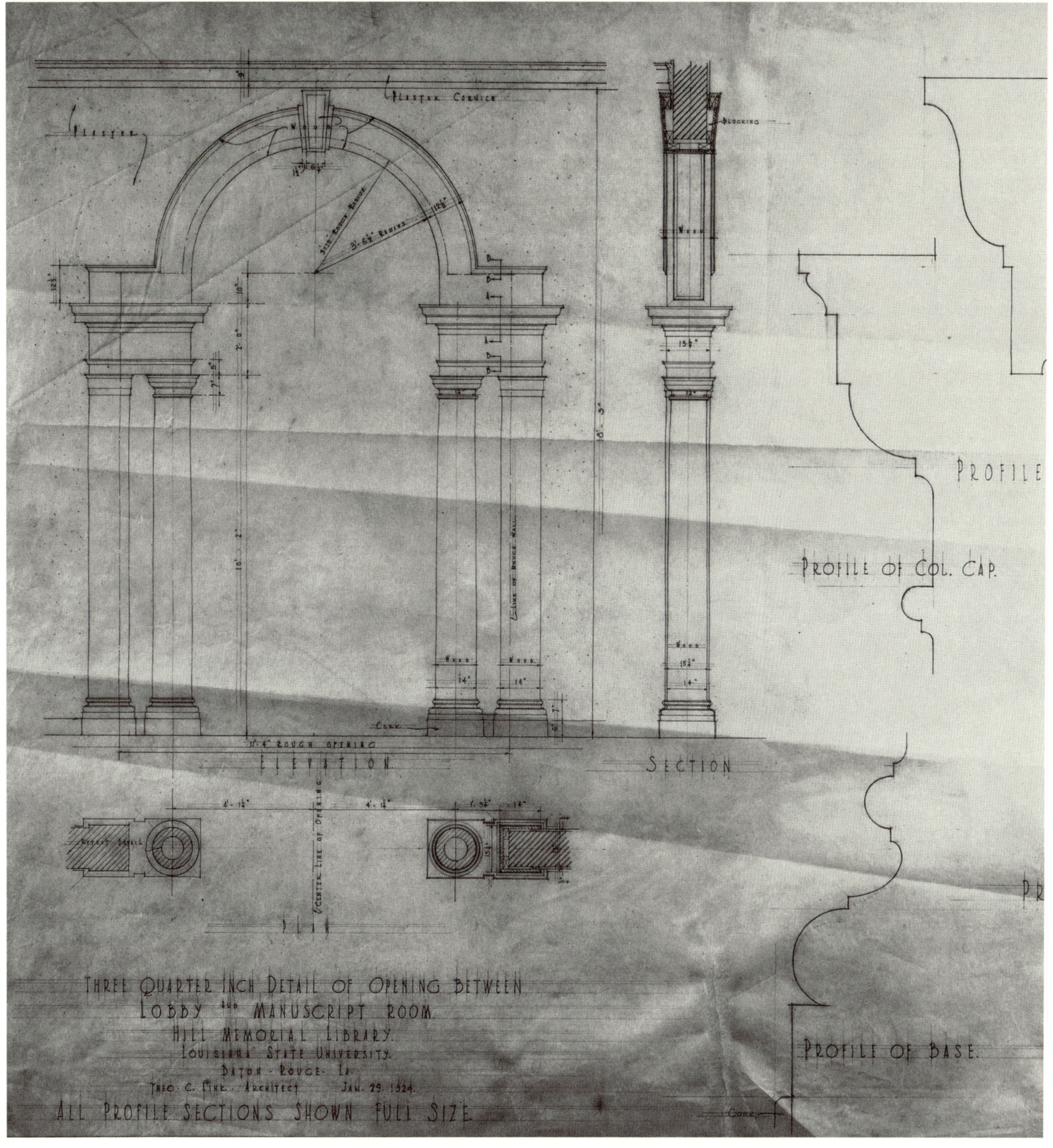

FIG. 4.30. Use of the "Palladian motif" by Link at the entry to Hill Memorial Library's now-lost Manuscript Room. The architectural device of flanking an arched opening in an otherwise solid wall with symmetrical lesser openings was adapted by Palladio from Roman examples, where it was a key component in triumphal gateways and other emblematic representations of the emperor and the empire. It appears many times on the LSU campus in the buildings designed by Link and later architects. Office of the President's Records, RG #A0001, Louisiana State University Archives, LSU Libraries, Baton Rouge, LA.

a version of the "Palladian motif" found at the beginning of the sequence on the Memorial Tower terrace, here executed in wood (fig. 4.30). Directly ahead, as one walked into this room intended to hold the university's most valuable library possessions, would be the form of Memorial Tower seen through the arched window at the center of the Library's main façade, offering a point of reflection.[20] It is as if this sequence of architectural forms says that at Memorial Tower you enter the public university, and in the Library you reach its highest function.[21]

The wide expanse of the great reading rooms in Hill Memorial complement the vertical emphasis of Memorial Tower, giving balance to the overall composition. The tower and the hall are two of the most fundamental archetypes in Western architecture. The hall is where people gather; the tower typically makes reference to that to which their gathering aspires. At a time when Louisiana had no state library or state archives, this building enabled the university to serve these roles, and consequently to be seen as the repository of knowledge for the state and its peoples.

CAFETERIA HALL

If the east-west axis of entry established a set of forms that relate the university and its mission to the people and institutions of the state, the other primary axis is a more internal one, relating to issues basic to the operation of the institution itself. These are represented most strongly by the two terminal buildings, Cafeteria Hall (Foster) and the Main Engineering Building (Atkinson), the flagship academic structure.

The Cafeteria was perhaps the most unique new campus structure (figs. 4.31–4.34). The building contained two large dining rooms, one on either side of a columned central hall. Kitchens and other service rooms were behind the dining rooms, on the northern side of the building, con-

FIG. 4.31. Cafeteria (now Foster) Hall, ca. 1925, just after its construction. Al Alleman Collection, Mss. 2877, Louisiana and Lower Mississippi Valley Collections, LSU Libraries, Baton Rouge, LA.

FIG. 4.32. Foster Hall in 1947, after the initial campus landscaping scheme had matured. Courtesy of LSU *Gumbo,* 1947.

FIG. 4.33. Side entry to Foster Hall. Courtesy of State Library of Louisiana.

FIG. 4.34. One of the two great two-story interior dining rooms in the Foster Hall cafeteria, showing the arched steel trusses and interior brick walls. Courtesy of LSU *Gumbo.*

nected to a sunken service drive. The dining rooms were spanned by a series of open, arched steel trusses supported by engaged brick piers along the side walls. The two front corners of the building step out in small pavilionlike structures that mark the entries just behind. Students would enter by either of these side doors, pick up a tray, and walk along a serving counter toward the center of the building, where drinks and cutlery were to be found, before moving into the dinning rooms themselves. On completion of their meal, they exited the building through the central arched opening along the main north-south axis of the campus.

This building and Atkinson Hall, at the other end of the axis, do not engage the adjacent structures to form larger compositional groups as do Hill Memorial and Memorial Tower. The Cafeteria itself is dominated by a central templelike face with its large, arched opening and circular window above. The body of the building, made up of two-story halls, is seen on the sides of this dominant central portion, with the two small, pavilionlike entry arcades at the corners.

The body of the Cafeteria resembles a traditional basilican hall, a form used extensively in early Christian and Roman architecture and among the oldest architectural forms in Western culture (fig 4.35). It is still utilized by most Western Christian churches, wherein one enters along the major axis of the building. The Romans used this building form in a perpendicular orientation, however, so that one entered into the large interior space through a small opening in what appears to us today to be a side wall. This Roman basilican form was also frequently used in conjunction with the open court of a forum and with a temple, as seen in the plans of Trajan's Forum in Rome and the Severan Basilica in the North African town of Lepcis Magna, to cite but two examples (see fig. 4.36). Re-creations of the design of the original, fourth-century basilica of St. Peter's in Rome indicate how that later complex continued the older Roman traditions by including a forecourt, or forum, as a part of the church's entry sequence (see fig. 4.37).

In providing this kind of design for the Cafeteria at the head of the major internal axis of the campus, Link appears to have collapsed these three architectural forms—the open court of the forum, the basilica, and the templelike façade—into a unique composition.[22] The open space of the quadrangle here, labeled "cloister" in his early drawings, serves in the place of a forum, as it did at St. Peter's and in

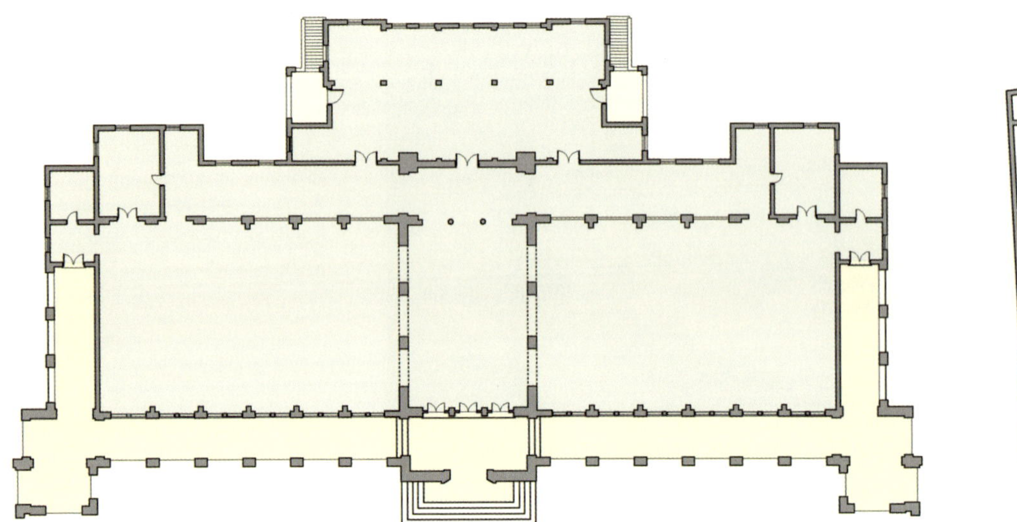

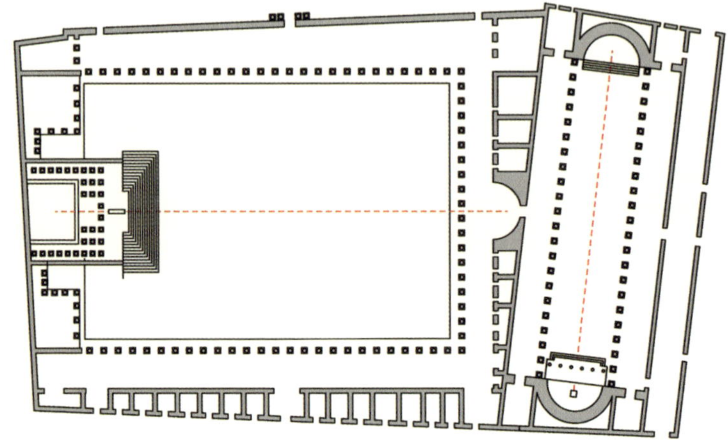

CLOCKWISE:

FIG. 4.35. Original floor-plan layout of Cafeteria (Foster) Hall, showing two large truss-roofed dining rooms, one on either side of a projecting central bay, with kitchens to the rear. Plan drawn by the author.

FIG. 4.36. Plan of the Severan Forum and Basilica, in the North African Roman town of Lepcis Magna, showing the typical ancient sequence of a basilican hall at right angles to the main axis of the forum and its temple. Link appears to have based his design of Cafeteria Hall and its relationship to the arcaded cloisters, or quadrangles, on this historical form. Plan drawn by the author.

FIG. 4.37. Reconstruction of the original fourth-century St. Peter's Cathedral in Rome, showing its use of a Roman forum coupled with a rotated basilica. The cathedral was demolished in the sixteenth century to make way for the current structure. Plan drawn by the author, adapted from Kenneth Conant, *Carolingian and Romanesque Architecture.*

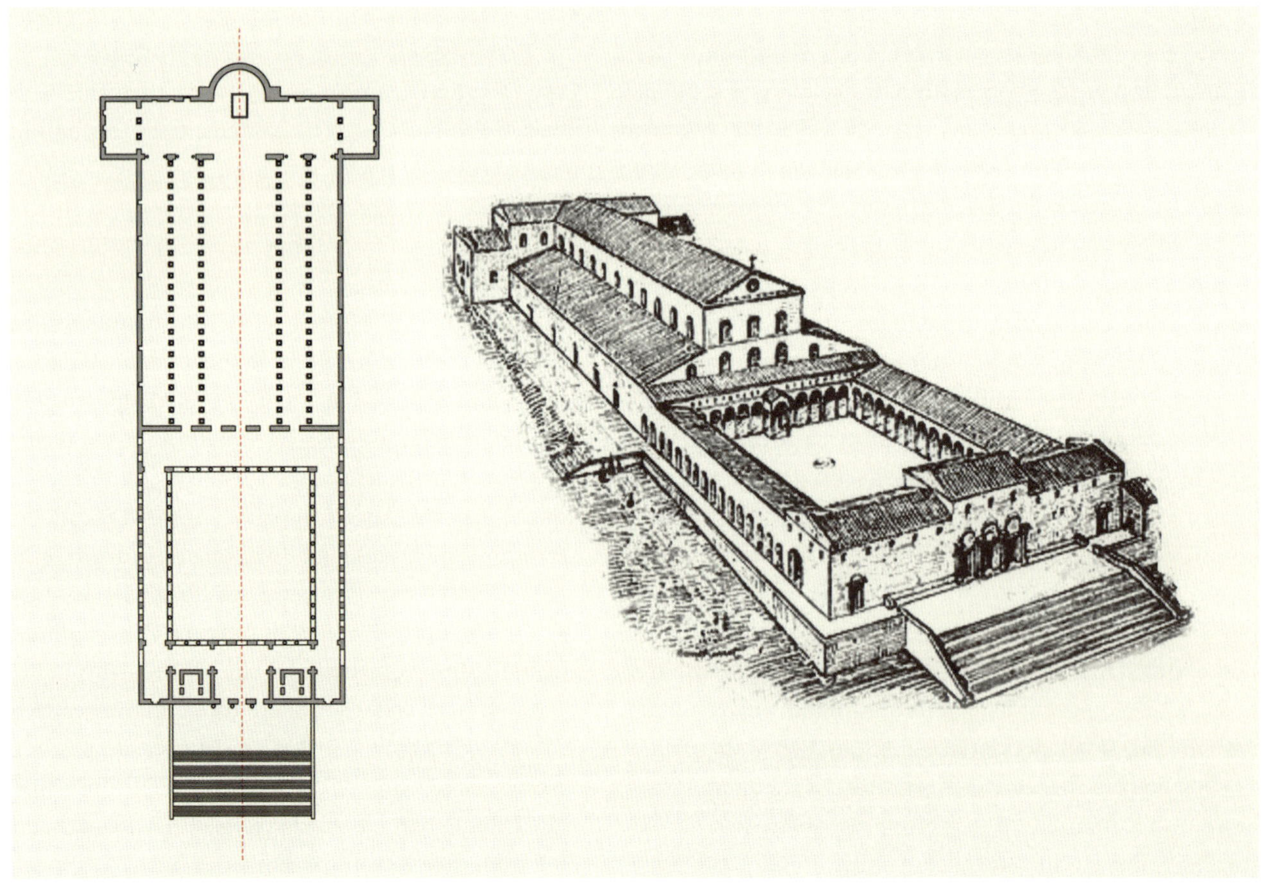

such medieval monasteries as that of St. Gall in Switzerland, for example, where one can see a similar arrangement of forum and basilica at the origins of the cloister tradition.

The templelike façade that the Cafeteria projects is the most striking in the entire campus design. Its vertical mass is composed of an arched doorway, flowing steps, and a simply indicated elegant roof protecting one from the sun and rain. Occupying the center of the building at the head of the campus plan is the large oculus; as the most prominent circle to appear in the architecture of Link's campus, it takes on a significant symbolism. The circle is a common architectural symbol in cultures around the world, typically taken to represent the embracing whole. The single arched opening at the center of the building's façade strikes a tone meant to resonate down the length of the Main Quadrangle (see fig. 4.32).

To the sides of this powerful frontal form are the campus arcades. By placing these arcades here, as the only ones incorporated into one of the four primary architectural figures at the ends of the two primary axes, the architect created a symbol of informality and repose associated with the idea of individual students gathering before and after meals to socialize. The presence of benches in these openings furthers this effect. From this building the arcaded passageways seem to flow outward and around the campus, embracing, guiding, and sheltering students through their academic days, furthering the effect of unity in the composition and in the student experience.

THE MAIN ENGINEERING BUILDING

At the opposite end of this north-south internal axis lies the Main Engineering Building, now Atkinson Hall (fig. 4.38).[23] Like that of the Cafeteria, the quadrangle façade of this building is divided into five sections, dominated by its central portion. The central portion of this building is more complex than that of the Cafeteria, however. It recalls the double groupings of Tuscan columns on Memorial Tower. On the second-story balcony, three arches supported on paired smaller columns bring a degree of refinement to the façade. This open central portion is flanked by walls containing four faculty-office windows that are richly framed with cast stone surrounds, projected grilles, and ornamental light fixtures.[24] The body of the building can be seen behind this central portico with the regular rhythm of windows marching off to either side. The façade is composed largely of these steady, even rows of windows, articulating the role of the classrooms in the dialogue of forms describing campus activity. These windows are regularly spaced and repetitively organized, not unlike the arrangement of student desks in the classrooms within. This is the only one of the four terminal buildings in which the façade facing the quadrangle features the regularity of classroom windows or clearly articulated faculty offices.

The central balcony opens off of an interior lobby with two sets of stairs symmetrically placed, as in Hill Memorial Library. These bring the student up to faculty offices and out onto the balcony with its spectacular second-floor view back down the axis to the single large arch of the Cafeteria in the distance. The Cafeteria, Hill Memorial Library, and the Main Engineering Building are the flagship academic buildings. Each has an interior spatial sequence that encourages the user to move inside before being turned around to face the larger axial composition on the exterior. Each of these buildings accomplishes this differently. In the Engineering Building, the central entry brings one into the heart of the building to a secondary axis expressed by the central hallway running the length of the building. The tripartite body of the Main Engineering Building is re-expressed in its central opening with a loggia and a colonnaded balcony.

Like the façades of all the other buildings in Link's design, that of the Main Engineering Building is a model of symmetrical, neoclassical composition. The central mass is framed by wings that are terminated by smaller units. Inherited from Rome, this centering technique was devel-

FIG. 4.38. The Main Engineering Building, now known as Atkinson Hall, at the southern end of the Main Quadrangle, as it appeared soon after completion in 1926. Like the other major buildings in Link's design for the campus, it utilizes bilateral symmetry, hierarchy, and a variety of architectural elements. Office of the Chancellor Records, RG #A0001, Louisiana State University Archives, LSU Libraries, Baton Rouge, LA.

oped most spectacularly in the sixteenth century by Palladio in the series of villas in the Veneto mentioned above. As compositions, these villas are frequently composed of arms of complementary architectural units, suggesting both the various activities of the estate and the unity of the entire concept. They represent, among other things, some of the first attempts to unify landscapes and architectural compositions around a working institutional form, in their case a working farm. This is another way in which Palladio's villas offer a precedent for A&M colleges such as LSU (see figs. 4.13 and 4.39).

The overall design of Palladio's villas typically developed along two perpendicular axes. In some cases, the approach leads up to the villa through the estate before continuing behind through an enclosed exedra and grotto, which take the composition from the far vista up to the *piano nobile.* Complementing this axis, the villas frequently extend outward at right angles to various smaller structures in a symmetrical embrace of the landscape and the processes of its working—wholes upon wholes upon wholes. The Main Engineering Building also follows this formal pattern of expansion from a central mass. Unlike the Palladian villas, however, it does so within the frame of the South Quadrangle. This is because Link's composition is an internally focused one. Palladio's villas opened outward to engage and dominate their landscapes. Although the façade here suggests openness and embracement through scale and reference to its precedent, its presence is projected, not outward across a landscape, but forward down the quadrangle to the Cafeteria in the distance. The central mass is wide enough to take an authoritative stance. It is a complex and detailed complement to the Cafeteria's narrow, direct, vertical massing with large-scale elements. Whereas the Tower and the Library address broad themes, the Cafeteria and the Main Engineering Building address the inner workings of a university.

A further nobility is added to the Main Engineering Building by the two small, pavilionlike projecting ends. This Palladian gesture helps the building to comfortably dominate the end of this 1,000-foot axis. As the culmination of this series of major campus buildings, the Main Engineering Building presents a more complex face. It also has a small campanile of its own atop the central portion of the building. This is a cubic mass topped by an even smaller mass that is penetrated by arches in each of the four cardinal directions and crowned by a small dome with a short spire and ball. Here at the end of the sequence of primary architectural forms on Link's campus plan, this cupolalike top recalls the form of Memorial Tower and makes a reference to the vertical dimension. It is a Renaissance symbol of wholeness or completion that runs through a series of forms, from square to circle and sphere held up to the sky. All around the campus, looking upward one sees circles: the face of the clock and dome of the Campanile, the colored roundels of the flanking buildings, the large round window of the Cafeteria, the small circles on the four corner pavilions marking the crossing of the primary axes, and finally this small sphere held aloft.

Many of the details of the design and construction process are still unknown. For example, the construction draw-

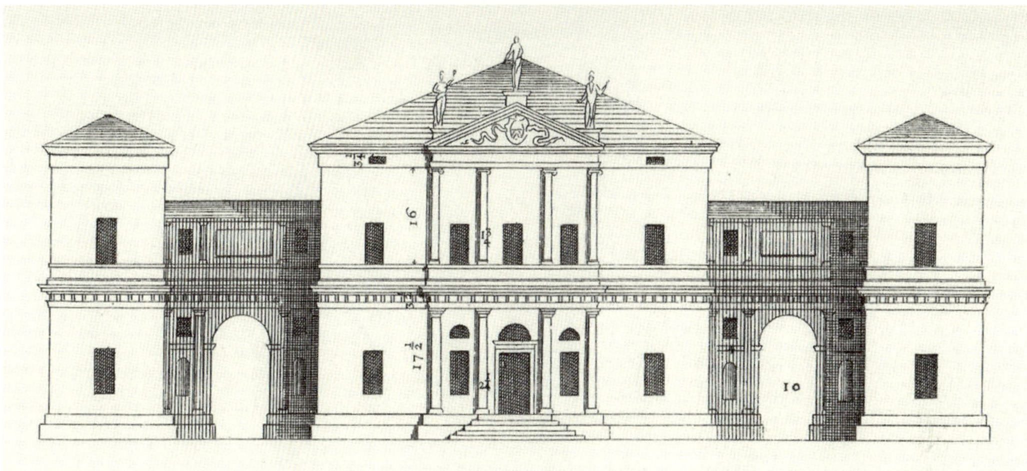

FIG. 4.39. Design of the Villa Pisani from Andrea Palladio's *Four Books of Architecture,* showing a use of architectural elements and compositional strategies similar to those used by Link at LSU.

ings for this building do not show it elevated by its grand, expressive front steps. At some point after the drawings were finished but before construction began, the decision was made to raise the building some 3 to 4 feet. The front and smaller rear stairs were added, and the interior hallway was given sets of stairs just inside the end doors. As is characteristic of Link's campus design, each of these was handled differently, and each was expressive of the status and location of the element. In the case of the Main Engineering Building, the front was given an almost monumental stair. It floods outward and recalls the steps of the Tower and Library terraces. Just inside the front door, one finds a lobby with the side stairways leading to the second floor. Straight ahead are three short steps giving onto the central hall through a series of three arched openings. This entire central section of the building, from the lobby through to the central portion of the hallway, is floored in marble. The hallways leading off in either direction are floored with terra-cotta tiles. The side entryways bring the visitor directly into the building at the level of the connecting arcades; it is only inside that the steps are encountered.

The compositional scheme of the Main Engineering Building and those of all of the buildings of the plan have roots in deeper aspects of Western culture. Like any good expression of the planning order of the Western neoclassical traditions, this building has an opening at the center of its main face. The main floor of this building is raised well above the ground. As in other buildings on the original campus master plan, this feature accommodates a utilitarian basement level beneath the main floor. This detail reflects the construction techniques of an earlier era, raising the main floor structure above the reach of groundwater. It also encourages the viewer to see the first floor as the *piano nobile.* If one looks around the southeastern corner of the Agricultural Administration Building just to the west of Atkinson, one will see a break in the side brickwork about four feet from the ground, where the plane of the wall steps back slightly. This feature can also be seen clearly at the rear of the building.

This expression of a base, which architects such as Palladio inherited from Roman and Greek sources, plays a subtle but important role in the overall language of campus buildings. It clearly indicates that the main floor is raised above the ground. The three-step stylobate of a Greek temple situated the building form as a representation of the activities it housed in proper relationship to the earth and the sky. Stepping up into such a temple, one leaves the ground, the everyday, and moves toward the religious. The Romans framed this effect within a more narrowly defined context by means of axes. This simple lifting device, one of the oldest and most fundamental in traditional Western architecture, is meant to ennoble the activities inside the building by disengaging them from the specifics of the everyday environment outside. By contrast, the utilitarian Mechanical & Civil Engineering Laboratory and the Engineering Shops, which complete the Engineering Quadrangle in Link's General Plan, were not given this ennobling feature. Another indication of their lower status is that they were built of exposed brick rather than the unique stucco finish of the main campus buildings.

FIG. 4.40. The main north-south axis of Link's original campus design, showing the view of Foster Hall from the balcony of the Main Engineering Building (now Atkinson Hall) in the early 1950s. LSU University Relations, photograph by Elemore Morgan.

In addition to its raised *piano nobile,* the design of the Main Engineering Building builds upon another ancient architectural commonplace in an even more fundamental way. Any Greek or Roman temple expresses its ontological status by providing a space for human activity protected from the unpredictability of the natural world. The protective character of this central open place is articulated through symmetry, with architectural devices on either side. A consequence of this is that any good neoclassical building has at its center an open space surrounded by solid elements expressed in a symmetrical form. This idea is expressed in the temple façade of four or six columns. How often does one find a temple with five or seven columns along the front, an arrangement in which the center is blocked? This rhythm of element-space-element separates, binds, and protects a place for human activity. The architectural commonplaces of a stylobate and pediment act similarly in the vertical dimension. Recall the effective simplicity of the indication of a pediment and the wide, floating steps of the Cafeteria Hall façade. These are the minimum elements needed to provide a whole or complete image in this style.

The exterior loggia and balcony on the northern façade of the Main Engineering Building lead to an open space in the middle of the building. A central framed hallway inside is accessed after passing through an internal loggia. This open space is located at the crossing of the major north-south axis of the campus with an interior hallway, one of several minor axes in the campus plan. At both sides of the central upper balcony are faculty offices articulated by singularly framed windows. To access these offices, a student must step outside of the second-floor lobby onto the balcony. They must come into contact with, and indeed move along, this major axis of the campus composition.[25] From here one sees the figure of Foster Hall in the distance, but now in its proper attitude and scale. This bringing a student out of the building and into contact with a distant image while on the way to a faculty member's office is a symbolic gesture of some beauty, suggesting that one can use the university's resources to find oneself and one's role in life (fig. 4.40).

THE AGRICULTURE GROUP

The secondary buildings making up the west side of the South Quadrangle in Link's campus design are the Language, Home Economics, Animal Industry, and Biology Buildings, the Ag Auditorium, and the Forestry & Horticulture Building (Allen Hall, Prescott Hall, Stubbs Hall, Dodson Auditorium, Audubon Hall, and the Agricultural Administration Building today). Prescott, Stubbs, and Audubon, together with Dodson Auditorium, were conceived and executed as a group, referred to as the "Agricultural Group" (see fig. 4.41). Although the group is composed of symmetrical building units, together they form a delightfully asymmetrical grouping that provides a clever counterpoint to the formal symmetries used at the axis ends (fig. 4.42). The halls along this side of the South Quadrangle are rather typical two-story classroom structures, with each floor composed of a central corridor with classrooms, offices, and other service rooms on either side. This simple arrangement provided the rooms with ample natural light and ventilation. The eastern end of each of these buildings was designed with a turned massing profile facing the South Quadrangle. The buildings are several feet wider at this end and yet have a simple, single roof slope toward the quadrangle.

The Animal Industry and Biology Buildings (Stubbs and Audubon Halls) were linked by the original Ag Auditorium (Dodson Hall). Dodson is a semicircular building hidden from the quadrangle behind an ornamental fountain. These structures, the classroom buildings, the auditorium, and the fountain were also conceived as a single design unit. Two of the classroom buildings repeat the motif of paired Tuscan columns on either side of a central entry. In contrast to the use of these columns as a traditional entry portico on the Tower and the Main Engineering Building, here the open space of the campus arcade continues behind the front face of the buildings. The openings between and alongside these paired columns provide a repetition of solid to void in the rhythm of the arcades. The front doors of the buildings, on the ground floor, are held to the back of this arcaded passageway. On the second floor, the interior rooms are pulled all the way out to the face in a more normal manner. These buildings are adorned by small pediments at the center and ornamental panels at each side; the circular motif is repeated on the second floor.

The quadrangle face of the Home Economics Building (Prescott), although the same size as the other buildings in this group, was treated differently. Here the façade is understood as one single plane with a set of three arched openings at the center. On the second floor, there is a central arched window flanked by two smaller rectangular ones. Together, these three windows are gently reminiscent of the Palladian motif found elsewhere on campus. As on the other buildings, the arcade continues behind the ground-floor face, repeating the rhythm of solid to void. Two metal grilles on the ground floor give the building added distinction. The architect's goal seems to have been to continue a recognizable pattern of familiar forms and to provide variations for interest and identity, as is the case with the buildings along the Lawn at Jefferson's University of Virginia.[26]

FIG. 4.41. The rhythmic façades of the Agriculture Group, along the western side of the Main Quadrangle, in 1932, before the live oaks were added to the landscape, showing Prescott, Stubbs, and Audubon Halls. Courtesy of LSU *Gumbo,* 1932.

Along this eastward-facing group, the fountain in front of the Ag Auditorium and between the Animal Industry and Biology Buildings (Stubbs and Audubon) forms a unique composition that is perhaps the most florid baroque element in Link's campus design.[27] A broken curved pediment and a semicircular niche, along with the variety of stucco and stone finishes, give this fountain a touch of elegance, providing a contrast to the restraint of the buildings around it. The western ends of these buildings, facing away from the quadrangle, line up with similar imposing, massing pro-

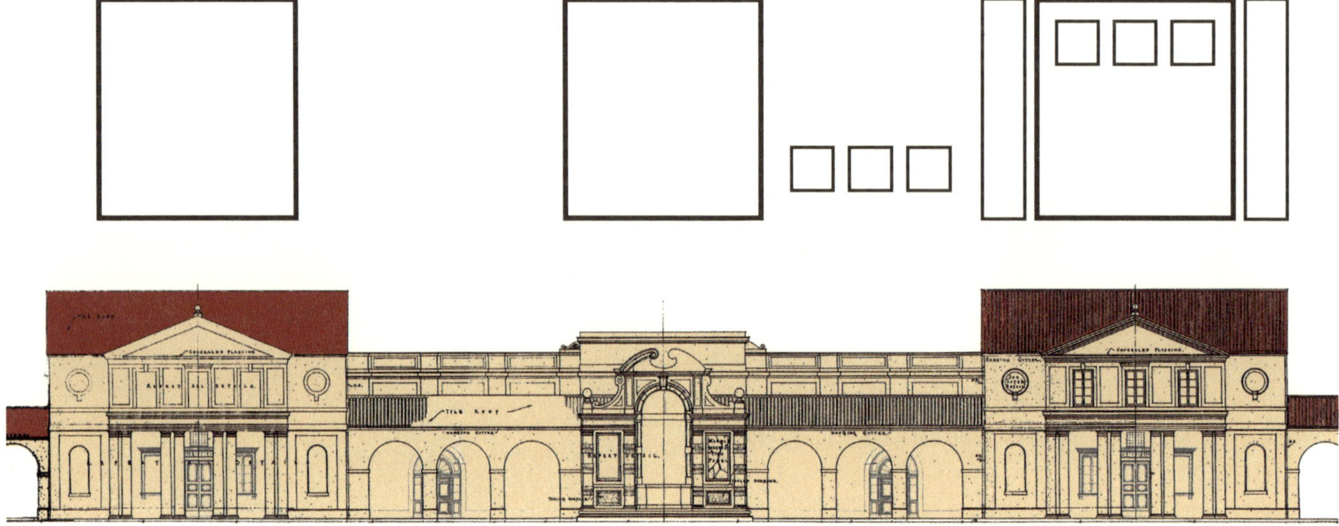

FIG. 4.42. East-facing quadrangle elevations of the Agriculture Group by Link, showing the use of rhythm and repetition to tie the different buildings into one overall composition. By Michael Roper and Anthony Threatt after Theodore Link, with overlay by the author.

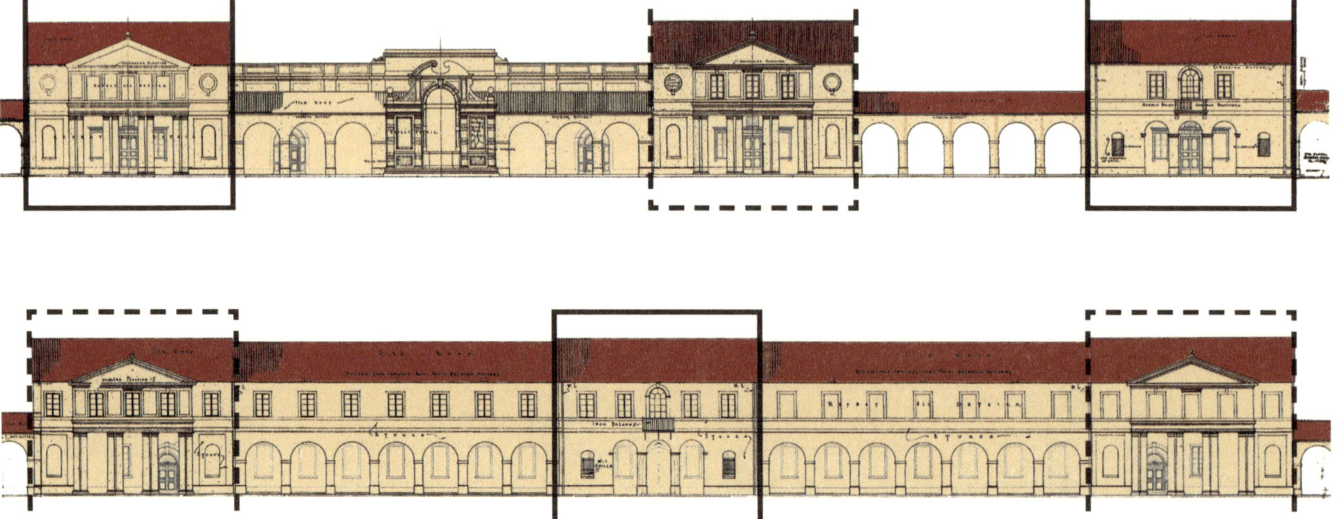

FIG. 4.43. Comparison of the Agricultural Group, on the western side of the Main Quadrangle, with the Chemistry Group, Coates Hall, on the eastern side in terms of repetition of element. By Michael Roper and Anthony Threatt after Theodore Link, with overlay by the author.

files that were visible from the fields below the bluff toward the river when the buildings were constructed.

THE CHEMISTRY GROUP

On the opposite side of the South Quadrangle are Boyd Memorial Alumni Hall, the Chemistry Laboratory, and the Physics Building (Himes, Coates, and Nicholson Halls). The center of this eastern side was originally known as the Chemistry Group, with the central building larger than the flanking buildings. As with the Ag Group across the quadrangle, this building was designed to look like three separate buildings joined together. The primary difference, however, is that the Chemistry Group is actually one large, single structure rather than three separate masses. This building is essentially one body that runs along the quadrangle; it contains a large central portion that extends back to the east. These differences in massing reflect the internal arrangements for needed space in both cases. Whereas the Ag Group can be seen as three separate structures connected in various ways, the Chemistry Group is one building divided on its face to give the appearance of three buildings connected by arcades. Like the Ag Group, the Chemistry Group has three protruding building façades. The two on the ends are very similar in composition to those of the Biology and Animal Industry Buildings on the other side. The central apparent building face is similar to that of the Home Economics Building (Prescott) across the quadrangle. The rhythms here can be expressed as the symmetrical A-B-A, compared with the syncopated A-c-A-B of the buildings opposite (see fig. 4.43).

This repetition of similar elements furthers the conception of the campus as a set of harmonically repeating buildings and architectural elements with local variations to meet functional requirements. The Ag and Chemistry Groups have the same overall width. The three protruding façades on the Chemistry Building are located so as to compose a clearly ordered set, with a unique façade in the center and two flanking ones matching each other. This is not the case with the Ag Group, directly across the quad, where the distance between the buildings varies. This arrangement is such that the differences between the internal compositions of the Ag and Chemistry Groups create a sense of variety within unity. While the façades repeat across the quadrangle, they do not do so methodically; there are subtle variations from one side to the other. In the Chemistry Group, the arcade runs along the entire length of the ground floor, again creating an alternating pattern of solid to void. The arcades running through the façades tie the buildings together in an ensemble. Their façades are composed of variations on the architectural elements found throughout the campus plan. By keeping the pedimented pavilion fronts to the ends, the design avoids creating too strong a centerpiece. Rather, the arcades mark the length of the quadrangle (figs. 4.44 and 4.45).

A very interesting unbuilt alternative design for the eastern façade of the Chemistry Group appears to be the closest thing to a direct quotation from a Palladian design that we have. Link intended the central portion of the eastern face of the Chemistry Building to be given a face similar to that used by Palladio in his Villa Saraceno, near Vicenza (see figs. 4.14 and 4.15).

ALLEN AND HIMES HALLS

Link's design for the campus called for four buildings to occupy the corner, or crossing, positions. Each of these was intended to hold the corners by means of a small pavilion, as was seen in the design for Peabody Hall. The second and third of these structures were built as Allen and Himes Halls, both completed by WDS. The open second-story porch of Peabody was not repeated in the design of these two buildings. In the design of Allen Hall, the first of the two to be built, the image of this porch was maintained on the northern façade. Small second-story columns in the form of engaged pilasters were included. Today, after the

FIG. 4.44. A mid 1920s view of the Main Quadrangle from Memorial Tower before the live oaks were planted, showing the Sugar House in the distance. Jasper Ewing & Sons Photograph Files, Mss. 3141, Louisiana and Lower Mississippi Valley Collections, LSU Libraries, Baton Rouge, LA.

FIG. 4.45. The expanse of the Main Quadrangle from the Chemistry Group, with Peabody and Foster Halls in the distance, 1927. Courtesy of LSU *Gumbo,* 1927.

enclosure of the porch on the southern façade of Peabody, these two facing elevations have a similar appearance. In the design of Himes Hall these façade details were omitted entirely. The corner-pavilion designs are essentially the same on these three buildings, providing some of the uniformity they were originally conceived to offer. For some reason, Himes Hall was placed some ten feet farther south than Allen, which put their corner pavilions out of alignment. Another effect of this misplacement is the narrow, single-archway passage between Himes and the Chemistry Group to its south. This contrasts with the two arches separating Allen and the Ag Group. The 1928 plan shows that these passageways were originally intended to be the same.

The fourth of these corner buildings was built in the 1950s as the Thomas Boyd Annex. Both the design and the position of this building were compromised; while it was built with a weakened version of the corner tower, it does not hold the corner in the way it was intended to do. It steps back to the north from the face of the Tower group and to the west, so that its corner pavilion does not line up with those of Peabody and Himes Halls.

NICHOLSON HALL AND THE AGRICULTURAL ADMINISTRATION BUILDING

The southernmost buildings on the sides of the South Quadrangle are the Forestry and Horticulture Building (Agricultural Administration) on the western side and the Physics Building (Nicholson) opposite. These two buildings were designed and executed by WDS after Link's death. The location and general massing of the buildings was set by Link's General Plan, but the specific design of these two structures is the work of WDS. They have many of the same details and surface materials as Link's buildings. The ends facing the quadrangle are slightly larger both horizontally and vertically than the adjacent Link designs. The second-floor offices are pulled to the face, and the arcade continues on the ground floor. They appear as terminating buildings and were given unique ornamental details and more grillwork than the others along the quadrangle sides. The architectural expression of these two buildings also differs from that of the other buildings lining the sides of the South Quadrangle in having a higher base and more steps on the entry façade (see fig. 5.26).

THE ENGINEERING GROUP

The only other buildings from the Link General Plan that were executed are those forming what was sometimes referred to as the Engineering Group.[28] Along with the Main Engineering Building (Atkinson Hall), this group includes buildings initially intended to serve as a Mechanical and Civil Engineering Laboratory, the Engineering Shops, a Future Engineering Extension, and a southern "future extension" to the Main Engineering Building, which was not built. By the time the Wogan & Bernard campus plan was made, ca. 1928, these had been designated as a Steam and Hydraulic Engineering Laboratory (today the School of Art) and an Electrical Engineering Building (Howe-Russell-Kniffen Geoscience West). The Engineering Shops remained the same. In both versions this was an interconnected group of structures dedicated to the study and practice of engineering and its applications, complementing the campus resources dedicated to chemistry and to the agricultural sciences.

The South Quadrangle, in contrast, was clearly intended to be a state-of-the-art center for the study of agriculture, chemistry, and engineering. Drawings prepared by Link established a precedent for the Engineering Shops and the adjacent Laboratory building. These two structures are faced with a common red brick, not the more expensive Earley stucco. Both have a symmetrical design centered on secondary axes within the overall complex, as well as small amounts of carved stone ornamentation. In these ways they seem to express a more utilitarian usage than do the finely detailed buildings defining the major quadrangles.

THE RICHNESS OF THE OVERALL PLAN ORGANIZATION

A further example of the thoroughness of Theodore Link's original plans for the core of the campus is the original treatment of the exterior doors. The plans for the various buildings designed by Link specify a great number of door types. While Link conceived of the plan and the profile of the buildings surrounding the North and South Quadrangles and personally oversaw the drawings for many of them, not all of the core buildings had been completed when he died. The New Orleans firm of Wogan & Bernard eventually took over as the campus architects. Wogan & Bernard's development of details and drawings for Link's buildings deviated from those he had completed, almost always simplifying formal relationships and eliminating detail. Neither that firm nor later architects appear to have fully understood Link's overall concept and its intricacies. The design of exterior doors is a case in point. There is a great diversity of originally built exterior door designs among the buildings lining the quadrangles today. These include the bronze gates to Memorial Tower, the original 10-foot-high front doors to Hill Memorial Library, the glazed doors of Cafeteria Hall, the ensembles of doors and sidelights for the buildings in the Ag and Chemistry Groups, the almost 10-foot-high front door to Atkinson Hall, and many others.

This range of door types was initially baffling, but the historic-preservation study of the LSU campus conducted in 2006 enabled us to understand much more about Link's thoroughness as a designer and the ways in which he uti-

FIG. 4.46. Overall view of Theodore Link's design for the campus core as it would appear today without the intrusion of Middleton Library blocking the architectural and spatial relationships. Courtesy of Professor Van Cox, FASLA, LSU Robert Reich School of Landscape Architecture.

lized the formal attributes of architectural massing, ornamentation, color, and detail to provide emphasis at different levels in the overall composition. Putting all of these different door types in their places on a campus plan allowed us to see that indeed they formed an important part of his design strategy. They helped to establish a sense of hierarchical order among the many various buildings, while giving each a sense of uniqueness. The most ceremonial doors are the bronze gates to the dedication room at Memorial Tower. The second most imposing are the original doors to Hill Memorial Library, the next building in the hierarchy. Cafeteria Hall exhibits three sets of glazed doors, emphasizing the openness and accessibility of the cafeteria as the center of student life and facilitating the building's more intense daily use. A thousand feet away, the Main Engineering Building also has a very imposing front door, almost 10 feet high with an overhead fanlight, scaled to fit in with its imposing façade, while the balcony door just above it does not have a fanlight.[29]

REFLECTIONS ON A MESSAGE

The LSU campus as designed by Theodore Link was dedicated on April 30, 1926. While all of the buildings surrounding the central quadrangles would not be completed for another thirty years, the defining structure and the crucial elements were all in place. The great sweep of the Parade Ground, the broad, inviting entry terrace, the east-west and north-south axes, the cruciform northern and southern quadrangles, and the four significant buildings acted as anchors. Each of the four buildings that acted as ends of this grand composition was given an architectural form symbolizing one of the main aspects of the university (fig. 4.46). Foster Hall, the original Cafeteria, with its places for casual gathering, represents the social side of campus life. At the opposite end of the long internal axis, the Engineering Building represents the purpose and accomplishments of the academy. Presiding as it does over the circular sweep of the present-day Parade Ground, the Soldiers and Sailors Memorial Tower raises itself to the sky, to nature, and to the authority of a higher purpose. Hill Memorial Library completes the quartet, as the muses of knowledge are called upon to complement the appeal of Memorial Tower and the great open sweep of the Parade Ground to the sky. Student life (Cafeteria Hall) and the rigor of academics (Main Engineering), knowledge (the Library) and heavenly inspiration are all evoked. Further, the North, or "Fine Arts," Quadrangle, with its Library and gestures of openness to the people of the state, describes the critical function of what we have come to call the liberal arts—history, literature, the social sciences, and the fine arts. In contrast, the South Quadrangle is defined by the natural sciences—biology, chemistry, agriculture, forestry, and horticulture. LSU is one of a number of state and A&M colleges around the country that arose in the nineteenth century with the aim of applying science to agricultural production. In the progression developed in the Link plan, these academic disciplines follow and enrich those of the North Quadrangle.[30] At the end of the progression lie the Main Engineering Building and a smaller group of associated laboratories and shops, as if to suggest that these disciplines provide a way for the knowledge produced in the university to be adapted and applied to the needs of the people of the state.

5

Growth beyond the Core

It was desired that these buildings should be an intuitive course in architecture for the students, and that they should take home improved standards in architecture to be reflected in the architecture of the state when these young people in turn began to build. That this hope might be well founded, simplicity permitting intimacy, encouraging emulation and making the buildings a part of the life of the people, was preserved.

—JOHN JOSEPH EARLEY, "Architectural Concrete"

The history of the current LSU campus in Baton Rouge has been layered with intention and possibility. It began at a time when large parcels of good outlying lands were still available near the growing state capital, lands enough to provide a prominent site with ample room for the agricultural experimentation central to the university's mission. The vision and sensitivity of Rick Olmsted raised the prospect of the new university well above the ordinary. Indeed, his Preliminary Plan would have put LSU among the finest architectural, planning, and landscape projects in the nation. Not hiring Olmsted Brothers to continue full services was an undeniable loss for the state, given the quality of the built environments that the firm did carry through to completion in other places.[1] Olmsted Brothers' plan was broad in scope yet attentive to detail. It skillfully and persuasively integrated the various aspects of the university into the existing landscape. In this way it was as visionary as that of any American university in existence.

The campus plan as adapted by Theodore Link is more insular and self-referential, ignoring the better parts of the site in small detail (the mounds and the magnolias) and in large (the vista to the Mississippi River). Nevertheless, it has much to recommend it. Link's consummate skill as an architect is nowhere more evident. He was prepared by a first-rate technical education, had decades of experience in architecture and management, and had performed a singular role in helping an adjacent state expand and modernize its own university system. His choice of Italian Renaissance architecture for LSU gave him an opportunity to address the local, or southern, connections to mission style while drawing on the history, range, and details of the broadest and deepest reservoir of architectural form in Western culture. It was a choice implemented with great attention to both concept and detail (fig. 5.1). There was nothing like it in the South at the time, really nothing anywhere. The people of Louisiana could hardly have asked for more.[2]

The singular flaw of Theodore Link's plan, in hindsight, has to do with the difficulty of expansion. As a closed quadrangular system of cloistered greens with terminal buildings, it did not suggest an obvious method of growth, a typical problem with this kind of closed-end plan. But then, in 1922 no one dared think that this college for fifteen hundred students would one day serve twenty times that number. Although this may have eventually been the case with the Olmsted plan as well, its variety of differently defined quadrangles may have provided a glimpse of a solution to growth.

The campus that Link designed was pedestrian oriented, whereas today the automobile has become a more dominant and necessary aspect of planning. Today, eighty years later, as one drives through the center of LSU along Louisiana State Highway 42, better known as Highland Road, one encounters an idyllic landscape marked by live oaks, broad lawns, and notably uniform buildings. The dark and light greens of the oaks and grasses contrast beautifully with the terra cotta and pebbly stucco of the red tile roofs and building façades (fig. 5.2). Link's Soldiers and Sailors Memorial Tower is centrally located and framed by a broader campus environment, itself demarcated from the everyday world by noble campus gateway pylons (fig. 5.3). Yet this vision of the broader campus experience was not entirely the result of either the Link or the Olmsted plan. It emerged during the 1930s, chiefly under the stewardship of the New Orleans architectural firm of Weiss, Dreyfous & Seiferth and the Avery Island landscape service of E. A. McIlhenny, with many other hands contributing (fig. 5.4).

The Highland Road corridor and the spacious campus vision it presents evolved between the opening of the new campus in 1926 and the beginning of the Second World War. Although during much of this time the nation suffered through the Great Depression, the impact of state investment spearheaded by the newly elected governor Huey Long and various federal public-works projects begun under Roosevelt's New Deal made this one of the most definitive periods in the development of the campus. Long, elected in 1928, arranged a creative mechanism whereby the state "bought" the downtown campus site and its existing buildings from the university for the development of a new State Capitol complex, providing LSU with funds for a major building program.[3] These and other state funds financed the construction of Smith Hall (1931, now Pleasant Hall), a Fine Arts Building (1931, Music & Dramatic Arts), Dalrymple Hall, a Home Economics training cottage, the Huey Long Field House and Pool (1931), a graduate women's dormitory (1935), Highland Hall (1935), Annie Boyd Hall (1936), the Formal Gardens at the Greek Theater (1938), a new men's dormitory north of the Pentagon

FIG. 5.1. Memorial Tower and the Administration entry group from the Parade Ground in the late 1920s. LSU Photograph Collection, RG #A5000, Louisiana State University Archives, LSU Libraries, Baton Rouge, LA.

FIG. 5.2. The Parade Ground today. Courtesy of Jim Zietz, LSU University Relations.

FIG. 5.3. The entrance gates at Highland Road and Chimes Street soon after they were built in the mid-1930s, marking the boundary of the campus environment and continuing the architectural language selected for the initial design of the core. LSU *Gumbo*, 1940, Courtesy of Special Collections, LSU Libraries, Louisiana State University, Baton Rouge, LA.

complex (1934), a Hospital where Broussard Hall now stands, the men's dormitories under the Stadium grandstands (1932), Leche Hall (1937, now the Old Law School), the French House (1935), and the Pan American House (1941, now Acadian House).

The other major contributor to the campus building boom of the 1930s was the federal government through its series of Depression-era agencies: the Public Works Administration, or PWA (1933–41); the Works Progress Administration, or WPA (1935–43); and the Civil Works Administration, or CWA (1933–34). Buildings funded by these agencies began to complete Link's quadrangles and filled out the Highland Road corridor during this decade. These included Evangeline Hall (1936), Grace King and Louise Garig Halls (1937), Parker Coliseum (1937), the Faculty Club (1938), the Geology Building (1938), the Commerce Building (1939, now Himes Hall), the Physics & Math Building (1937, now Nicholson Hall), new dorm rooms enclosing the northern end of Tiger Stadium (1936–37), Alex Box Stadium (1937–38), the Panhellion, or Panhellenic Building (1938), a new Infirmary (1937?), and the Forestry, or Agricultural Administration, Building (1938).[4] These building projects extended the new campus well beyond the scope of Link's plans.

LINK'S GENERAL PLAN AND THE GROWTH OF THE CAMPUS

One of the weaknesses of Link's General Plan for LSU was its lack of a clear strategy for building beyond the inner core. Link had been asked to reduce the size of the campus proposed by Olmsted Brothers, and the order of the plan he produced was largely internal, as we have seen. Such expansion as was indicated on Link's plan was directed by an eastern continuation of its main east-west axis across Highland Road for a group of Women's Dormitories in the location first suggested on Olmsted Brothers' Preliminary Plan of 1921. The Link plan also indicated a continuation of the main east-west axis beyond Hill Memorial Library to a Gym Armory, to be placed at the bluff. This westward extension of the axis would not have been obvious on the ground, as it was broken by Hill Memorial and then not supported by flanking buildings or other landscape features. Link's depiction of the Gym Armory on the General Plan, his only known representation of it, seems to indicate a building facing west onto an exterior terrace with stairs leading down to a lower Stadium in the floodplain below, whose 50-yard line would have been along this main campus axis.[5] The final marking of this axis in Link's plan was to be a swimming pool beyond the football field. Although these western extensions were coordinated with the main axis, they would not obviously have extended its experience or its message (see fig. 3.5).

Apart from the alignment of the Gym Armory, the Stadium, and the Swimming Pool, the arrangement of all the other structures and functional uses indicated for this side of the campus was rather haphazard. An Open Air Theater is shown, though not in the precise location indicated on the Olmsted Brothers plans, its eventual location. No less

FIG. 5.4. Map of the core campus area, showing the original buildings defining the quadrangles in red, along with the additional buildings in brown, contributing to the National Register Historic District shaded in beige. Other buildings mentioned in the text are shown in dark gray. Provided by the author, courtesy of the LSU Facility Planning database.

FIG. 5.5. "Aeroplane View of the Campus." Rendering of Link's 1923 campus design, showing the tightly organized academic core facing the Parade Ground surrounded by a range of loosely placed outlying buildings. Office of Public Relations Photos, Jack Fiser Collection, RG #A5000.0020.1, Louisiana State University Archives, LSU Libraries, Baton Rouge, LA.

than six dormitories are shown in inexplicable arrangements. A Student Union is obliquely angled parallel to a face of the bluff in the northwestern corner of the site plan. To the southwest, a cluster of utilitarian structures surrounds the Sugar House experiment station. Three of these buildings are oriented with reference to rail lines, while the orientation of the fourth seems to be determined by nothing more pertinent than a drainage canal.

Link's General Plan indicates an arboretum-like Botanical Park riding the crest of the bluff above these buildings and near the Gym Armory. A Parade Ground is shown south of the Stadium, adjacent to an extensive University Lake in the floodplain (containing a Boat House) that would have had to be entirely excavated. Besides the existing New Orleans–Baton Rouge rail lines to the west, a spur into the campus, and the new drainage canal at the foot of the bluff, the plan shows a picturesquely curving series of roadways surrounding the Parade Ground and the Lake, contrasting with the tightly coordinated, hierarchical planning axes of the core plan.

The treatment of other parts of the campus is almost as haphazard. To the extreme south, the Dairy Barn, the Stock Judging Pavilion, and the Beef Cattle Barn appear in their present locations on the General Plan, as they were already under way during Link's time at LSU, the one concrete vestige of Olmsted Brothers' work.[6] A mix of other agricultural buildings appear strewn across the landscape near Highland Road at the southern end of campus. An Auditorium and a Fine Arts & Music Building flank the semicircular area in front of Memorial Tower. A President's Residence is shown at the northern end of today's Tower Drive, and a Faculty Residence is shown along Highland Road in the location of what is known today as the Old President's House. Most of these were never built, but their legacy of haphazard planning was influential and has not yet been fully overcome. It seems clear that in Link's brief time in Baton Rouge he focused on the basic structure of the plan for the central buildings and on their designs and that other than the suggestions made in the General Plan, he did not spend much time on the design and/or coordination of the outlying buildings.

PLANNING AFTER LINK

The most decisive contributions to campus architecture in the years immediately following Link were made by the successor firm Wogan & Bernard, of New Orleans.[7] The 1928 "Map of Campus" by Wogan & Bernard shows finished and projected buildings up to that point (see fig. 4.7). This plan is essentially what is shown in the "aeroplane" rendering of Link's plan produced in 1923 (fig. 5.5). Although we do not have a comprehensive campus plan by Link after his initial General Plan of April 1923, this rendering and the corresponding Wogan & Bernard plan may represent Link's intentions at his death in November of that year.[8] By the time of the 1928 plan, the four dormitory buildings marking a reference of the Pentagon Barracks on the downtown campus had been built, and construction on the Stadium in its present location had begun. The proposed location of a future Gym Armory had shifted off of the main axis, with a smaller Museum building shown awkwardly placed between it and the rear of Hill Memorial Library.[9] The Women's Dormitory group moved from across Highland Road to the northern side of the present Parade Ground, here labeled "Lawn." An expanded Auditorium has moved opposite this to the south, to the site occupied by the Fine Arts & Music Building in Link's plan. Thus the aerial rendering and the 1928 plan, while similar, are not identical.

Link's plan indicated a continuation of the curving roadway behind the earlier location of the Women's Dormitories, creating in effect the great circle that defines the present-day Parade Ground. This eastern drive is omitted on the 1928 plan. The Women's Dormitory complex just east of Highland Road has been replaced here by four Student Church Centers lined up along Highland Road opposite Memorial Tower, with tennis courts behind them, each building anticipated as a different design. The plan shows a group of Fraternity and Sorority Houses in the northeastern corner of campus, along Highland Road and Dalrymple and south of the Faculty Residence (Old President's House).[10] A President's, or Commandant's, House is shown along a newly proposed road that would become Infirmary Drive. In the same general part of campus are shown other residences that Link had suggested but are here depicted much less ceremoniously. In general, however, this plan indicates a first attempt to rethink the role of Highland Road as a forecourt to the campus, using the student religious centers as a kind of complement to Link's entry group, with Memorial Tower at its heart, giving the buildings along the newly paved road an independent order not deriving from Olmsted Brothers' vision or the Link campus as built.

On the other side of campus, the current Gym Armory was being built directly on axis with the rear of Hill Memorial, although as mentioned above, this arrangement is not obvious on the ground (fig. 5.6). Locating the building here, facing east, was the final step that prevented the campus plan from acknowledging the bluff (Olmsted Brothers) or any suggestion of a westward continuation of the main campus axis toward the river (Link). The location of the

FIG. 5.6. The Gym Armory, built in the late 1920s, showing the use of the utilitarian St. Joe brick to create a sense of expressive architectural details in a building lying just outside the academic core. Courtesy of East Baton Rouge Parish Library.

FIG. 5.7. The Pentagon Dormitory, by Wogan & Bernard, utilizing St. Joe brick combined with scant, classically inspired details in a configuration reminiscent of the Pentagon Barracks on the old downtown campus site. Office of Public Affairs Photos, RG #A0020, Louisiana State University Archives, LSU Libraries, Baton Rouge, LA.

FIG. 5.8. The architects for the outlying LSU Sugar House constructed in the 1920s also used a utilitarian brick with white stone details to give the administration building a distinctive character over the more industrial use of brick without such details on the process units behind. Courtesy of State Library of Louisiana.

FIG. 5.9. The Huey P. Long Field House, built with brick of a finer quality and white stone neoclassical details, in contrast to the utilitarian materials used on the Gym Armory next door. Courtesy of East Baton Rouge Parish Library.

Gym Armory on the bluff was used purposely in another practical way, however, with the lower floor opening unceremoniously outward to the fields to the west for use as marshaling grounds and the upper floor opening to the east for use by students as a gymnasium.

By the time this plan was drawn, Wogan & Bernard had produced the design for the Men's Dormitories (Pentagon) on the northwestern edge of Link's campus (fig. 5.7). While this building group was meant to evoke fond associations with the original Pentagon Barracks on the downtown campus, it continues a distinction in the use of materials and architectural language developed by Link, who differentiated between what might be called primary and secondary campus buildings. The core buildings defining Link's quadrangles utilized J. J. Earley's pebble stucco as an exterior coating for the molded fine architectural columns and other details, as discussed in chapter 4. For more utilitarian buildings, Link used a simple, economical treatment of buff-colored St. Joe brick with occasional white trim pieces for emphasis. The buildings around his Engineering Shops, for example, had been designed in this way, as had those for the Sugar House (fig. 5.8). Wogan & Bernard used this treatment in much of the work they did on campus during this period.[11] Their design for the Gym Armory pushes this "utilitarian" language by adding more stone and brick details, one way of suggesting its significance. The first floor is heavily rusticated, with the brick pulled out to suggest stone coursework laid in horizontal layers and articulated as voussoirs for the arches above the doors. On the upper floor the brick is used with stone pieces to create the pilasters and entablatures typical of neoclassical architecture. This treatment was used across Europe in the Renaissance for urban façades; the ground floor was made to look fortified and protective, while the upper floor represented the finer activities conducted within.

Treating the first floor as a platform that in some way raises the body of the building above the ground was commonplace in classical and neoclassical architectural design. Link's use of this treatment at LSU was both subtle and pervasive, being most obvious in the most significant buildings. For the Gym Armory, Wogan & Bernard abandoned this subtlety in favor of a more formulaic treatment. Their use of the material palette of Link's "utilitarian" buildings, but with intensified detail, separates this building from others on campus.[12]

The location of an Alumni House (today the Journalism Building) on the corner opposite the Gym Armory is first noted on a 1934 WDS study of campus-expansion options, one of a series of studies done over the decade. This building was taken apart on the downtown campus and rebuilt and expanded here in 1933–34 with funds provided by the CWA. The WDS design of the Huey Long Field House followed the example of the rebuilt Alumni Hall in creating a third, intermediate material palette based on a finer yellow, more closely resembling the tan stucco of the core campus, with more articulate stone trim and ornamental pieces (fig. 5.9). These two buildings became models for the larger buildings built in the late 1940s—Johnston, Hodges, and Hatcher Halls, by the Baton Rouge firm of Bodman & Murrell, and East and West Laville Halls, by the New Orleans firm of August Perez & Associates. Altogether these postwar dormitory groups create a kind of layering of campus buildings with regard to brick and neoclassical detailing, which becomes less evident as one moves out from the core to, for example, the 1970s CEBA Building.

In the northwestern corner of the campus, Link's General Plan shows a Hospital, projecting out from the Native American mounds. Nearby, a future Student Union follows the irregular character of the topography as the northernmost campus structure. In the 1928 Wogan & Bernard plan, the Hospital has been moved to the east to make room for a future Men's Dormitory north of the Pentagon complex. The Student Union has been placed where Link's Hospital was located. Olmsted Brothers had suggested that a low area, or slough, just to the west of the adjacent bluff become the location of a "Sunken Garden," perhaps the origin of the Greek Theater garden. The site north of the theater itself was identified as swampy on the initial site survey, and Olmsted Brothers suggested that it be developed as a picturesque series of ponds and walks behind the theater stage. The first indication of a campus swimming pool on the 1928 Wogan & Bernard plan is in the low area below the bluff where Olmsted Brothers had suggested the Sunken Garden. That pool was eventually included in the building that WDS designed as the Huey Long Field House (fig. 5.10). This low area was excavated to create a pond that existed there into the 1960s, and the Garden was later reconceived behind the Greek Theater.

FIG. 5.10. The Swimming Pool at the Huey P. Long Field House, facing west looking over the floodplain, a center of campus recreation for decades. LSU Photograph Collection, RG #A5000, Louisiana State University Archives, LSU Libraries, Baton Rouge, LA.

© 1929

The 1928 Wogan & Bernard document indicates that the architects were contemplating broader additions and changes (see fig. 4.7). Link's quadrangles, for example, are shown with projected wings and additions meant to provide more academic space within the inner core of the General Plan. The Chemistry Group (Coates Hall) is depicted with wings extending back, and the southernmost buildings on the eastern and western sides of the Main Quadrangle have L-shaped wings, as does Link's Peabody Hall. A new Electrical Engineering Building completes the southernmost Engineering Quadrangle on the plan. Greenhouses and an "Insectary" surround a formal garden behind Dodson Auditorium, perhaps as a complement to the Botanical Garden that Link intended for the area just to the west. A Social Science Building mirroring Peabody Hall is also indicated in line with Link's plan. These few suggested additions and extensions included on the 1928 plan follow Link's vision without adding major new buildings or grappling with significant new planning issues (fig 5.11).

WEISS, DREYFOUS & SEIFERTH, E. A. MCILHENNY, AND THE HIGHLAND ROAD CORRIDOR

By 1932 Weiss, Dreyfous & Seiferth had taken over as campus architects, and the Baton Rouge landscaper Steele Burden had been hired to coordinate and develop campus plantings. WDS, hired by Governor Huey Long to design the new Governor's Mansion on North Boulevard and the State Capitol building on the old downtown campus site, garnered a great deal of further state work during the following years. During the 1930s, WDS designed quite a few buildings on the LSU campus, more than any other architectural firm except Link's, leaving a strong imprint.[13] For the most part, these WDS buildings on campus are larger outlying buildings oriented to roadways and set back varying distances as they continue around to the east and the south from the Gym Armory and get larger and more complex in their arrangements.

Along with drawings of these various buildings, WDS produced a sequence of planning studies that make it clear that the campus was evolving and that these architects were searching for an overall ordering concept. Among other things, these studies demonstrate a consistent effort to complete Link's central quadrangles with compatible buildings, while highlighting various efforts to add more academic space. The steady addition of auxiliary buildings of all kinds outside the core is reflected in each of these several studies as well. Along with the Gym Armory, the Field House, the Pentagon dorms, the Fine Arts Building, and Smith Hall, these studies include a few smaller structures mostly devoted to agriculture-related uses immediately south of the Engineering Quadrangle and a full range of building types, uses, and locations along the eastern side of Highland Road and on the open ground beyond. These include new dormitories, mostly for women, on the eastern side of campus and various locations for individual faculty houses. These planning studies also detail the evolution of ordering ideas for buildings facing Highland Road. Most of the issues in these plans can be found developing in the 1928 Wogan & Bernard plan, but they took on more urgency in the WDS campus studies. During this period a pattern developed for organizing the buildings along Highland Road, proposals were made for a Romance Languages group, and various landscaping and garden design plans were developed, including plans for the Formal Garden behind the Greek Theater, gardens surrounding the French House, and a new Arboretum.

One of the most interesting aspects of these various WDS campus studies is the proposal for a new academic quadrangle anchored to the southern end of Link's plan and extending east into the block occupied by the Memorial Oak Grove shown on the 1934–35 plan (fig. 5.12). This would have substantially expanded the academic space of

FIG. 5.11. (*facing page*) Aerial photograph of the new LSU campus in 1929, showing the recently completed Gym Armory, the Sugar House, and the beginnings of Tiger Stadium surrounded by agricultural lands yet to be developed, with the tree-filled swamps that would become the future University Lakes in the distance. Courtesy of East Baton Rouge Parish Library.

FIG. 5.12. Mid-1930s working plan of the campus, showing built structures in black and proposed new buildings in gray. This plan study, one of several Weiss, Dreyfous & Seiferth studies for the campus, shows an investigation of extensions to the use of quadrangles as a way of organizing academic expansion. This tightly organized grouping contrasts with the buildings on the western side of campus along the bluff and those proposed east of Highland Road. Plan redrawn by the author. The original is in Collection 53, Weiss, Dreyfous & Seiferth Office Records, Southeast Louisiana Archives, Tulane University, New Orleans.

the early campus and suggests an interest in doing so in a way that would be compatible with Link's work, something that has not occurred in the time since. This plan also suggests a more southerly location for a campus Auditorium, interacting spatially with this new quadrangle extension and still on a secondary axis with Smith (Pleasant) Hall to the north. Another interesting aspect of this planning study is that while it shows the same kind of expansion to the rear of the Chemistry Group (Coates) seen in the 1928 Wogan & Bernard plan, it also shows an enlargement of the eastern end of the North Quadrangle accomplished by the removal of two of Link's buildings with their corner defining towers. This idea was not followed, as eventually the Commerce Building (Himes Hall) was built in roughly the same location as Link intended. Its complement, the Thomas Boyd Annex, did not appear until the 1960s as a weakly executed reflection of the slowly degrading Peabody, Allen, and Himes model.

All of these WDS planning studies explore a variety of approaches to the campus east of Highland Road, most of which suggest using this area for individual faculty houses in differing arrangements.[14] The picturesque arrangement of men's and women's housing units is all that remains in these studies of Olmsted Brothers' romantic Arboretum layout on this side of campus, providing a contrast to the more institutionalized forms of the campus itself, as had Link's suggestions for the development of the western lowlands. During this time the Episcopal Church Student Center was built at the southeastern corner of Highland and Dalrymple, and a Graduate Men's Dormitory, sometimes known as the Law Dormitory, was built on a diagonal orientation behind that.[15] These two buildings were the first to be constructed within the eastern half of the circular loop drive, which reappeared from the Link General Plan. The idea of repeating the forms of these two buildings on the opposite side of the east-west axis as a frame for a central building in line with Memorial Tower set the stage for the eventual placement of the Law School here. The footprint of the Faculty Club would roughly mirror that of the Episcopal Student Center. The second diagonally oriented building was never built, and this men's dorm was eventually demolished.

The Music & Dramatic Arts Building, Smith Hall, and the core of the Women's Dormitory group along Highland Road (Highland, Evangeline, and Annie Boyd Halls), all initially designed by WDS, set a new pattern in planning, being placed in relation to roadways with varying degrees of setback. These forms progressed from a single recessed building with a dominant central pavilion (the Music & Dramatic Arts Building, figs. 5.13 and 5.14) to a more complex, three-part building with a recessed central façade pavilion (Smith Hall, figs. 5.15 and 5.16), to an even more recessed composition of several buildings including an access drive (the dorm group, fig. 5.17). The Music & Dramatic Arts Building uses a Brunelleschian arcade and repeats the della Robbia roundels on an otherwise economical fa-

FIG. 5.13. Postcard view of the newly constructed Music and Dramatic Arts Building, utilizing a brick of finer quality and lighter color than the earlier LSU brick buildings with more selective stone trim. LSU Photograph Collection, RG #A5000, Louisiana State University Archives, LSU Libraries, Baton Rouge, LA.

FIG. 5.14. The Music and Dramatic Arts Building, with Smith (Pleasant) Hall in the distance, showing their use of similar architectural elements. LSU Photograph Collection, RG #A5000, Louisiana State University Archives, LSU Libraries, Baton Rouge, LA.

FIG. 5.15. Photograph of Smith (Pleasant) Hall in the mid 1930s, showing the use of symmetry, hierarchy, and various architectural elements in one large building framing its own entry court. LSU Photograph Collection, RG #A5000, Louisiana State University Archives, LSU Libraries, Baton Rouge, LA.

FIG. 5.16. The design of the Pleasant Hall entry façade combines many of the architectural elements of the core campus and its pebbly stucco in different ways. LSU *Gumbo*, 1940, Courtesy of Special Collections, LSU Libraries, Louisiana State University, Baton Rouge, LA.

çade. The scale of the central entry pavilion at Smith Hall matches that of the single arch of Foster Hall, a large feature meant to be seen from a distance, and the connecting Palladian arcades of Link's entry group with their broken entablatures (see figs. 4.30 and 4.32). Thus, while the coordination of building detail and planning order of this dorm group begins to reflect the richness of Link's design efforts, the variations among these buildings and their orientation to the street did not provide the kind of unified composition Link had achieved. Rather, the location of each responded primarily to the immediate context. The Music & Dramatic Arts Building and Smith Hall were designed to stand on their own. Highland and Annie Boyd Halls were conceived as two parts of an evolving ensemble forming a horseshoe-shaped complex closed off at the end by Evangeline Hall (fig. 5.18). This last building, as well as Grace King and Louise Garig Halls, along Highland, the final buildings to be added to this group, were the work of Edward F. Neild, of Shreveport. WDS had prepared drawings for Evangeline Hall as part of their work on Highland and Annie Boyd Halls the year before. Their design for Evangeline Hall, which was a better fit with the two adjacent dormitories, was not built, however, the one by Neild being favored. Across the street behind this group, the Panhellenic Building, for

FIG. 5.17. Rendering of the proposed Women's Dormitory Group (showing Grace King and Louise Garig Halls in front), 1937, by Edward F. Neild, D. A. Somdal, and Edward Neild Jr., of Shreveport. Courtesy of LSU Shreveport Archives, Noel Memorial Library, box 55-2a.

FIG. 5.18. Evangeline Hall, situated at the head of the Highland Road Dormitory Group, comprising Annie Boyd, Highland, Grace King, and Louise Garig Halls, all executed in the LSU pebbly stucco surface with Italian Renaissance–inspired architectural details. Courtesy of LSU Public Affairs.

sorority offices, existed for years, until it was demolished in the 1980s to make way for the East Campus Apartments.

Significantly, these new buildings, along with the Faculty Club by WDS and the three dorms by Neild, continued Link's Italian Renaissance–based architectural language and utilized the same pebble stucco as his primary buildings.[16] The five-building Women's Dormitory group, designed by WDS and Neild, represents a successful collaboration of two independent architectural firms in the development of a unified group that extends the architectural language of the Link campus along the lines established by the 1931 WDS interpretations of the Music & Dramatic Arts Building and Smith (Pleasant) Hall.[17] If one compares the dormitory group with these earlier buildings, one can see a steady elaboration of architectural form and detail toward a courtyard concept not unlike the original Link quadrangles; unfortunately, these spaces were also progressively given over to the automobile (fig. 5.19).

The most significant new vision that emerges in the WDS planning studies is the spacious Highland Road corridor, defined by a relatively consistent building setback on its eastern side and a steady rhythm of live oaks (fig. 5.20). This setback was defined by Leche Hall (the Old Law School), the Episcopal Student Center, and the new Fac-

FIG. 5.19. Plan diagrams of the Music and Dramatic Arts Building, Smith (Pleasant) Hall, and the Evangeline Dormitory Group, showing progressive clustering of form and detail around the central entry of each. Diagrams by the author.

FIG. 5.20. Early aerial view of Smith (Pleasant) Hall landscaping (*upper left*), live oak plantings, and the religious centers along Highland Road. Fonville Winans Aerial Photographs, Mss. 4605, Louisiana and Lower Mississippi Valley Collections, LSU Libraries, Baton Rouge, LA.

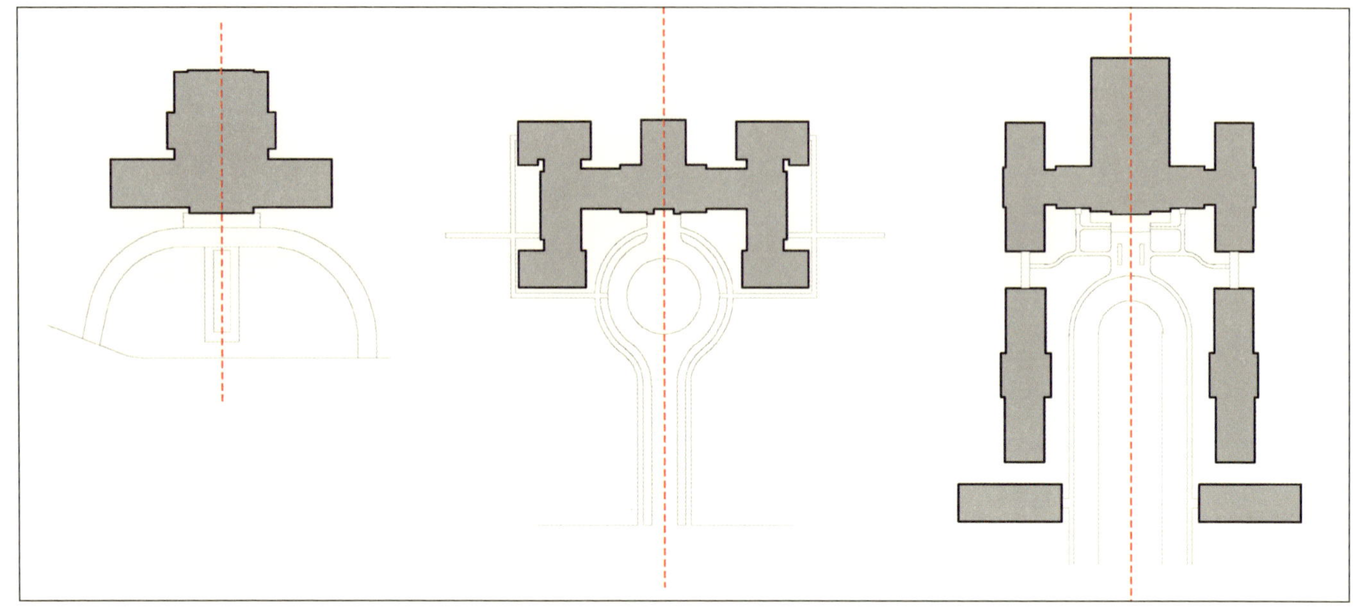

ulty Club, all more or less following the location strategy of the first Faculty Residence built by Link more than a decade earlier. The new Women's Dormitory complex and the French House sit farther back from the street. What is now the Old Law School building, originally known as Leche Hall, was conceived as a replica of the recently completed U.S. Supreme Court building in Washington, DC, designed by Cass Gilbert. That building had been modeled after Thomas Jefferson's replication of the Roman temple known today as the Maison Carrée in Nimes, France, for the Virginia State Capitol in Richmond. Jefferson considered the architecture of republican Rome to be an appropriate model for the new American democracy, and his use of this form has been widely influential throughout the United States. In their design of this prominent campus building, WDS followed Link in using eclectic models with a history of associations; even their replication of such a model here is more direct and less skillfully layered than most of Link's work at LSU (figs. 5.21–5.25).

The pattern of coordination between architecture and planning that began with Link and was weakly carried out in the majority of these WDS buildings came to an end with the French House, in several ways. This curious building, originally conceived as a part of a Romance Languages group indicated on several of the WDS campus studies, was eventually built as a separate, stand-alone structure. Although also designed by WDS in these years, it was conceived as a reflection of Louisiana's French heritage and modeled in a general way after chateau design from rural France. It thus represented a break with the mission-style ambience first suggested by Olmsted and reinterpreted by Link as southern European, or Italian (see fig. 5.36). The French House was not the first building on campus to break with the earlier style, as the Field House, the Pentagon Dorms, the Episcopal Center, the Gym Armory, Leche Hall (built at roughly the same time as the French House), and even Link's "utilitarian" buildings had followed other sensibilities. But the French House was the first to abandon

FIG. 5.21. LSU's Old Law School, known originally as Leche Hall, designed by Weiss, Dreyfous & Seiferth in 1936. Courtesy of LSU *Gumbo,* 1936. LSU "Highland Road Photos."

FIG. 5.22. The U.S. Supreme Court Building, in Washington, DC, designed by Cass Gilbert and completed in 1935, modeled after Thomas Jefferson's Virginia State House. Wikimedia Commons.

FIG. 5.23. Jefferson's Virginia State House, completed in 1792 and modeled after the Maison Carrée. Postcard in author's personal collection.

FIG. 5.24. The Maison Carrée, in Nimes, France, dating from ca. 16 BC. This, the best preserved Roman temple, through Jefferson's Virginia State House became a model for many buildings across the United States representing institutional order. Wikimedia Commons.

the symmetrically conceived, neoclassically inspired model so central to these other campus buildings. Its conception was still eclectic, as was almost all academic architecture in the United States during these years.[18] Design in the French House building was considered a way of invoking historical traditions to create an atmosphere conducive to teaching and learning. The vision for the Romance Languages group faded as the building was placed along Highland Road in a manner similar to the other buildings there.

THE EMERGING CAMPUS LANDSCAPE

The designs of these buildings and the efforts of Weiss, Dreyfous & Seiferth to tie them together in a unified campus plan are complemented by a series of plans produced by the landscape architects working for E. A. McIlhenny, of Avery Island, during the same period.[19] These documents included planting layouts that were drawn over base plans provided by WDS. During the years that WDS was doing so much work for the state, McIlhenny developed a close working relationship with the firm's senior partner, Leon Weiss, providing the plant materials for the new Governor's Mansion, the State Capitol, and the approaches to the Mississippi River Bridge in Baton Rouge, among many other projects. By the end of 1936 these two men had discussed the need for a comprehensive relandscaping of the LSU campus, with McIlhenny commenting that "the planting that is there now is badly overgrown, and most of it should be eliminated."[20] The basic planting scheme for shrubs on campus up to that point had been primarily the "foundation" planting that occurred in the 1920s, very soon after the first wave of buildings along the main South Quadrangle was built. The plants and the planting design had been provided by the E. A. McIlhenny Landscaping Service but had not been adequately maintained in the years since.[21]

Beginning in 1937, McIlhenny opened a branch office in Alumni Hall on the LSU campus (now the Journalism Building, moved from the old campus in 1931) to coordinate the replanting design. Initially this office was staffed by the landscape architect Ralph Ellis Gunn, who was later joined by Harry Baker, from Pennsylvania, also a trained landscape architect.[22] Over the next year they produced a wide array of planting designs for a full range of campus settings that included the first known plans for putting live oaks in Link's quadrangles; for planting in the courtyard behind Dodson Auditorium and the passageways between the adjacent buildings in the Ag Group on that side of campus; for the other buildings being added to the core, such as the Commerce Building (Himes), the Physics & Math Building (Nicholson), and the Geology Building; for the Pentagon Dorms and the new Infirmary; for the Faculty Club and Leche Hall; and for landscaping around the Football Stadium.

Their plans for the eastern side of campus included landscaping around the Panhellenic Building and a vegetable and flower garden behind what was by this time two home economics training cottages on Raphael Semmes Drive. Gunn produced at least two designs for gardens surrounding the recently completed French House and plans for a new campus arboretum between these and University Lake, recently created from swampland cleared by the WPA. Baker produced an extensive landscape design,

FIG. 5.25. (*facing page*) Typical Weiss, Dreyfous & Seiferth construction drawings for the Old Law School, showing the richness of detail that went into the building. Courtesy of LSU Facility Services.

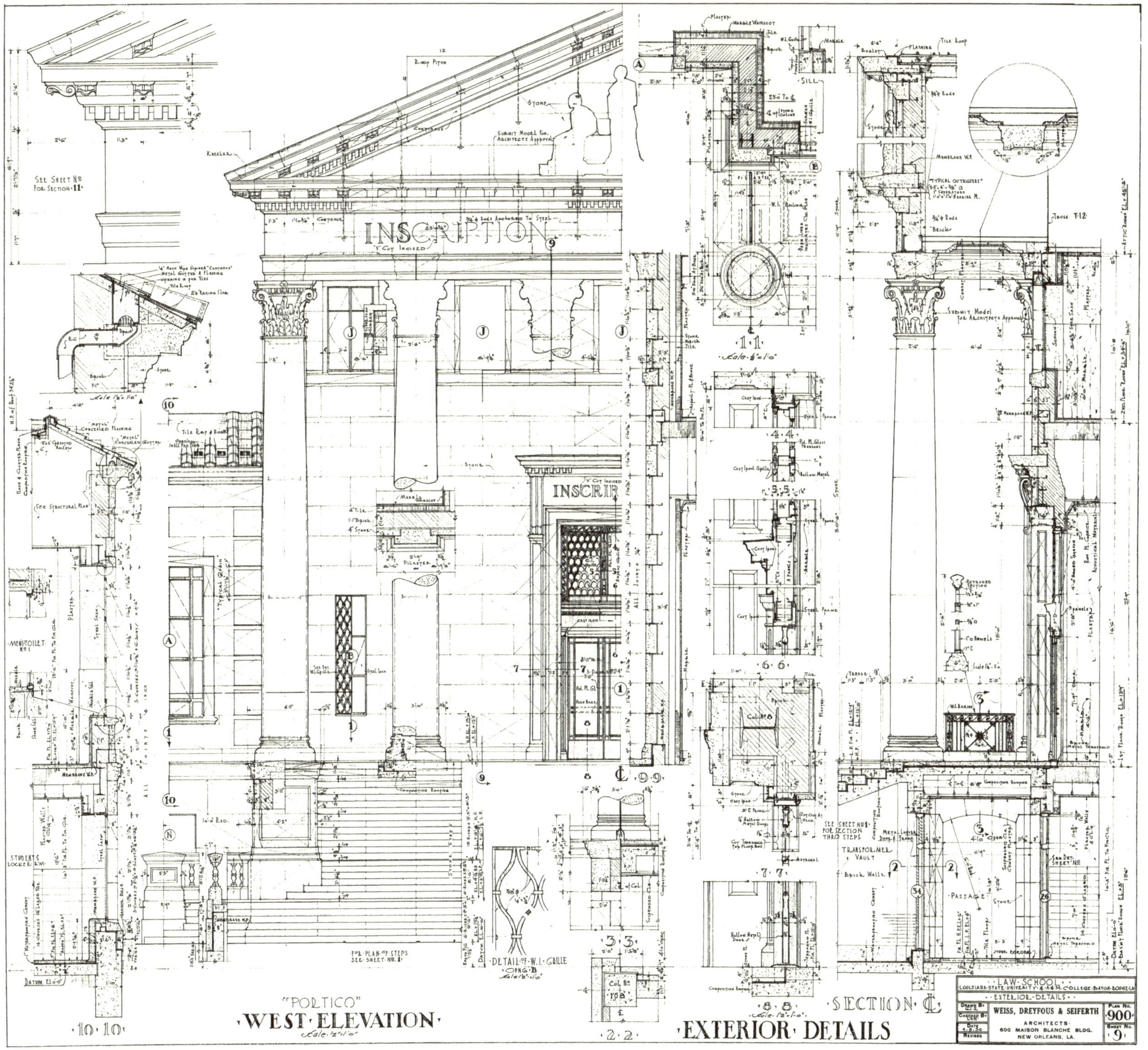

INSCRIPTION
"PORTICO"
WEST ELEVATION
10 10
2 2
EXTERIOR DETAILS
SECTION ℄
DETAIL OF W.I. GRILLE
LAW SCHOOL
LOUISIANA STATE UNIVERSITY & A & M COLLEGE BATON ROUGE LA
EXTERIOR DETAILS
WEISS, DREYFOUS & SEIFERTH
ARCHITECTS
600 MAISON BLANCHE BLDG.
NEW ORLEANS, LA.
PLAN NO. 900
SHEET NO. 9

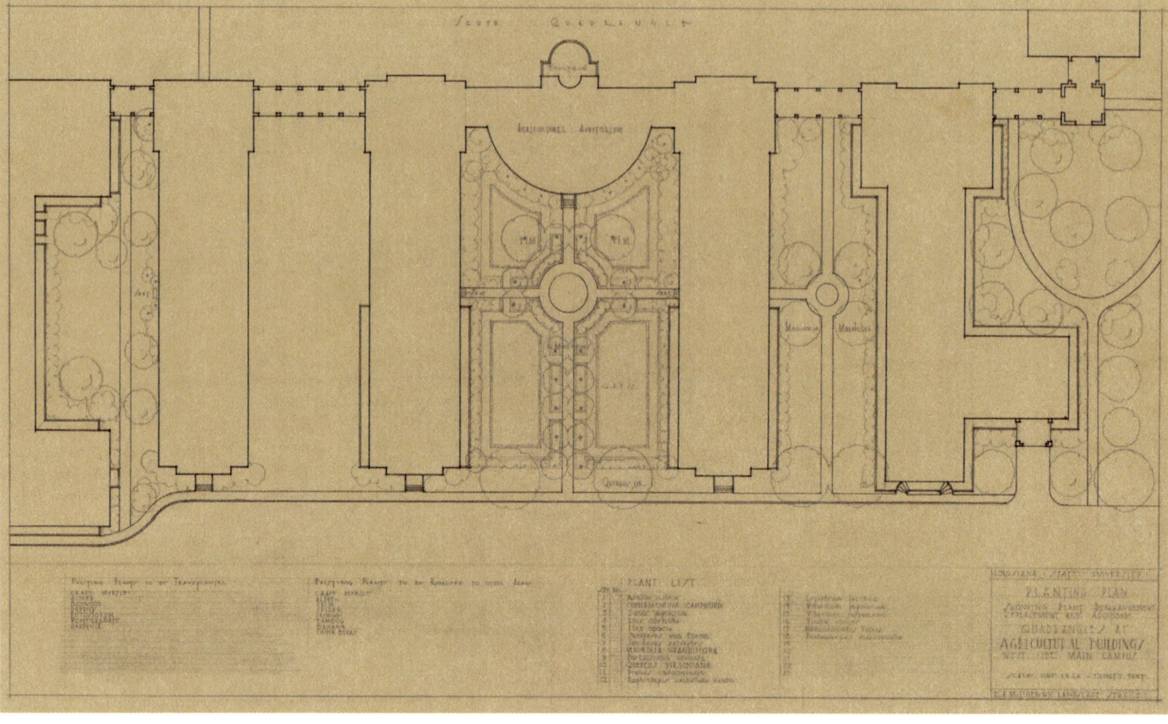

FIG. 5.26. The Physics & Math Building, now Nicholson Hall, on the eastern side of the Main Quadrangle in February 1938, showing one of the newly planted live oaks. The building was designed using an austere version of Link's architectural language. Courtesy of State Library of Louisiana.

FIG. 5.27. "Planting Plan showing Plant Rearrangement, Replacement and Additions," landscape plan for the courtyards between buildings in the Agricultural Group, by E. A. McIlhenny, 1937–39. Courtesy of E. A. McIlhenny Enterprises, Inc., Avery Island, LA.

FIG. 5.28. (*facing page*) "Planting Plan for the Formal Garden at the Greek Theater," 1938, by Harry Baker for E. A. McIlhenny. Courtesy of E. A. McIlhenny Enterprises, Inc., Avery Island, LA.

including a reflecting pool, for the newly conceived Formal Garden behind the Greek Theater. Most of these various planting and landscape designs are reflected on the first and most comprehensive map of campus showing the architectural developments in place and planned by 1938, entitled "Proposed Landscape Development," the most beautiful campus-plan drawing up to that time.

While the planting plans for the Physics & Math Building and the Commerce Building in the Main Quadrangle, along with those for the Geology Building and some of the new buildings along Highland Road, generally show a continuation of the foundation-planting scheme used initially on campus, this period saw the development of a more spatially assertive planting pattern in the courtyards between the buildings on the western side of this quadrangle (fig. 5.26).[23] An undated landscaping plan by McIlhenny's office entitled "Planting Plan showing Plant Rearrangement, Replacement and Additions," for the "Quadrangles at Agricultural Buildings, West Side Main Campus," indicated a range of conceptions for the spaces between Allen, Prescott, Stubbs, Dodson, and Audubon Halls and the recently added Agricultural Administration Building (fig. 5.27).[24] While all of these, except the larger space behind the Agriculture Auditorium (Dodson), were conceived as primarily pedestrian passages, each was treated differently. Most interesting, perhaps, were the transverse walkways made possible by the doorways in the middle of the northern and southern façades of the buildings flanking the Auditorium. The large courtyard behind the Auditorium was also designed with a cruciform pattern of four sidewalks lined by trees leading to a small circular lawn in an arrangement that closely follows Link's intentions for the space.[25] The two side doors are shown here with seats in front of them, suggesting that they had already been closed off. A corresponding seat is shown at the center of the northern façade of Prescott, indicating that that door too had already been closed off.

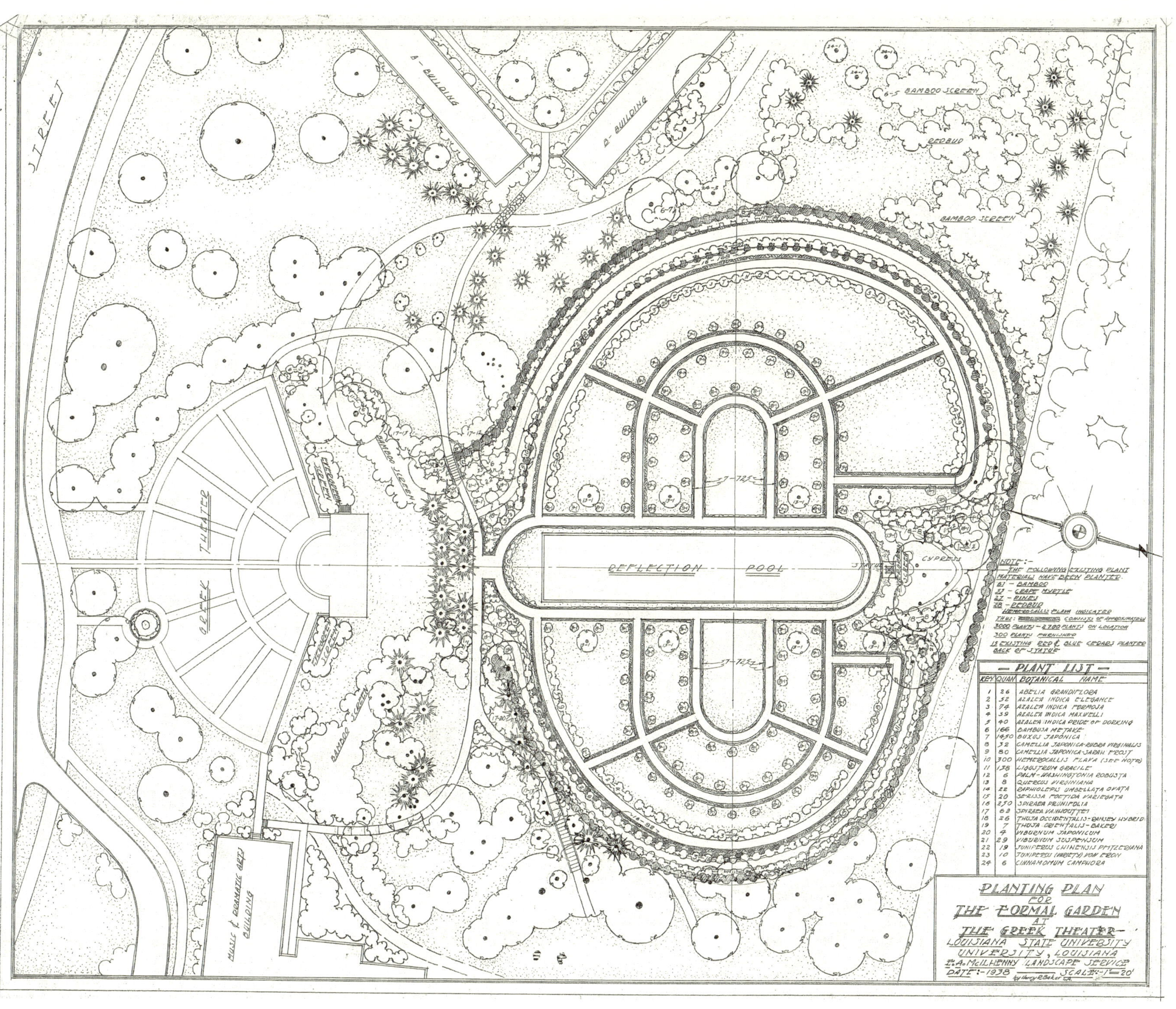
STREET
B-BUILDING
A-BUILDING
BAMBOO SCREEN
REDBUD
BAMBOO SCREEN
GREEK THEATER
BAMBOO SCREEN
BAMBOO SCREEN
DEFLECTION POOL
STATUE
CYPRESS
MUSIC & DRAMATIC ARTS BUILDING
N
NOTE:-
THE FOLLOWING EXISTING PLANT MATERIALS HAVE BEEN PLANTED.
61 - BAMBOO
57 - CRAPE MYRTLE
27 - PINES
28 - REDBUD
HEMEROCALLIS FLAVA INDICATED THUS: CONSISTS OF APPROXIMATELY 3000 PLANTS - 2700 PLANTS ON LOCATION 300 PLANTS FURNISHED
15 EXISTING RED & BLUE CEDARS PLANTED BACK OF STATUE
— PLANT LIST —
KEY QUAN BOTANICAL NAME
1 26 ABELIA GRANDIFLORA
2 52 AZALEA INDICA ELEGANCE
3 74 AZALEA INDICA FORMOSA
4 39 AZALEA INDICA MAXWELLI
5 40 AZALEA INDICA PRIDE OF DORKING
6 166 BAMBUSA METAKE
7 1450 BUXUS JAPONICA
8 32 CAMELLIA JAPONICA-RUBRA VIRGINALIS
9 80 CAMELLIA JAPONICA-SARAH FROST
10 300 HEMEROCALLIS FLAVA (SEE NOTE)
11 138 LIGUSTRUM GRACILE
12 6 PALM-WASHINGTONIA ROBUSTA
13 8 QUERCUS VIRGINIANA
14 22 RAPHIOLEPIS UMBELLATA OVATA
15 20 SERISSA FOETIDA VARIEGATA
16 250 SPIRAEA PRUNIFOLIA
17 62 SPIRAEA VANHOUTTEI
18 26 THUJA OCCIDENTALIS-RAMSEY HYBRID
19 7 THUJA ORIENTALIS-BAKERI
20 4 VIBURNUM JAPONICUM
21 29 VIBURNUM SUSPENSUM
22 19 JUNIPERUS CHINENSIS PFITZERIANA
23 10 JUNIPERUS (VARIETY) VON ERON
24 6 CINNAMOMUM CAMPHORA
PLANTING PLAN
FOR
THE FORMAL GARDEN
AT
THE GREEK THEATER
LOUISIANA STATE UNIVERSITY
UNIVERSITY, LOUISIANA
E. A. McILHENNY LANDSCAPE SERVICE
DATE:-1938 SCALE:-1"=20'
by Harry R Baker L.A.

FIG. 5.29. Postcard view of Gardens and Reflecting Pool behind the Greek Theater (no date). LSU Photograph Collection, RG #A5000, Louisiana State University Archives, LSU Libraries, Baton Rouge, LA.

FIG. 5.30. Statue of the Spanish explorer Hernando de Soto that stood for years at the far end of the now-filled-in Reflecting Pool behind the Greek Theater. LSU Photograph Collection, RG #A5000, Louisiana State University Archives, LSU Libraries, Baton Rouge, LA.

Originally these midrange entries into Link's buildings had been designed with more formality than might have been typical, with double doors at the first-floor level approached by stairs recessed in arched alcoves. This drawing is a design study and not a construction drawing, and there is only slight evidence that any of the ideas expressed in it were carried out. In fact, the remnants of older plant materials in these locations suggest slightly that different schemes were followed.

The most complete drawing in the McIlhenny series is the one titled "Planting Plan for the Formal Garden at the Greek Theater," prepared in 1938 by Harry Baker (fig. 5.28). This drawing describes a pattern of regularly spaced plants of various kinds following rings of semicircular walks surrounding a Reflection Pool on axis with the theater. The gardens were structured around a lawn, which together with the pool re-created the cruciform shape of Link's quadrangles. The rounded northern end of the pool focused attention on an unspecified statue framed by an evergreen screen (fig. 5.29). To the north of this the plan calls for cypress trees, but given the size of the trees in early aerial photographs, they may well have been here already in the low swampy area noted on the Olmsted Brothers survey.[26] For years a statue of Hernando de Soto stood here (fig. 5.30).[27]

The plants list for the Formal Gardens includes camellias, azaleas, and ligustrum, all species that have become common in southern Louisiana garden landscapes. The liberal use of McIlhenny's trademark bamboo was called for

FIG. 5.31. Aerial photograph of the campus from the north in the late 1930s, showing the Greek Theater Gardens and Reflecting Pool, the Pentagon Dorms, the Music & Dramatic Arts Building, and the new buildings along Highland Road. Courtesy of www.FonvilleWinans.com.

in landscape screens. Evenly spaced live oaks are indicated for both sides, forming an allée framing the pool that leads back from the theater stage. The landscaping of the entire area was intended to be continuous with that proposed to surround the adjacent Pentagon Dorms (fig. 5.31). The next year this office also produced a landscape plan for the new Infirmary building by Neild, on the opposite side of the gardens.

It appears that while this sequence of planting plans was prepared by the landscape architects working for McIlhenny, the plans were actually carried out by Steele Burden, who made alterations and adaptations of his own. Burden played a large role in the conceptual development and planting of many other landscaped spaces on the campus. Having grown up southeast of campus, on Windrush Plantation, Burden had a lifelong involvement with Louisiana landscapes. Hired by LSU in 1930, he was perhaps the most consistent influence on the development of the campus landscape until his retirement some forty years later. According to James Stakely, Burden "attended LSU for a couple of years on and off before taking on a job landscaping City Park (in 1928) in Baton Rouge. . . . He served as superintendent after 1929 and began his lifelong association with tree-planting in Baton Rouge."[28]

The exact nature of the working relationship between Burden and McIlhenny's designers and the plans they produced is not clear, as very little documentary evidence is available. Anecdotally, Burden had the reputation of being strong willed, not one to follow plans made by others. In point of fact the plan for the Formal Gardens at the Greek Theater appears to be the only McIlhenny planting plan carried out pretty much as drawn.

Of all the plant materials on campus, the live oaks leave the most indelible impression; along with Memorial Tower and Tiger Stadium, they have become the university's most enduring symbols. Live oaks were a salient feature of the old downtown campus, especially in the area surrounding the Commandant's, or President's, House (see fig. 1.9). Oaks were planted on the current campus as early as 1922 along the soon-to-be-paved Highland Road. In 1924 some 260 trees were planted by the LSU Forestry Club, many of them oaks. The grove of live oaks memorializing fallen Louisiana soldiers behind the current LSU Union was dedicated in 1926. Thus, by the 1930s oaks were the dominant tree type on campus. This is perhaps not surprising, as these magnificent trees had long been an important part of the culture of southern Louisiana, where they appear naturally on the highland sites first chosen by early European planters for their homes. Before that, the Native Americans had an established tradition of building mounds and villages on the elevated ground preferred by these trees. As far back as we can trace, they seem to have been markers of human ambition in the region. Burden's oft-quoted sentiment that "the live oak is the most beautiful thing to come out of the ground" captures something of this timeless connection, and it was natural that they assumed a key role here.[29]

The plan produced by the McIlhenny LSU "field office" for planting live oaks is the first known drawing to show oaks inside the quadrangles (fig. 5.32). Although the actual plantings followed the general pattern of the plan, their locations do not correspond exactly to the locations suggested there. In the plan, a relatively regular spacing of seven trees along each side of the South Quadrangle is broken on each side to frame the primary architectural features, the fountain by Dodson Auditorium on the west and the center pavilion of the Chemistry Group (Coates Hall) on the east. The plan shows a continuation of this regular spacing around the inner core area for a total of thirty new trees. Today the spacing is less regular, and there are only twenty-two live oaks in all.[30] These oaks were planted in the South and North Quadrangles by February 1938, just as the new Physics & Math Building was being finished. A few trees remaining from the pre-campus period in the northern part of the quadrangle were left in place.

The most unique, most richly conceived, most beautiful of all the landscape proposals prepared by the McIlhenny

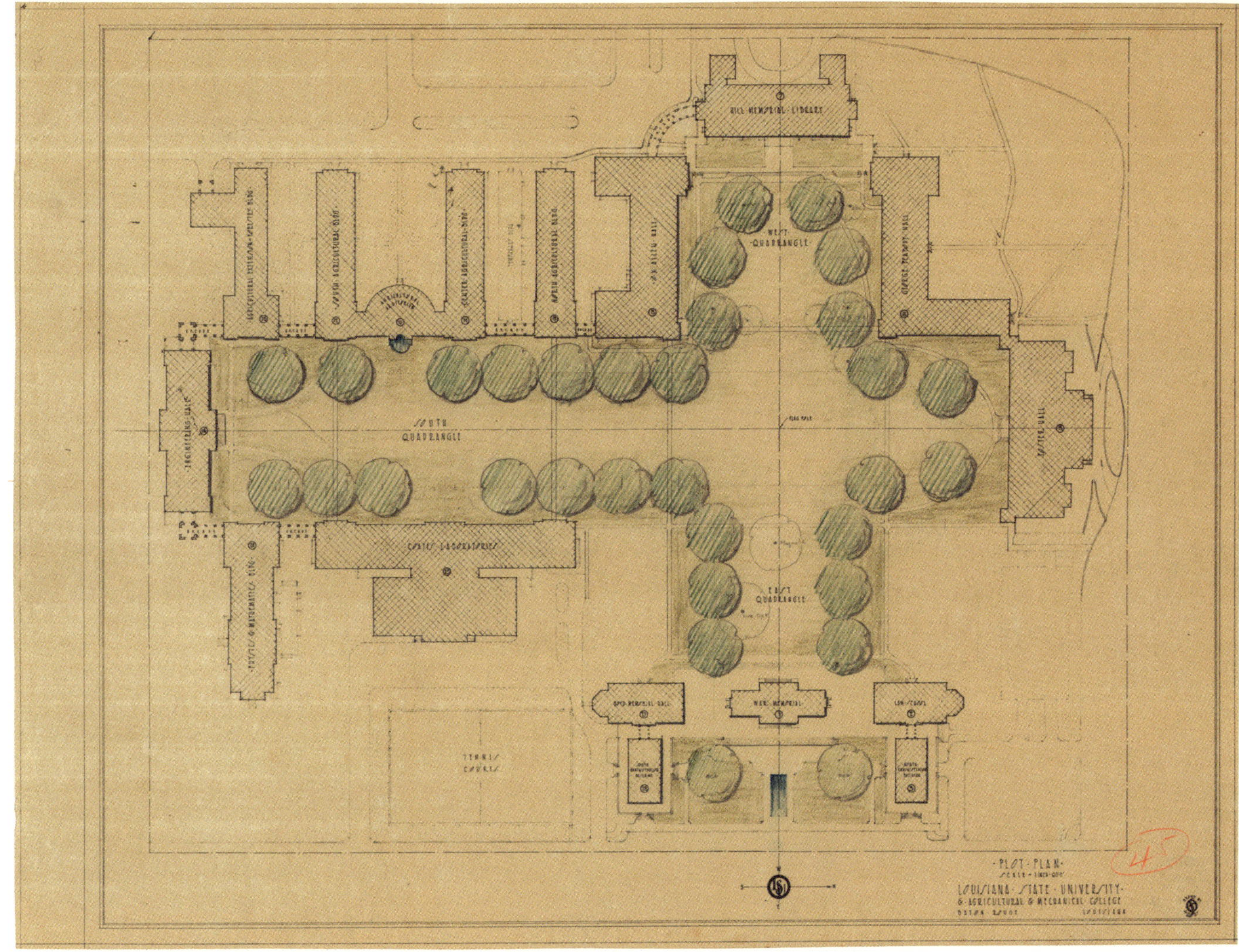

FIG. 5.32. Original planting plan for live oaks in the LSU quadrangles, produced by E. A. McIlhenny, April 1937. Courtesy of E. A. McIlhenny Enterprises, Inc., Avery Island, LA.

field office, however, was the initial design for gardens surrounding the Maison Française, or French House. This building went through several phases in its conceptual planning, first as one of a number of buildings devoted to a Romance Languages group located in various places on the different WDS campus plan studies before it appeared in the plan by Gunn (figs. 5.33 and 5.34). These changing locations, that it was grouped with other buildings meant to serve similar purposes, the extensive gardens designed for it, and its different architectural inspiration all contribute to its uniqueness on the campus. In the Gunn design for "Gardens and Horticultural Experimental Plots," we see the French House embedded in a variety of different garden types worthy of the kind of French country chateau it emulates, distinctly different from anything else on campus. Directly in front, facing Highland Road, appear a pair of low clipped-hedge fleurs-de-lis on sculpted lawns and bounded by a squared topiary grove of trees on either side, reflecting a kind of formality and the celebration of the French cultural heritage that this facility was meant to

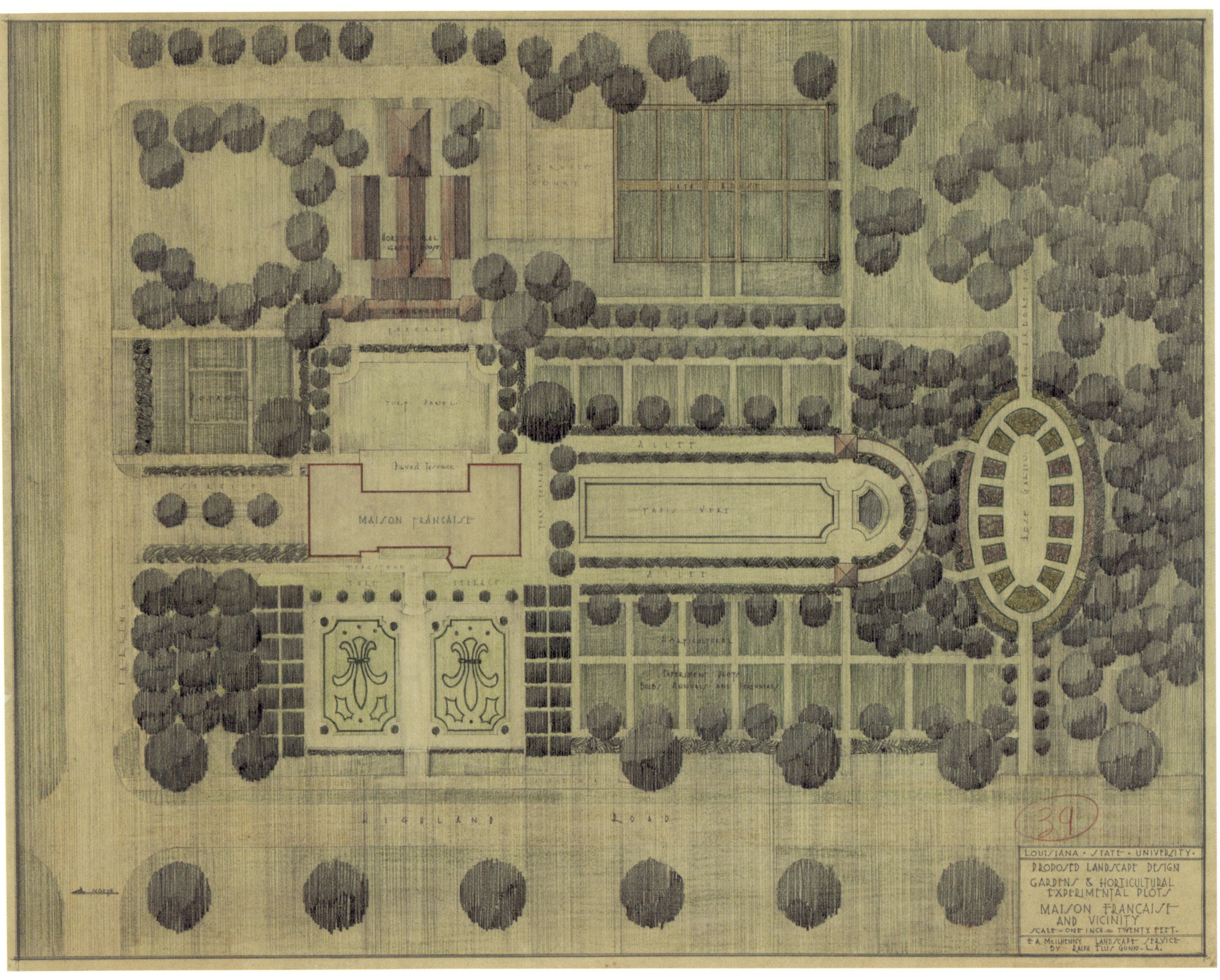
39
LOUISIANA • STATE • UNIVERSITY •
PROPOSED LANDSCAPE DESIGN
GARDENS & HORTICULTURAL EXPERIMENTAL PLOTS
MAISON FRANCAISE AND VICINITY
SCALE – ONE INCH = TWENTY FEET.
E. A. McILHENNY LANDSCAPE SERVICE BY RALPH ELLIS GUNN – L.A.
Paved Terrace
MAISON FRANCAISE
TAPIS VERT
TURF PANEL
ALLEE
ROSE GARDEN
HIGHLAND ROAD

FIG. 5.33. (*facing page*) "Proposed Landscape Design, Gardens and Horticultural Experimentation Plots, Maison Française and Vicinity," by Ralph Ellis Gunn for E. A. McIlhenny, winter 1938–39. Courtesy of E. A. McIlhenny Enterprises, Inc., Avery Island, LA.

FIG. 5.34. Rendering of the "Proposed Garden Development" for the Maison Française, or French House, by Ralph Ellis Gunn for E. A. McIlhenny. Courtesy of E. A. McIlhenny Enterprises, Inc., Avery Island, LA.

evoke. To the south along Highland Road is an extended series of manicured experimental plots for bulbs, annuals, and perennials. Extending south from the building itself to a pool and arbor is a *tapis vert,* an extended expanse of lawn, lined with trees on either side. Beyond this is an oval Rose Garden composed of various beds for different species, eventually leading to a pathway that heads east to the Arboretum, intended to be located along a reshaped Campus Lake to the south. Behind the house, accessible from its large central living room, a paved terrace gives way to a gravel walk and shrub-framed lawn. On the eastern side of this outdoor extension of the building is a proposed assembly of horticultural greenhouses faced by a shelter and toolhouse pavilion. The northeastern corner of the immediate site was to include a *potager,* or kitchen garden, for the chefs of the Maison Française. All in all, it was conceived as a rich and elegant representation of French cultural and horticultural traditions compatible in a general way with Link's goal of a teaching role for the architecture of the campus.

As plans for this extensive landscaping evolved with the changing conception of this part of campus, the design of the proposed French House gardens was simplified (figs. 5.35 and 5.36). The Vegetable and Cutting Gardens were relocated, and the design of the formal garden was reworked.[31] The second scheme featured a broad front lawn framed by sculpted hedges facing Highland Road. Behind the house a formal lawn reaching out from a paved terrace remained, with a raised terrace ending in a hint of

FIG. 5.35. Alternate planting plan for the Maison Française, January 1939, by E. A. McIlhenny Landscape Service. Courtesy of E. A. McIlhenny Enterprises, Inc., Avery Island, LA.

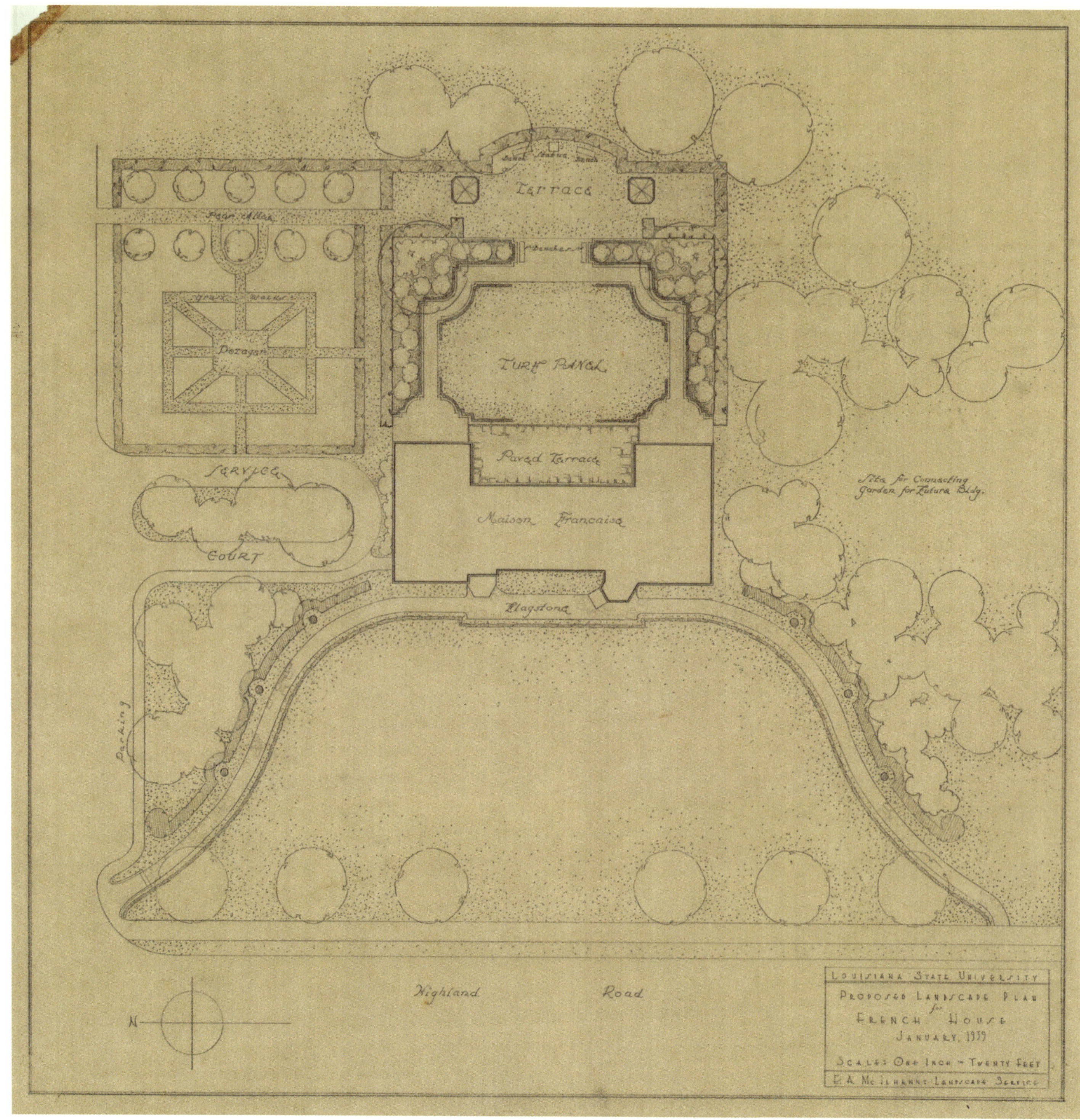

an exedra with benches and an unspecified statue. To the north of this, an allée of pear trees and a landscaped service drive framed a small formal garden with a network of gravel walks. To the south of the French House is indicated a "Site for Connecting Garden for Future Building," with no indication of what that building might be. At least portions of this design were carried out, as the broad front lawn flanked by sculpted hedges, an altered formal rear garden with a more extensive planting palette, and the landscaped side service court appear in early aerial photographs of the building (see fig. 5.36). Virtually nothing of this remains today. In years to come, greenhouses not associated with the French House would be built further to the east of these locations.

For many years, both before and after the construction of the Laville dormitories in 1947, a large collection of camellias grew to the east of the French House.[32] Camellias played a special role in the campus landscape between the 1930s and the 1970s, when many of them were removed. McIlhenny, who was attracted to Asian landscapes, developed a large collection at Avery Island and was influential in promoting their distribution and use in gardens throughout the state. In the 1930s and 1940s this interest was supported by many in the LSU horticultural and agricultural departments, who also collected and experimented with numerous camellia types. They were favorites of Burden as well, who not only used them in his work at LSU but included them in gardens he designed throughout the region. Although many of the once-extensive colonies of camellias on campus no longer exist, traces of this diversity are still visible near Himes and Peabody Halls.[33]

By 1941 the southernmost end of this expanded French House garden site had given way to the Pan American House, apparently something of a return to the Romance Languages group idea of almost a decade earlier (figs. 5.37 and 5.38). The Vegetable and Cutting Garden designed in the spring of 1938 for the area behind the university's new Home Economics training cottages contained distinct areas for vegetables, fruit trees, and several species of roses surrounded by a bamboo hedge. That garden functioned in this location until it was removed to make way for the Highland Dining Unit that stands there today. The inclusion of vegetable and cutting gardens, experimental plots, and greenhouses in these places ultimately reflects the decisions made by Rick Olmsted to use the uplands at the southern end of campus for agricultural and horticultural purposes (fig. 5.39). "So far as I can judge it is as nearly ideal as could possibly be found for demonstration farming for the State of Louisiana, embracing as it does the problems of the 'hill-farmers' of the northern part of the state and those of the bottomland farmers of the southern part."[34]

Beginning in 1927, the large open fields in this part of campus were developed as the Hill Farm for agriculture, horticulture, and agronomy research (fig. 5.40). Over the next sixty years an extensive range of research was conducted here that included the development of new and productive varieties of potatoes, pears, peppers, okra, cabbage,

FIG. 5.36. Aerial photograph of the Maison Française (undated), showing aspects of the alternate planting plan by E. A. McIlhenny Landscape Service. Fonville Winans Aerial Photographs, Mss. 4605, Louisiana and Lower Mississippi Valley Collections, LSU Libraries, Baton Rouge, LA.

FIG. 5.37. Architect's 1941 rendering of the Pan American House (now Acadian House) on Highland Road. Courtesy of LSU Office of Resource Services.

FIG. 5.38. Ornamented entry façade of the Pan American House on Highland Road. Courtesy of LSU *Gumbo.*

FIG. 5.39. Agricultural research on the eastern side of campus, behind the Maison Française and the Pan American House on Highland Road, with Parker Coliseum just visible to the south. Fonville Winans Aerial Photographs, Mss. 4605, Louisiana and Lower Mississippi Valley Collections, LSU Libraries, Baton Rouge, LA.

strawberries, shallots, lima beans, collards, and tomatoes. The area also became an important testing site for breeding programs for hibiscus, lilies, daffodils, camellias, and various types of fruit trees. The extensive testing areas for the American Rose Society and other horticultural uses have since been moved to outlying university lands, including the Burden Research Plantation, and today only a small portion of these uses remain in this location as the Hill Farm Community Garden.[35]

The use of this side of campus for horticulture-related uses also inspired the "Proposed Landscape Design for Arboretum Lake and Language Houses in area between Ag Center and Women's Dormitories," produced by the McIlhenny field office in 1938. In this proposal we see the development of a full Arboretum along the northern side of the small Campus Lake. McIlhenny's drawing indicated that this body of water be reshaped to provide a variety of settings for the Arboretum. Olmsted Brothers' Arboretum had been located north of this spot, backing up to the swampy area marking the eastern border of the campus at the time. But the plans changed as WPA improvements turned it into a more desirable area. The Arboretum drawing, done before the Pan American House on Highland was conceived, also suggested that the other language houses be located along a gently curving roadway here. On the southern side of this Campus Lake the Agricultural Coliseum, designed by Ed-

FIG. 5.40. Agricultural research in the Hill Farm area along the eastern edge of campus in the 1970s.

ward F. Neild, in 1937, was named for Governor John Parker, known as the "Father of LSU" for his political and financial support of the move to this campus. It was touted as "the largest domed structure in the South at the time" (fig. 5.41).[36]

Many of these various planting designs were brought together in McIlhenny's "Proposed Landscape Development" plan, made over the winter of 1937–38 (fig. 5.42). Not only does this drawing present the most complete view of how these various McIlhenny projects would fit together but it was the most comprehensive map of campus produced up to that time, chronicling not only the planting proposals but also the majority of the buildings built in the boom of the 1930s.[37] Here we see the cruciform core designed by Theodore Link surrounded by a steadily growing

FIG. 5.41. Parker Coliseum, designed by architect Edward F. Neild. Courtesy of Baton Rouge Room, East Baton Rouge Parish Library

array of buildings representing the successful expansion of the university's abilities. At its core the designs of Olmsted Brothers and then Link had created a pedestrian-scale campus of closely related buildings and open spaces. The university had continued building the missing buildings along of Link's quadrangles, and by this point the only open space was the northeastern corner, adjacent to Thomas Boyd Hall, which was eventually completed by the Thomas Boyd Annex.[38] With the exception of the football and baseball stadiums and some research buildings, almost all of the significant new buildings were aligned with roadways. A careful look back at Olmsted Brothers' Preliminary Plan of 1921 shows a very different vision (see figs. 2.16 and 2.25). There, the extended structure of interrelated quads anticipated, and would have provided for, much of the expansion that occurred over the 1930s. More importantly, the great majority of outlying buildings in the Olmsted Brothers plan fit the design vision in ways that would have made them integral to the plan's success.

Notice on Olmsted Brothers' Preliminary Plan how the Women's Dormitory group east of Highland Road is composed of no less than seven separate buildings surrounding an open green lawn on axis with the North Quadrangle. This ensemble continues the main features of the overall campus plan, with primary and secondary axes, hierarchical massing, and the integration of outlying gardens and structures.[39] Notice too the Men's Dormitory group at the northwestern corner of campus, again composed of seven buildings, which here work together with the topography and existing tree groups to create an ensemble that could begin with one or two buildings and grow in a planned way over time, enhancing the overall sense of campus unity. Even the outlying agricultural structures on this plan reflect similar ordering concepts. The placement of the Campus Chapel, seemingly isolated from the overt order of the campus plan, actually would have offered an antidote by overlooking the facility for student assembly in the natural bowl of the adjacent Open Air Theater and the picturesque network of ponds and garden paths. This natural topographical feature, if developed in this way, would have offered a restful and contemplative balance to the more structured aspects of campus life, with the Music Auditorium and housing for the president and for faculty participating at a slight distance. The ritual of assembly and performance in the Music Auditorium is projected along a secondary axis through the Fine Arts Quadrangle and across the Parade Ground to the Armory and all its associated activities. And so it goes throughout the marvelous Olmsted plan. This layered interaction between buildings and planning themes was something Link's General Plan did not accomplish as effectively beyond the core. It is a dimension absent from the 1928 Wogan & Bernard plan and from most LSU plans since.

In the overall pattern of order that the McIlhenny and WDS plan portrays, a coordinated pedestrian core of interrelated buildings is surrounded by a series of roadways that became the planning armature of the campus—today's South Campus Drive, Field House Drive, Dalrymple Drive,

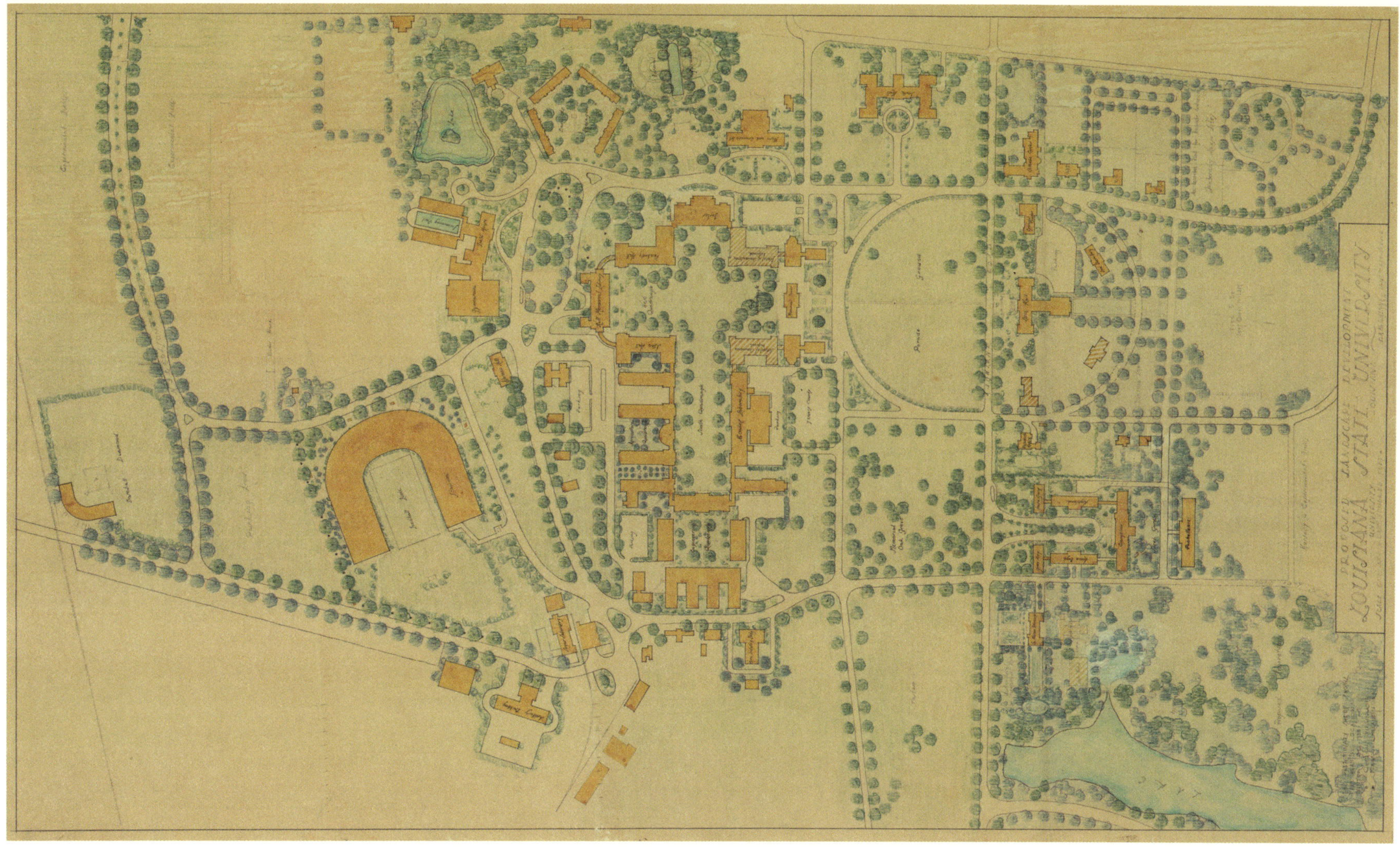

FIG. 5.42. “Proposed Landscape Development,” by E. A. McIlhenny Landscape Service in 1938, showing the role of live oaks in unifying the campus landscape. By the mid-1930s the policy of even setbacks along Highland Road had been established. Courtesy of E. A. McIlhenny Enterprises, Inc., Avery Island, LA.

and Highland Road. Along these roadways major buildings of various uses and massing strategies sprung up, from the relocated Alumni Hall (1931) and Gym Armory (1927) to the French House (1935) and Parker Coliseum (1937). The only one of these to interact with the Link plan was Leche Hall, the Law School. The location of this building along Highland Road directly opposite Memorial Tower adds to its prominence in the campus environment, placing law and its traditions (American and Roman) opposite sacrifice in the collection of associations. It is the most overtly Roman building on campus, and the only one that interacts with Link’s scheme in this way.

The large number of existing and proposed live oaks shown on this plan illustrates the important role of this species in the campus landscape. They line every roadway, as was common at the time on large streets in Baton Rouge (fig. 5.43). Although Baton Rouge lost much of its live-oak canopy to street widening in the 1960s, New Orleans has retained its distinctive live oak–lined streets. They are also to be found in the quadrangles, along with a few other spe-

FIG. 5.43. Live oaks along Highland Road. Courtesy of Jim Zietz, LSU University Relations.

FIG. 5.44. *(facing page)* The 1948 General Development Plan, by Swanson Associates, of Bloomfield Hills, Michigan, showing a strategy for expanding the academic core eastward toward the University Lakes. Courtesy of LSU Office of Facility Development.

cies distributed loosely around campus. There is even a suggestion on the plan of a widening allée of oaks from the rear façade of Leche Hall eastward toward the new University Lake. What we do not see at the large scale of this map is the other plant materials—primarily camellias, azaleas, and eventually crepe myrtles—that fill out the campus landscaping.[40]

One other key component of this emergent campus landscape experience worth noting is the entrance gates designed by WDS in 1936 (see fig. 5.3). These noble structures demarcate the university and all it represents as they intensify the experience of difference created by the controlled palette of color and form on the campus. Such gateways have been a part of the academic environment for centuries, with many striking examples in the colleges of Oxford and Cambridge, when the university grounds were not only entirely pedestrian but completely separated from the outer city. The downtown LSU campus hosted brick gateways reminiscent of Johnston Gate at Harvard (1889) or the Van Wickle Gates at Brown University (1901). The new LSU gates by WDS utilized the same pebble stucco found on the major campus buildings. And since they were built across a state highway, they do not include a closable metal gate apparatus; they are symbolic in nature.

THE IMPACT ON LATER ARCHITECTURE AND CAMPUS PLANNING AT LSU

While the essential structure of the more memorable parts of the LSU campus and its landscape were in place by the time the United States entered the Second World War, there was another master plan in the years immediately following that anticipated the explosive growth of the campus to come. The General Development Plan (1948), by Swanson Associates, Architects & Planners, was done before there was any dramatic expansion out from the university's initial core (fig. 5.44). Swanson Associates was formed in 1947 by J. Robert Swanson, of Bloomfield Hills, Michigan.[41] This plan proposed directing growth in an easterly direction toward the University Lakes. This area of campus had been designated in Olmsted Brothers' Preliminary Plan as the location of an Arboretum and adjacent various agricultural uses, backing up to the then-wooded edge of the swamp. The Arboretum was never executed, but the area has supported various, though decreasing, agricultural and horticultural uses since that time. While Link's General Plan did not extend this far to the east, it had broken with the Olmsted Brothers vision of a westward focus to the campus. This focus to the east had begun when Link effectively closed off Olmsted Brothers' western axis by the design and placement of Hill Memorial and by the location of the Gym Armory on the bluff but facing eastward. The eastward focus picked up, in planning at least, after the WPA work in 1936 opened up the lakes along the eastern edge of campus.[42]

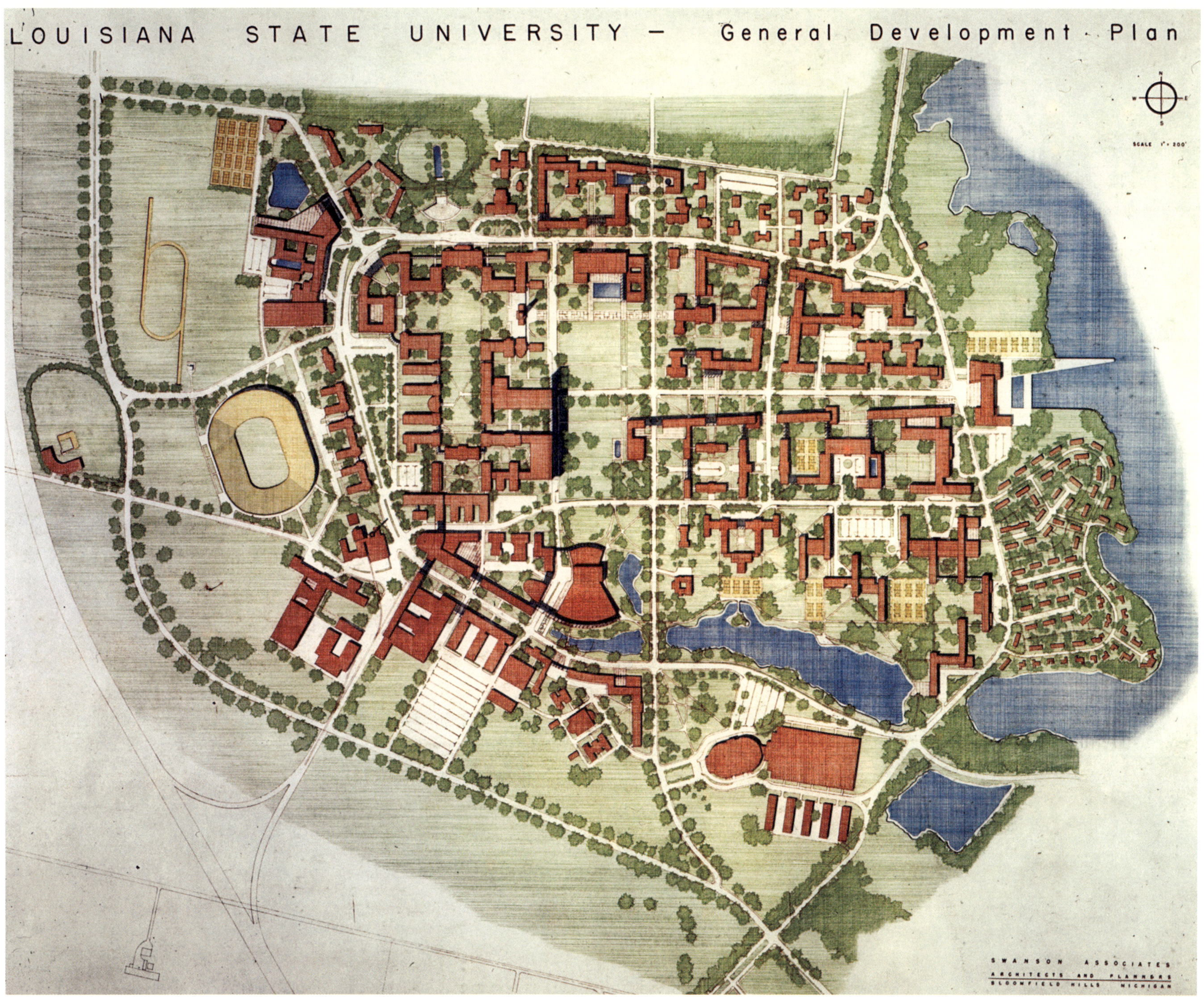
LOUISIANA STATE UNIVERSITY — General Development Plan
N
W
E
S
SCALE 1" = 200'
SWANSON ASSOCIATES
ARCHITECTS AND PLANNERS
BLOOMFIELD HILLS MICHIGAN

FIG. 5.45. Hatcher Hall, designed by the Baton Rouge architects Bodman & Murrell in 1947 and one of three men's dormitories built along the bluff facing the campus core. These buildings follow the use of a finer blond brick and articulate stone details. Office of Public Relations Records, Historic Photograph Files, RG #A0020, Louisiana State University Archives, LSU Libraries, Baton Rouge, LA.

FIG. 5.46. East and West Laville Halls, originally built as women's dormitories by August Perez & Associates, of New Orleans, in 1947. Office of Public Relations Records, Historic Photograph Files, RG #A0020, Louisiana State University Archives, LSU Libraries, Baton Rouge, LA.

The Swanson plan was the most complex and ambitious one prepared for LSU up to that time, anticipating a university with more than twice the classroom capacity it had then.[43] It was a highly organized vision that could have provided a guided development path well into the future. While not following Link's hierarchical pattern of primary and secondary axes coordinated with architectural detail, it did tie the location, mass, and orientation of future buildings into a sensible and dramatic plan diagram that accommodated automobile planning at a new scale. It was the proper successor to the Olmsted and Link plans for LSU.

Here growth was organized through a proposed series of almost Oxford-scale courtyard groupings extending eastward from Highland Road in perspectivally diminishing lines along Raphael Semmes Drive to a new "Club for Faculty and/or Students" on the Lakes. These courtyards would have been dedicated to academic clusters that could have been built up over time. Existing buildings such as the Law School, Pleasant Hall, and the Field House were also woven into new groups by the addition of adjacent buildings. The plan includes the suggestion of an addition behind Hill Memorial Library, perhaps doubling its capacity.[44] To the south of South Stadium Drive the Swanson plan depicts clusters of new dormitories in a somewhat looser configuration that also could be added to over time without losing the overall conception. The Arboretum McIlhenny had projected along the northern shore of Campus Lake is not present in the plan, but the reshaped shoreline was still being envisioned as a parklike complement to the adjacent student housing. There is even a suggestion to expand the small lake across Highland Road into an existing depression to frame a new, large campus Auditorium. Along the edge of University Lake itself the plan suggested a more suburban pattern of single and double family houses. The Parade Ground would have lost much of its familiar feel with the elimination of its memorable circular drive, the imposition of a Campus Art Museum on its northern edge, and a Student Union bridging Highland Road on the south, announcing the new eastward pattern of development.

The character of the Highland corridor as an organizing feature that had been evolving through the 1930s is here displaced by the more purposeful concept of Raphael Semmes in organizing the eastward growth. This Swanson plan pays better attention to traffic and parking organization throughout than did the WDS work of the 1930s. A "loop" road helps to rationalize campus traffic, something the university still struggles with, and the placement of university services and some engineering disciplines beyond it to the south.

This plan represents not only the fourth generation of plans for LSU but also the fourth broad-scale style of planning seen on campus in the twenty-seven years since the Olmsted Brothers firm had been hired. That firm's romantic planning methodology, which sought to integrate buildings into a picturesque whole and in which the designer's skill was subordinated to whatever beauty and inspirational values were inherent in an existing landscape, had been displaced by Link's more neoclassical pattern. In that more architectonic system, an imposed planning armature of hierarchical axes had taken center stage in organizing the relationships between buildings and the landscape. The 1930s had seen the synthetic, or piecemeal, planning efforts of WDS. Here in the Swanson plan of 1948 we see the first impressions of modernist European-style planning ideas.[45]

While in the Swanson plan the present iconic, circular Parade Ground would have lost much of its force, the planned strategies for extensive, long-term growth represent the first time this problem had been approached at LSU. It was a compromise between the necessity of an automobile-savvy approach and one organized around pedestrian-scale enclaves. Although it was not followed, it did plant the seeds for a broad southward expansion of the College of Engineering along with and adjacent to the university's maintenance facilities. It also was the first plan to suggest housing along the southern portion of the new campus lakefront for faculty and female students. Male student housing was to grow along what has since become Fraternity Row, along Dalrymple Drive. The plan also acknowledged earlier intentions for growth along the western bluff by showing the series of easterly facing buildings growing southward from the relocated Alumni Hall, designed by Bodman & Murrell in 1947—Johnston, Hatcher, and Hodges Halls (fig. 5.45). These buildings, the first on campus designed by a Baton Rouge firm, struck a functional intermediary between the materials palette begun by Link and that used by Wogan & Bernard in the Gym Armory. They were rapidly followed by the somewhat similar material strategy used for East and West Laville Halls by Perez & Associates (figs. 5.46 and 5.47).

FIG. 5.47. Architect's rendering of the new women's dormitories and cafeteria behind the Maison Française to the east of Highland Road. Courtesy of LSU Office of Facility Development.

Conclusion

In the earliest years of the republic, the college filled an important gap in America's social structure, but it was, in the large part, a devout sectarian effort, steeped in missionary purposes and structured to create America's clergy. Institutions such as Harvard and Yale would transform themselves beyond this singular purpose, becoming homes for classical training and for educating the sons of America's elite. New experiments also blossomed in the post-Revolutionary period, notably the publicly funded and nondenominational University of Virginia—the direct outgrowth of the passions of Thomas Jefferson and his acceptance of the Enlightenment.

—JOHN AUBREY DOUGLAS, "California and a Great American Movement"

The story of the development of the university in the United States has been one of opening up opportunity to increasingly wide sectors of society while spreading across broadening landscapes. Jefferson's role in this process was momentous. The publicly owned, nonreligious University of Virginia, with its pavilions housing different academic disciplines focused on a central library surrounded by an expansive lawn, has become the primary example of what the architectural historian William Pierson described as a "controlled environment . . . essential to the rational pursuit of knowledge" (fig. C.1). Pierson called it "one of the most enlightened and visionary conceptions in the history of Western Man."[1] From this beginning, the university campus in the United States has developed into a widely used cultural form allowing the reinterpretation of historical models toward new and evolving social agendas, becoming the basis for many further innovations (fig. C.2).[2]

The campus has become a key component in the broader American effort to build an Enlightenment-inspired liberal society dedicated to the rational use of evolving bodies of knowledge toward the increase of freedom and prosperity widely defined. In fact, the term *campus* as it is used here is largely an American invention, its first known uses being in the early nineteenth century and referring to a university green.[3] The Latin root of this term, *camp,* in addition to its more familiar meaning as a place where an army is housed in tents, also refers to a field of contest, such as the Campus Martius in ancient Rome, a place for games, athletic practice, and military drills, a sense still carried today in the idea of a parade ground. At the University of Virginia and subsequent American campuses, we see this sense develop through the adaptation and reuse of two other historical archetypes, the cloister and the lawn. At LSU we have seen the role of the cloister in Olmsted Brothers' and especially Link's work and that of the lawn in the development of the Highland Road corridor through the 1930s.

The medieval cloister was itself a reinterpretation of the Roman forum that survived in the early Christian basilica complexes as a symbol of monastic devotion and self-discipline. The monks would use their rosary beads and the cloistered walks to mark the regularity of their steps in prayer. The ideal square pattern of the cloister, typically with a tree or pool in the center, became a symbol for their devotion, a symbol of an ordered universe excluding and contrasting with the unpredictability of the everyday world. This form was adapted in the English university towns of Oxford and Cambridge as a controlled open space at the heart of each college, set apart from the outer economic and social world of the town, a model of the reflective self-discipline required of academic pursuit, based on the monastic model. The separation of town and gown was ritually reinforced by sometimes elaborate gateways and gate-closing ceremonies marking the threshold of demarcation.

We have seen Link's use of the idea of the forum-become-cloister at LSU, making this reference central. Outside of that cloistered, inner core the LSU campus developed in the 1920s and 1930s in line with the idea of the lawn, a more recent invention. As far back as Jacobean England, the manor house surrounded by a manicured field of green had been a symbol of prestige. At first these manicured fields were simply the result of grazing herds, but as they were brought up to and around the manor house, they

FIG. C.1. Thomas Jefferson's architectural design for the public University of Virginia, a hallmark of the Enlightenment search for a disciplined liberal society, set a precedent that has been widely followed. This design combined unique pavilions for separate academic disciplines and connecting arcades with a broad central lawn presided over by a library, all modeled after Roman examples, marking the first "teaching campus" in the United States. Detail from *A map of the state of Virginia . . . from the late surveys authorized by the Legislature and other original and authentic documents,* by Herman Boÿe, 1825 (G3880 1859 .B615 1859). University of Virginia Library.

FIG. C.2. The architect's rendering of the LSU Campanile, which invokes the shared values of sacrifice and service as it reaches for the heavens in front of the sweeping expanse of the Parade Ground at the entry to the sheltered quadrangles of the university. Courtesy of LSU *Gumbo*, 1924.

eventually became a defining feature of the British aristocratic landscape.[4] These lawns were expensive to maintain without the constant presence of livestock, and the middle class did not adopt them until the invention of mowing machinery in the nineteenth century.

But like the regularized green space of the cloister, the lawn is also a controlled and disciplined space. It became an expression of Enlightenment social order in the broad green open spaces that separated many public and government buildings from the street. There is a religious reference here as well. Unlike the Continental practice of locating the primary church or cathedral in the center of the town, frequently adjacent to the market, the English developed the use of a "close," or enclosed green, to surround the church or cathedral and set it apart in an idealized way from the secular space of the town. This is still exemplified today at Westminster Abbey in London and even more so at Salisbury Cathedral. The practice of setting other kinds of government institutions apart in the same way followed and became an important part of the colonial British experience in North America. Thus, when Jefferson called for an open green space at the center of his university plan, he may have been recalling the Palace Green in Williamsburg or crystallizing the New England ideal of the village green, as well as adapting the older form of the cloister to the public purposes of his university.[5]

The effective merging of these two archetypes, lawn and cloister, was solidified, as universities began to expand in size and scope, by the use of campus gates such as those designed by Weiss, Dreyfous & Seiferth for LSU in 1936. These noble structures demarcate the measured space of the university, as they intensify the experience of difference created by the controlled palette of color and form one finds on campus. The downtown LSU campus had brick gateways reminiscent of the Johnston Gate at Harvard, and many other campuses across the country also followed that example. The difference between Ivy League examples and those at state universities such as LSU is that the latter gates serve primarily a symbolic function, as there is no wall.[6]

What all of this demonstrates is a steady, thoughtful adaptation of significant cultural forms to changing social needs through invention and planning. Among the hundreds of examples across the country in these years, some of the most innovative were those by Ralph Adams Cram at Rice, Cass Gilbert and others at Yale, and Myron Hunt at Pomona College in California. These and other examples range from Jefferson's inspirational model, through the grandiose Beaux Arts "White City" of the Chicago 1893 Exposition, to the more romantic neo-Gothic examples, with Georgian and many other less distinct influences thrown in. The results of this process are among the finest accomplishments of the great American experiment.

Seen in the context of these broad historical processes, the work of Rick Olmsted in identifying and interpreting Louisiana landscapes and Theodore Link in combining and reinterpreting key architectural traditions appears to have been not only inventive but engaged with a central theme in modern Western civilization, the creation of an open, educated, and increasingly prosperous society, bringing the state university of Louisiana to this task. The work of WDS in the 1930s continued this effort.

The opening of American universities to the middle class, which began with the Morrill Act of 1862, necessitated a great increase in the number and size of campuses to accommodate the larger student populations. In particular, the period following the First World War saw explosive growth at colleges and universities across the nation, accompanied by many new conceptions of order, planning, and campus architecture. While the best of these public campuses began with a coherent and adaptable campus plan, very few have been able to maintain the order of the initial vision over the subsequent decades of growth and change. Even with a coherent master plan, coordinating and controlling large numbers of buildings commissioned by different administrations, designed by different architects, and built over a wide span of time are difficult tasks. This is true when a university understands the challenge and develops a culture of planning within the institution; the situation can become even worse when it does not. When one considers the additional dilemma of individual automobile ownership and associated parking requirements, it is remarkable that the LSU campus has turned out as well as it has without the guidance of strong and comprehensive master plans or the commitment of the university to utilize one during most of the years since Link.[7]

The 1920s and 1930s saw the university struggle with growth and order. This led to recognition of the need for further planning, which resulted in the sweeping vision of the Swanson Plan of the immediate postwar years. In less than thirty years, between 1921 and 1947, a diverse array of planners utilized methodologies from Olmsted Brothers' romantic and Link's neoclassical ones, through an ad hoc process, to the modernist planning of Swanson. But in the following decades neither the university nor the state developed a culture of planning or a general recognition of its value, and the great disaster of unplanned growth that followed this lost opportunity created problems for LSU that unfortunately were typical of those faced by many public institutions of similar size around the country. These include traffic and pedestrian overlaps (already an acknowledged problem in 1947); random placement of large buildings, uncoordinated with more broadly conceived growth and circulation strategies; the hodgepodge development of lesser buildings; and overreliance on existing streets as planning corridors, to name a few of the most prominent issues facing campus planners. The tragedy of locating a large interruptive structure such as Middleton Library in

FIG. C.3. Middleton Library, built in the 1950s. The library interrupted Link's architectural relationships and obscured their historical references. Office of Public Relations Records, Historic Photograph Files, RG #A0020, Louisiana State University Archives, LSU Libraries, Baton Rouge, LA.

the center of the historical Main Quadrangle is a consequence, indicative of a pattern of thinking in the 1950s and 1960s in which the value of integrated planning coordinated with older architecture was not seen critically (fig. C.3).[8] We can do better.

Citizens and public servants must find opportunities to provide well-designed public environments in which architecture and planning are coordinated in the service of the broadest goals and ambitions of the state and its people. Louisiana has many beautiful neighborhoods, urbane districts, and delightful "main streets," but other than the university campuses, very few outstanding public environments celebrate the common commitments and shared opportunities these provide. The core of the LSU campus is an example of what we can do when we set our sights high. It stands out today as one of the most successful and inspiring examples in the state, one meant by its architect to become "an intuitive course in architecture for the students," spreading the influence of its ideals and inspirations across the highlands and lowlands of Louisiana.

APPENDIX

Chronological Development of the Site through 1926

(based on dates of construction contracts)

1918

Twelve hundred acres purchased

1922

November 23, 1922	Warehouse (rail)	$10,319.36
November 23, 1922	Dairy Barn	$52,128.78
November 23, 1922	Beef Cattle Barn	$42,669.70
November 23, 1922	Dairyman's Residence	$8,075.41
December 18, 1922	Engineering Shops	$184,135.66
December 18, 1922	Powerhouse	$70,042.96

1923

January 12, 1923	utility tunnels	$204,220.00
January 12, 1923	Engineering Laboratory	$115,907.93
January 12, 1923	Laundry Building	$19,358.39
March 12, 1923	Main Engineering Building	$240,948.93
March 12, 1923	Agricultural Group	$477,278.33
April 24, 1923	South Administration Building	$54,843.98
April 24, 1923	North Administration Building	$54,843.98
April 24, 1923	D. F. Boyd Memorial Hall	$102,788.98
April 24, 1923	Law Building	$102,726.50
May 9, 1923	sanitary sewers	$43,320.85
June 26, 1923	George Peabody Hall	$290,034.70

July 9, 1923	Hill Memorial Library	$330,275.31
August 9, 1923	Stock Judging Pavilion	$62,492.43
August 14, 1923	storm sewers	$55,099.50
December 22, 1923	Residence, Dean of Agriculture	$22,447.02
1924		
January 7, 1924	Chemical Laboratory (Chemistry Group)	$471,074.29
February 18, 1924	Sugarhouse	$99,591.54
July 14, 1924	Hog Barn	$10,116.10
November 26, 1924	Dining Hall	$323,489.02
[*erected in 1924*]	Athletic Stadium	$130,087.70
[*no date given*]	Campanile	$211,625.16
1925		
June 17, 1925	Dormitories for Men (Pentagon)	[*no cost given*]
October 5, 1925	Band Practice House	$3,533.30
December 16, 1925	Greek Theater	$22,500.00
December 22, 1925	Poultry Plant	$11,182.00
1926		
February 26, 1926	Residence for Manager of Dining Hall and	$17,326.41
	Residence for Commandant	[*no cost given*]
	Early finish on eleven academic buildings	$404,940.11
	landscaping	$50,000.00

Source: New Campus and Buildings of the Louisiana State University, pamphlet (1926?), Louisiana and Lower Mississippi Valley Collections, LSU Libraries, Baton Rouge, LA.

NOTES

1. THE DOWNTOWN CAMPUS

1. The Journalism Building on campus today occupies this historic Alumni Hall, which was dismantled and rebuilt in an enlarged form in its present location in the 1930s.

2. Hill Memorial Library, Alumni Hall, Garig Hall, and Peabody Hall were among the buildings that had been donated to the university. See Ruffin, *Under Stately Oaks;* and Thomas Boyd to Charles A. Favrot, 3 November 1920, Boyd Papers.

3. The Harvard campus had been given its distinctive red-brick Georgian-style gates beginning in the late 1890s, with the McKim design of Johnson Gate in 1889. These, along with the eventual iron fence, helped to establish the identity of Harvard Yard as a precinct set apart, and the gates became a model for campus designs around the country. See Stern, "University Campus."

2. FREDERICK LAW OLMSTED JR. AND THE GREATER UNIVERSITY

1. See untitled digital scan of newspaper clippings in the Michael Desmond Collection.

2. Upon the death of his elder brother, John Charles Olmsted, in 1920, Frederick Law Olmsted Jr. became a senior partner, just before his work for LSU began. See Klaus, "Frederick Law Olmsted, Jr."

3. Olmsted, "Report to Newspapers." The next several quotations are from this same source.

4. See "History of Gartness." The city of Baton Rouge had offered land along Perkins Road for the university's dairy operations as early as 1878.

5. See Boyd to Favrot, 3 November 1920, Boyd Papers.

6. For the Olmsted Brothers firm's copy of the survey, see fig. 2.3; the student survey in the Olmsted Archives is essentially the same. The Olmsted Archives is now part of the National Park Service.

7. The engineering students' survey utilizes a datum 21 feet higher than that of Olmsted Brothers' commissioned survey. Although the relative elevations differ because of this, the two surveys are very similar, if not identical, in most other respects.

8. These lakes were created during the Works Progress Administration years.

9. See Foote, *Beleaguered City,* 143.

10. This graveyard appears in only one other drawing, the working study of the Olmsted Preliminary Plan (see fig. 2.16).

11. This slight pond was probably the result of removing earth to build the mounds so many centuries ago.

12. The three ditches on the site also follow this orientation, as can be seen in figs. 2.4 and 2.7.

13. On Frederick Law Olmsted Jr.'s planning philosophy, see www.aapra.org/Pugsley/OlmstedFrederickLaw.html and www.olmsted.org/the-olmsted-legacy/frederick-law-olmsted-jr.

14. Note that Olmsted Brothers' Preliminary Plan of October 1921 showed an electric streetcar or rail line along the eastern side of Highland Road (fig. 2.16).

15. The Preliminary Plan appears in the Olmsted Archives in several versions, fig. 2.16 perhaps being the clearest.

16. An aerial photograph of Macdonald College, in Ontario, in the Olmsted Archives files relating to LSU suggests that the kind of quadrangle arrangement over a bluff that it shows may have been an inspiration for the LSU plan.

17. Personal conversation with staff of Olmsted Archives, March 2008.

18. Although the arboretum was not part of the later campus plan by Theodore Link, these eastern parts of the property were initially developed for agricultural and horticultural uses. The decreasing "Hill Farm," behind the Lod Cook facilities, is all that remains today of Olmsted's vision of the appropriate use of this upland for agricultural research for Louisiana's hill country.

19. These barns flanking the Livestock Judging Pavilion were designed and provided through Olmsted Brothers by the Louden Machinery Company, of Fairfield, Iowa, a noted provider of such farm buildings at the time.

3. THEODORE C. LINK, ARCHITECT

1. Tetley, "Theodore C. Link Biographical Chronology"; personal correspondence with Gary Tetley, architectural historian, St. Louis, September 2008.

2. Gary Tetley to author, September 2008. "I have identified Link's projects in Mississippi during the construction of the State Capital Building from 1900–1903. At the University of Mississippi in Oxford he renovated and built wings on the Lyceum and designed and built Ricks Hall. He was also doing work for Oscar Johnson in Holly Springs. Then there is a 12 year period before he does anymore work in Mississippi. In 1916 he returns to Jackson to repair and renovate the long vacant 1839 Old State Capital. Then from 1918–1921 he is in change of a massive state building campaign that includes just about all state colleges and hospitals. I have identified some of the projects Link designed during this period but not all. He returned to the campus at Oxford for an additional wing and dining room to Ricks Hall and more renovation to the Lyceum. He also built a new chemistry building. At MSU he built Perry Hall."

3. According to an article from an unknown Mississippi newspaper in my possession, dated 5 August 1922, "Mr. Link . . . was selected chiefly because of the splendid record made by him in Mississippi as architect of the new capitol building, supervising architect of the rehabilitation of the old capitol, and his great work in directing the expenditure of the $5,000,000 for betterments at state institutions." Some of this work was done in association with a partner, Wilbur Trueblood, also from St. Louis.

4. Theodore C. Link to Governor John Parker, telegram, 6 February 1922, and letter, 11 February 1922, in Boyd Papers, digital scans in author's possession.

5. See Link to Parker, 25 March 1921, Boyd Papers, digital scan in author's possession. The next several quotations are from this same letter.

6. Article from unidentified newspaper, 3 August 1922. The article continues: "Louisiana architects expressed the feeling that the state board had not given the matter of availability of state architects qualified to undertake such an improvement, sufficient investigation and endeavored to show that the best interest of the commonwealth would be served in postponing the selection of an architect and a further consideration of the matter. . . . The board of administration plainly indicated that it did not feel an investigation necessary and with little discussion named Mr Linke [*sic*] as architect."

7. This firm had been known as Toledano, Wogan & Bernard until the death of Albert Toledano in 1923.

8. An article titled "Plans Materially Altered by Theodore C. Link, Architect," published in the *State Times* on 21 April 1923, contains perhaps the first public description of Link's design of the new university campus.

9. Link's General Plan, for example, also indicates that the building to be located at the site of what is today Nicholson Hall was to be a physics building and that the three buildings along the western side of the South Quadrangle were to be for agricultural sciences.

10. The form of what became Dodson Auditorium is shown but not labeled on Link's General Plan.

11. Only digital scans of rather small-scale reproductions of this originally large rendering are known to exist.

12. The earliest plan drawing in which these pavilions are indicated is a 1930s WDS plan, although Peabody Hall, designed and detailed by Link, has such pavilions, and one can therefore assume that he intended these four buildings to define the corners in this way.

13. Both of these porches were part of the original building but have since been filled in.

4. ARCHITECTURE OF THE CAMPUS

1. In a letter to William Thorton, Jefferson states that the pavilions were to present "a variety of appearance, no two alike, so as to serve as specimens for the Architecture lecturer." See Pierson, *American Buildings and Their Architects,* 1:327.

2. For other prominent sally ports in university campus design, see Reed College in Portland, Oregon, by Patterson & Beach (1912), and Washington University in St. Louis, Missouri, by Cope & Stewardson (1900), with whose plan Link surely would have been familiar, in Turner, *Campus,* 222, 226.

3. Although the Romans used concrete extensively, benefiting from its ability to make an architecture of rich spatial diversity possible, they always covered it with other decorative treatments.

4. See esp. Earley, "What Concrete Means to the Craftsmen."

5. See U.S. National Park Service, *Meridian Hill Park Cultural Landscape Report;* on Earley's contribution to Meridian Hill Park, see the National Park Service website, www.nps.gov/mehi/historyculture/jearley.htm.

6. Although Earley's work was mostly confined to the Washington, DC, area, he did have a hand in several significant projects in Chicago and a few elsewhere. For details, see Cron, *Man Who Made Concrete Beautiful.*

7. See www.myfranciscan.org/index.php?option=com_content&view=article&id=84&Itemid=1.

8. Forgey, "Concrete Proof of One Man's Legacy."

9. See Earley, "Architectural Concrete."

10. Ibid. As far as Link's role in the selection of this style, other than what Earley says here, we know only that it was one of the architectural idioms in whose use he was competent.

11. Ibid.

12. See Palladio's *Four Books of Architecture,* bk. 2, plate 35, and bk. 3, plate 20, for examples of his use of this motif.

13. The base of Memorial Tower is solidly built of reinforced concrete walls and structure, covered with the architectural stucco of Earley. The tower portion itself, however, has a concrete-enclosed steel frame with hollow clay tile that was reworked in the 1960s.

14. The building was altered in the mid-1940s. The gates were pulled out to the face of the exterior walls, and bronze doors were added so that the space could be closed off from the exterior, making it an interior room. This treatment unfortunately lessened the space's effectiveness as a memorial.

15. The young architect-in-training Charles Eames worked for the St. Louis firm of Trueblood & Graf from 1926 to 1929. Wilbur Trueblood and Theodore Link had at one time been partners.

16. The Cloister of San Lorenzo in Florence is one possible reference for this kind of elevation, with a porch and columns over an arcaded gallery wall. Cass Gilbert had made this association some years before in a letter to the architect Irving Pond regarding his designs for the University of Michigan campus master plan: "You may find that by a scattered, rambling low structure, each function housed in a separate wing or in a separate section, you could accomplish wonders. Is it not in fact a sort of brotherhood building? May it not therefore partake of the character of some monastic building with its cloister yard, its refectory, its meeting or council hall, its little cells or bedrooms?" Christen and Flanders, *Cass Gilbert,* 80.

17. The complete extent of these arcades, which is not clear on the General Plan, is shown more clearly in a "key plan" dated 19 June 1923.

18. See Palladio, *Four Books on Architecture.* These towers resemble an amalgam of various similar corner-marking towers shown in Palladio's bk. 2, plates 35, 38, 42, 44, and 45.

19. The influence of the Boston Public Library was widespread. Cass Gilbert had used a similar design for the new library at the University of Texas in Austin a few years earlier, for example.

20. The motif of a central arched window flanked by smaller rectangular openings or windows is repeated again in the center of the Library's east, or main, façade.

21. The utilitarian rear façade of Hill Memorial Library reveals the extent of the internal stack system in such a way that one may conjecture that the designer was allowing for future expansion of the collection.

22. It is important to say that we have no direct evidence that Link was using such references in his designs for the LSU buildings of this campus. Nor, for example, do we have direct evidence that he was using Palladio as a reference. The symbolic interpretations are conjectural only.

23. Atkinson Hall held the School of Engineering until it was moved out to the Center for Engineering and Business Administration (CEBA) Building in the 1970s. Today the School of Architecture occupies this noble structure.

24. In recent years I have been fortunate to have one of these offices as my faculty office on campus.

25. It is the acts of coming and going to the cafeteria with friends or going to meet a professor that bring the student ritually into direct contact with this axis.

26. Jefferson's design was meant to instruct; details of the various pavilions were taken from his knowledge of Roman buildings.

27. On the copy of Link's General Plan held by LSU, a second, perhaps similar feature is shown directly across the quadrangle from the fountain; it does not appear elsewhere and was never built.

28. Except for Atkinson Hall, the buildings in this group fall outside of the Getty-sponsored historic-preservation study of the LSU core campus.

29. The complexity of door types is exacerbated by the fact that over the decades many of the original wooden doors have been replaced by modern aluminum and glass doors. This has been done to increase visibility and door life, as the original wooden doors were very heavy and not able to stand up to the intense daily use. The campus was designed for fifteen hundred students, and enrollments passed that number long ago. But the replacements do not necessarily acknowledge the original intent of the door designs.

30. I thank LSU professor Paul Hoffman for this observation.

5. GROWTH BEYOND THE CORE

1. The Olmsted Brothers had developed plans and reports for dozens of educational institutions by this point in its history, as noted in a list of more than seventy-five sent to LSU in 1921.

2. It is impossible to determine whether Link's arguments against hiring Olmsted Brothers were based solely on his stated convictions or perhaps on his desire to influence the outcome of the selection process in his favor. But his comments certainly seem to indicate a disregard, if not a lack of understanding, of what Olmsted Brothers had accomplished, of what the legacy of the senior Olmsted really was.

3. See Williams, *Huey Long,* 517–21.

4. See Leighninger, *Building Louisiana.*

5. Memorial Coliseum in Los Angeles, designed in 1921 and complete by 1923 as a tribute to veterans of the First World War, has a somewhat similar mid-level entry, although there it is located at one end of the stadium, not along the 50-yard line.

6. These three buildings were, however, designed and provided by the Louden Machinery Company, of Fairfield, Iowa.

7. On the role of Clarence Link after his father's death, see chapter 3.

8. The many small "key plans" that show up in Link's working drawings for campus buildings do not show outlying structures.

9. Although by this time design had begun on the present Gym Armory in its current location on axis, the idea of an LSU Museum persisted.

It disappears in the WDS work of the 1930s, then reappears in the Swanson plan of 1948. It existed for many years in the base of Memorial Tower before eventually moving to the Shaw Center, in downtown Baton Rouge. At the present moment, just as the university is about to publish the LSU Treasures compendium, the very existence of its Museum is threatened by looming state budget cuts.

10. This structure, designed by Link as a one of a number of residences intended for faculty, was offered to President Boyd. When Boyd expressed his desire to continue living at the President's House on the downtown campus, William Dodson, the dean of agriculture, moved into this building for a time.

11. This palette was later used for a series of smaller buildings along South Campus Drive beyond the Engineering Shops known today as the Veterinary Science Building, Franconi Hall, the Food Science Building, and the Nuclear Science Building. Later a kind of hybrid of both materials was used by WDS on Audubon Hall, stucco in front, brick on the rear, again probably a cost-cutting measure.

12. Leche Hall also utilized a different, more overtly Roman version of this treatment, raising the main floor ceremoniously to the top of a grand entry stair. Compare this building's treatment with Link's treatment of the relation between the grand stair and the main floor in his Main Engineering Building (Atkinson Hall), for example.

13. The WDS work on campus during this period includes the Music & Dramatic Arts Building, Smith Hall (now Pleasant Hall), alterations to Foster Hall, a boys' dormitory, the Greek Theater, stadium work, a women's dormitory, the Huey Long Field House, an Animal Industry Building, Highland Hall, the French House, Annie Boyd Hall, Evangeline Hall, the Campus Gates, the Faculty Club, Leche Hall (the Old Law School), the Physics & Math Building (Nicholson Hall), the Panhellenic Building (now demolished), the Commerce Building (Himes Hall), the Geology Building, a senior graduate dormitory, and a dormitory for faculty.

14. Although these four drawings show the entire campus with existing and proposed buildings, there are inconsistencies. The first two, entitled "Layout of Louisiana State University," are dated 31 October 1932 and 31 October 1934. Both, however, show the Huey Long Field House, which was not completed until 1935, in its final form. These drawings, as well as the complete records of Weiss, Dreyfous & Seiferth can be found at the Southeast Architectural Archives, Tulane University, New Orleans.

15. The property occupied by the Episcopal Student Center and those occupied by the Catholic and Baptist Student Centers, to the north, are leased from the university. The eventual presence of a religious building, the Law School, and the Faculty Club, all ultimately unrelated uses, on this prominent block opposite Memorial Tower is the result of years of indecision. The Episcopal Student Center was designed by Wogan & Bernard in 1928, before the stock market crash the following year, but was not built for several years.

16. This stucco had also been used on the Faculty Residence built by Link on Highland, even though the building's design was not as ceremonial as the designs for the academic buildings.

17. The Huey Long Field House was built in a somewhat more yellow brick than the St. Joe used by Link and Wogan & Bernard. Its location and placement indicate a response to the adjacent Gym Armory and the Native American mounds opposite.

18. The style of this romantic building could be seen as LSU's nearest approximation of a medieval style, which was sweeping the country.

19. The plans are located in the McIlhenny Company Archives at Avery Island, La.

20. E. A. McIlhenny to Leon Weiss, 1 December 1936, McIlhenny Company Archives, folder 193, MA 038, Weiss, Dreyfous & Seiferth, New Orleans, LA.

21. See advertisement for McIlhenny's "Jungle Gardens" in the 1927 *Gumbo,* which reads: "We Furnished the Plants and Landscaped the New Louisiana State University Campus."

22. After leaving McIlhenny's field office, Gunn established a successful practice in Houston, where he executed many designs in the River Oaks area, returning to Louisiana in the mid-1950s to design the gardens at Rosedown Plantation near St. Francisville. See correspondence between McIlhenny and Baker beginning in July 1937 in the McIlhenny Company Archives, folder 25, EA, MA. According to McIlhenny company president Edward Simmons, the landscape architects also included Jan Garber, Neil Simmons, and John Kennedy, and there may have been others. See Cox, "Campus Landscape," n. 4.

23. This plan was preceded by more extensive, annotated plans for the main-quadrangles area showing intentions for reworking the entire core area, also present in the McIlhenny Company Archives. Although McIlhenny's "foundation" planting apparently continued into the late 1930s, today virtually no traces of this scheme remain.

24. The passage between Prescott and Stubbs was occupied for years by a "temporary building" and therefore was not included on this plan. The widened area between Allen and Prescott was later partially filled by an additional building.

25. This form shows up again in McIlhenny's "Proposed Landscape Development" plan, in the small circular feature with four walks in the center of the Engineering Quadrangle, behind Atkinson and at the entry to Smith (Pleasant) Hall.

26. This survey indicates a standing-water swamp here with cypress trees along the edges but does not cover the full area eventually incorporated into these Formal Gardens and their surrounding trees.

27. Anecdotal stories on campus attribute the design of these Formal Gardens to Dean Broussard, of the LSU Ag Center and to Steele Burden, but this drawing makes it clear that credit must be given to the landscape architect Harry Baker, working for McIlhenny.

28. Stakely, "Steele Burden and Windrush."

29. Cox, "Campus Landscape."

30. Correspondence in the McIlhenny Company Archives, folder 118, EA drawer, MA 045, indicates that the university ordered thirty live oaks for the "Main Quadrangle" in January 1938. But these oaks inside the quadrangles were probably planted by Burden. See also Cox, "Campus Landscape."

31. The second French House garden design is dated January 1939; the first is undated.

32. The two rear diagonal wings of these halls, like the main buildings designed by Perez & Associates, were added in 1954 and 1955. When these wings were added, the architects apparently studied the possibility of adding wings to the eastern side of Evangeline Hall as well. These wings added another level of spatial richness to the composition of the dormitory buildings. As afterthoughts, however, they could not have done so in a manner compatible with that initially proposed by the Olmsted Brothers' Preliminary Plan.

33. Besides the extensive collections on Avery Island, perhaps the finest collection of LSU-sponsored camellias from this period can still be found at the Hammond Research Station, on the Tangipahoa River east of Hammond. This collection, begun and developed by W. F. "Hody" Wilson Jr. from the mid-1930s, and today has more than 450 named cultivars among the more than 600 varieties to be found there.

34. Olmsted, "Report to Newspapers."

35. See "About Hill Farm," www.lsuagcenter.com/en/our_offices/departments/SPESS/Hill+Farm/.

36. See Leighninger, *Building Louisiana,* 25. The WPA provided funds for a number of projects on campus, including Alex Box Stadium, the northern end of the football stadium, a student health center, the Physics and Math Building, the Agricultural Administration Building, the Panhellion, and the University Lakes. See ibid., 103–4. Neild's other buildings on campus included the Infirmary and the two women's dormitories.

37. This plan appears to have been produced before the revisions were made to the designs for the French House, the Arboretum, and the Vegetable and Cutting Garden.

38. This building, which was not added until the 1960s, only loosely followed the example of Link's massing and architectural language. At first glance it seems to fit in, but a closer look reveals its faults, the most obvious of which is that its location, and the location of its corner tower, is not in line with the three other, older corner towers.

39. Over the years, the university has built equally large dormitories for women in the Highland and Laville complexes, but without the complementary richness seen in this plan.

40. Governor Huey Long's assassination in 1935 was followed by a period of unrestrained corruption after the boom years of state and federal largesse. Governor Richard Leche went to prison in 1940 for mail fraud, among other charges; LSU president James Monroe Smith was imprisoned for embezzling $500,000 in university funds to play the stock market, unsuccessfully; and some twenty other state employees were also indicted. Along with these scandals, the university sued McIlhenny in 1939 for overpayment, charging that as a personal friend of Governor Leche he had been given no bid contracts, in violation of state law, and that his work at LSU had gone unsupervised, by Smith's orders. The university charged that McIlhenny had been given the contracts illegally, because Smith and the executive committee of the LSU Board of Supervisions had not been given board approval and no bids had been taken. McIlhenny had been given two contracts to do work at LSU, the first in October 1937, to landscape the campus "in keeping with the dignity of the great university," and the second in December 1938. McIlhenny also had state contracts for landscaping work at Southeastern Louisiana College, in Hammond, and the University of Southwestern Louisiana, in Lafayette. In January 1940 the state attorney general refused to allow the state to pay McIlhenny the balance due on any of these contracts even though the State Board of Education requested permission to pay for work already done and to allow completion of the work at Southeastern. In September 1940 McIlhenny was indicted, along with Leche, for overcharging LSU. The former attorney general, James P. Ellison, and Smith were named in the indictment. In 1942 the Louisiana State Supreme Court ruled that competitive bidding had not been required and that the university had gotten its money's worth from McIlhenny, and the charges were dropped. However, these events effectively severed any further relationship between McIlhenny and LSU. See Hebert, "Remembering the Scandals"; "E. A. McIlhenny Indicted with Leche in L.S.U. Landscaping," and "Huge Overcharge for Landscaping Claimed by L.S.U.," unidentified newspaper clippings in the McIlhenny Collection, Hill Memorial Library; "Gardener Denies Permit to Settle McIlhenny Bills," *New Orleans Times-Picayune,* 24 January 1940, also in the McIlhenny Collection; and Roger M. Grace, "Edward A. McIlhenny: Businessman, Naturalist, Author . . . Fibber," Reminiscing, *Los Angeles Metropolitan News Enterprise,* 21 October 2004, www.metnews.com/articles/2004/reminiscing102104.htm.

41. Swanson had previously worked with Eliel Saarinen alongside the elder Saarinen's soon-to-be-famous son Eero and had married Eliel's only daughter, Pipsan.

42. After 1936, residential subdivisions began to expand along the opposite shores of University Lake.

43. Swanson Associates produced three, slightly different "option" plans in developing the final plan described here.

44. Although this particular configuration of an expanded university library also appears to have required the removal of the Native American mounds to make it possible, the idea of expanding Hill Memorial to the rear in some manner is certainly one of the best ideas proposed here.

45. See Le Corbusier's 1922 "Contemporary Plan for a City for Three Million Inhabitants" and his plans for Marseilles, with their towers-in-the-

park idea, similar to Swanson Associates' dormitory slabs in their parklike setting along Campus Lake. Boesiger and Girsberger, 316–19, 344–46. For the General Motors Technical Center in Warren, Michigan, being designed by Eero Saarinen at the same time that Swanson's General Development Plan for LSU was being prepared, see Temko 16–33.

CONCLUSION

1. Pierson, *American Buildings and Their Architects,* 1:317.

2. See Turner, *Campus;* Stern, "University Campus"; and Gaines, *Campus as a Work of Art.* Another crucial aspect of the growth of the university idea in the United States that influenced LSU was the Morrill Act, signed into law by Abraham Lincoln in 1862, during the Civil War. It resulted in the rapid establishment of almost seventy colleges and universities and ushered in a public policy that utilized public institutions "such as the university, to shape America's political, economic, and social experiment." It "forced the expansion of higher education toward an education and research model suitable for a changing national economy" and encouraged the addition of programs in agriculture and mechanical arts. This trend was extended by such federal legislation as the Hatch Act of 1887, which supported the teaching of science in agriculture and encouraged experimentation. These acts were part of a broad process that has continued to this day with the establishment of technical and community colleges across the nation. Even corporate environments have jumped on board, beginning with the General Motors Technical Center in Warren, Michigan, and including the suburban campuses of IBM and others companies in the 1960s and, most recently, the Microsoft campus in Redmond, Washington, to cite a few prominent examples.

3. See *Oxford English Dictionary,* s.v. "campus" and "camp."

4. In English garden history the invention of the ha-ha, a wall or other barrier set in a ditch so as not to mar the landscape, intended to keep cattle from entering the lawn immediately surrounding the manor, marks the controlled esthetic or leisure dimension. According to Horace Walpole, "The contiguous ground of the park without the sunk fence was to be harmonized with the lawn within; and the garden in its turn was to be set free from its prim regularity, that it might assort with the wilder country without." *Essay on Modern Gardening.*

5. See O'Malley, "Lawn in Early American Landscape." Note Ralph Waldo Emerson's similar sentiment as expressed in his Journals: "There is no police so effective as a good hill and a wide pasture in the neighborhood of a village . . ." Quoted by Lewis Mumford in *The City in History,* 495, and by Georges Teyssot in *The American Lawn,* 10. See also William H. Pierson Jr., "The University of Virginia," in Pierson, *American Buildings and Their Architects,* 1:316–34.

6. That Thomas Jefferson did not separate his "public" university from the people it was meant to serve by means of a wall is one of his most important contributions to the idea of the university in America, but keeping the sense of control and demarcation as the university expanded is what makes these mostly symbolic gateways useful.

7. This situation appears to have changed since the 2003 Campus Master Plan produced by SmithGroup/JJR and the range of subsequent plans that have followed, including the Residential Life Master Plan, the Union Master Plan, the University Recreation Master Plan, the Athletic Master Plan, the Parking Master Plan, the Veterinary Medicine Master Plan, and the Louisiana Emerging Technology Center District Master Plan.

8. Significant buildings of merit have been built on campus in the years since the campuswide plans discussed here, such as the LSU Union and Lod Cook. But in these cases the architects acted alone and were adept enough to take advantage of the unique sites they were given and the unique roles of the buildings they were asked to design. The LSU Union, designed by the Baton Rouge architect John J. Desmond, FAIA, is one of the few examples of modern architecture in Louisiana to achieve widespread acclaim nationally, winning the American Institute of Architects Regional First Honor Award shortly after it was built, and the only twentieth-century Louisiana building included in G. E. Kidder Smith's prestigious *Architecture of the United States.* One of many buildings that Desmond's office produced for the campus, it contrasts perhaps most strongly with the CEBA Building, also one of his. At CEBA the design turned inward away from the sea of parking that was its only context, creating a rather foreboding hulk. Locating such a large classroom building so far away from the core of campus and surrounding it with parking certainly represents a failure that contrasts with the comprehensive planning of groups of buildings shown in these earlier examples.

BIBLIOGRAPHY

ON BATON ROUGE AND THE LSU CAMPUS

Albrecht, Andrew. "The Origins and Early Settlement of Baton Rouge." *Louisiana Historical Quarterly* 28, no. 1 (1945): 5–68.

Bedsole, V. L., and Oscar G. Richard III, eds. *Louisiana State University: A Pictorial Record of the First Hundred Years.* Baton Rouge: Louisiana State University Press, 1959.

Bordignon Favero, Giampaolo. *The Villa Emo at Fanzolo.* Trans. Douglas Lewis. University Park: Pennsylvania State University Press, 1972.

Boyd, Thomas Duckett, Family Papers. Louisiana and Lower Mississippi Valley Collections, LSU Libraries, Baton Rouge, LA.

Burden, Steele. Oral history interview, session 1. 19 July 1993. Conducted by Suzanne Turner and transcribed by Melissa Perez. Mss. 4700.0318. Louisiana and Lower Mississippi Valley Collections, LSU Libraries, Baton Rouge, LA.

———. Oral history interview, session 2. 2 February 1994. Conducted by Kathy Grigsby and transcribed by Tara Zachary. Mss. 4700.0452. Louisiana and Lower Mississippi Valley Collections, LSU Libraries, Baton Rouge, LA.

Carleton, Mark. *River Capital: An Illustrated History of Baton Rouge.* Sun Valley, CA: American Historical Press, 1996.

Cox, Van. "The Campus Landscape." In Desmond and Cox, *Architecture of LSU.*

Dedication Exercises of the New Campus and Buildings. Louisiana State University and Agricultural and Mechanical College, April 30 to May 2, 1926, Baton Rouge. Dedication program, Special Collections, LSU Libraries, Baton Rouge, LA.

Desmond, J. Michael, and Van Cox. *The Architecture of LSU: Historic Preservation Study and Recommendations for the Core Campus Area.* Lulu Publishing, 2010.

Draughon, Ralph. *Down by the River: A History of the Baton Rouge Riverfront.* New Orleans: U.S. Army Corps of Engineers, New Orleans Division, 1998.

Fleming, Walter L. *History of Louisiana State University.* Sewanee, TN: University of the South Press, 1931.

———. *Louisiana State University, 1860–1896.* Baton Rouge: Louisiana State University Press, 1936.

Foote, Shelby. *The Beleaguered City: The Vicksburg Campaign, December 1862–July 1863.* New York: Modern Library, 1995.

Gaines, Thomas. *The Campus as a Work of Art.* Westport, CT: Praeger, 1991.

Hebert, Mary. "Remembering the Scandals." T. Harry Williams Center for Oral History, Louisiana State University, Baton Rouge. www.lib.lsu.edu/special/williams/newsletters/ohnewsletter7.html.

"History of Gartness." University Archives, Office of the President Records, Special Collections, LSU Libraries, Baton Rouge, LA.

Hoffman, Paul. "How LSU Got Its 'O' and Its Architect." Unpublished paper, 1999.

Homburg, Jeffery Alan. "Archaeological Investigations at the LSU Campus Mounds Site." *Louisiana Archaeology* 15 (1988): 31–204.

———. "Comments on the Age of the LSU Campus Mounds: A Reply to A. Jones." *Louisiana Archaeology* 20 (1993): 183–96.

Jeter, Marvin D., Jerome C. Rose, G. Ishmael Williams Jr., and Anna M. Harmon, eds. *Archeology and Bioarcheology of the Lower Mississippi Valley and Trans-Mississippi South in Arkansas and Louisiana.* Research Series No. 37. Fayetteville: Arkansas Archeological Survey, 1989.

Jones, Dennis. "Archaic Mounds in Louisiana: The Case of the LSU Mounds Report." *Louisiana Archaeology* 20 (1993): 169–78.

King, Edward. *The Great South: A Record of Journeys in Louisiana, Texas, the Indian Territory, Missouri, Arkansas, Mississippi, Alabama, Georgia, Florida, South Carolina, North Carolina, Kentucky, Tennessee, Virginia, West Virginia, and Maryland.* Hartford, CT: American Publishing, 1875. docsouth.unc.edu/nc/king/king.html.

Kingsley, Karen. *Buildings of Louisiana.* New York: Oxford University Press, 2003.

Leighninger, Robert D., Jr. *Building Louisiana: The Legacy of the Public Works Administration.* Jackson: University Press of Mississippi, 2007.

The LSU Campus Mounds: A National Treasure. Baton Rouge: Louisiana State University Museum of Natural Science, 1998.

Meyers, Rose. *A History of Baton Rouge, 1699–1812.* Baton Rouge: Louisiana State University Press, 1976.

Michel, John T. *Report of the Secretary of State to His Excellency W. W. Heard, Governor of the State of Louisiana, May 12th, 1902.* Baton Rouge: News Pub. Co., State Printers, [1902].

Neuman, R. W. "Report on the Soil Core Borings Conducted at the LSU Campus Mounds Site (16EBR6), East Baton Rouge Parish, Louisiana." *Louisiana Archaeology* 15 (1988): 1–29.

New Campus and Buildings of the Louisiana State University. Pamphlet (1926?). Louisiana and Lower Mississippi Valley Collections, LSU Libraries, Baton Rouge, LA.

Pringle, Heather. "Oldest Mound Complex Found at Louisiana State." *Science* 277 (1997): 1761–62.

Puppi, Lionello. *The Villa Badoer at Fratta Polesine.* Trans. Catherine Enggass. University Park: Pennsylvania State University Press, 1975.

Ringle, Andrew D. "Edward Avery McIlhenny, Pioneer Bamboo Planter." Unpublished paper, 2002.

Ruffin, Thomas F. "Before Long." *LSU Alumni Magazine* 70, no. 2 (1994): 17–21.

———. "The Greater University." *LSU Alumni Magazine* 70, no. 1 (1994): 24–28, 42.

———. "Land-Grant Colleges: Coming of Age." *LSU Alumni Magazine* 60, no. 3 (1993): 18–23.

———. "Land-Grant Colleges: Growing Pains." *LSU Alumni Magazine* 69, no. 2 (1993): 45–49, 56.

———. "Land-Grant Colleges: Louisiana Goes to College." *LSU Alumni Magazine* 68, no. 4 (1992): 20–23, 33.

———. "Land-Grant Colleges: The A&M College." *LSU Alumni Magazine* 69, no. 1 (1993): 25–29.

———. "Land-Grant Colleges: The Early Years." *LSU Alumni Magazine* 68, no. 3 (1992): 31–33, 47.

———. "Mr. Morrill's Dream." *LSU Alumni Magazine* 68, no. 2 (1992): 19–21.

———. *Under Stately Oaks: A Pictorial History of LSU.* Baton Rouge: Louisiana State University Press, 2002.

Saunders, Joe, and Thurman Allen. "The Archaic Period." *Louisiana Archaeology* 22 (1997): 1–30.

Saunders, Rebecca. "The Case for Archaic Period Mounds in Southeastern Louisiana." *Southeastern Archeology* 13, no. 2 (1994): 118–34.

Smith, Steven, Phillip Rivet, Kathleen Byrd, and Nancy Hawkins. *Louisiana's Comprehensive Archaeological Plan.* Baton Rouge: State of Louisiana, Department of Culture, Recreation and Tourism, Office of Cultural Development, Division of Archaeology, 1983.

Stakely, James Tracy. "Steele Burden and Windrush: A Historical Documentation of a Landscape Designer and His Garden." BA thesis, School of Landscape Architecture, Louisiana State University, August 1997.

Stringer, G. L., D. S. Frink, et al. "A Mound Complex in Louisiana at 5400–5500 Years before Present." *Science* 227 (1997): 1796–99.

Thom, Evelyn Martindale. *Baton Rouge Story: An Historical Sketch of Louisiana's Capital City.* Baton Rouge: Foundation for Historical Louisiana, 1967.

U.S. Geological Survey. *Baton Rouge, LA* (map). 1:62,000. 15-Minute Series. Washington, DC, 1908.

ON THEODORE C. LINK

Desmond, Michael, Collection, MSS 5084, Louisiana and Lower Mississippi Valley Collections, LSU Libraries, Baton Rouge, LA. A collection of random, frequently unidentified newspaper clippings about Theodore C. Link donated by Mr. Link's surviving family through the services of Mr. Gary Tetley, of St. Louis.

Tetley, Gary. "Theodore C. Link Biographical Chronology." Copy in author's possession.

ON FREDERICK LAW OLMSTED JR., THE OLMSTED BROTHERS, AND FREDERICK LAW OLMSTED SR.

Beveridge, Charles E. *The Master List of Design Projects of the Olmsted Firm, 1857–1950.* [New York]: National Association for Olmsted Parks with Massachusetts Association for Olmsted Parks, 1987.

Beveridge, Charles E., and Paul Rocheleau. *Frederick Law Olmsted: Designing the American Landscape.* New York: Rizzoli International, 1998.

Birnbaum, Charles A., and Mary V. Hughes, eds. *Design with Culture: Claiming America's Landscape Heritage.* Charlottesville: University of Virginia Press, 2005.

"In Memoriam: Frederick Law Olmsted (1870–1957)." *Landscape Architecture* 24, no. 1 (1958): 55–57.

Klaus, Susan L. "Frederick Law Olmsted, Jr.: Landscape Architect, Planner Educator, Conservationist (1870–1957)." www.olmsted.org/the-olmsted-legacy/frederick-law-olmsted-jr.

———. "Olmsted, Fredrick Law, Jr." In *Pioneers of American Landscape Design,* ed. Charles A. Birnbaum and Robin Karson, 273–76. New York: McGraw Hill.

Olmsted, Frederick Law. *Civilizing American Cities: Writings on City Landscapes.* Cambridge, MA: MIT Press. 1971.

———. *Frederick Law Olmsted: Essential Texts.* Ed. Robert Twombly. New York: Norton. 2010

Olmsted, F. L., Jr. "Report to Newspapers." Olmsted Associates Records, microfiche series B, reel 338, Manuscript Division, Library of Congress, Washington, DC.

Rybczynski, Witold. *A Clearing in the Distance: Frederick Law Olmsted and America in the Nineteenth Century.* New York: Scribner, [c. 1999].

Whiting, E. C., and W. L. Phillips. "Frederick Law Olmstead, 1870–1957: Appreciation of the Man and His Achievements." *Landscape Architecture* 48, no. 3 (1958): 145–57.

ON JOHN JOSEPH EARLEY

Aument, Lori. "Construction History in Architectural Conservation: The Exposed Aggregate, Reinforced Concrete of Meridian Hill Park." *Journal of the American Institute for Conservation* 42, no. 1 (2003): 3–19.

Avery, W. M. "Earley's Mosaic Concrete Opens Limitless Vistas in Products Field." *Pit and Quarry* 37, no. 3 (1944): 131–34.

Creighton, Wilbur F. *The Parthenon in Nashville.* Nashville, 1989.

Cron, Frederick W. *The Man Who Made Concrete Beautiful.* Fort Collins, CO: Centennial, 1977.

Earley, John Joseph. "Architectural Concrete." *Proceedings of the American Concrete Institute* 22 (1926): 513–34.

———. "Architectural Concrete of the Exposed Aggregate Type." *Journal of the American Concrete Institute* 30 (1934): 251–78.

———. *The Concrete of the Architect and Sculptor.* Chicago: Portland Cement Association, 1926.

———. "Introduction to Architectural Concrete." *Proceedings of the American Concrete Institute* 20 (1924): 157.

———. Method of Producing a Predetermined Color Effect in Concrete and Stucco. US Patent 1,376,748. Application filed July 6, 1920; patent issued May 3, 1921.

———. "Some Problems in Devising a New Finish for Concrete." *Journal of the American Concrete Institute* 16 (1918): 127–37.

———. "What Concrete Means to the Craftsmen Who Are Entrusted with Interpreting Architectural Design." In *Substance, Form and Color through Concrete,* by Atlas Portland Cement Company, 15–22. New York: Atlas Portland Cement, 1924.

Forgey, Benjamin. "Concrete Proof of One Man's Legacy to Washington." *Washington Post,* 31 March 2001. groups.yahoo.com/group/columbia_heights/message/4124.

Hart, Russell. "The 'Parthenon' Nashville." *Architectural Forum* 46 (May 1927): 433.

"John Joseph Earley (1881–1945)." www.myfranciscan.org/index.php?option=com_content&view=article&id=84&Itemid=1.

Pearson, J. C., and J. J. Earley. "New Developments in Surface Treated Concrete and Stucco." *Proceedings of the American Concrete Institute* 16 (1920): 70–86.

OTHER

Ackerman, James S. *Palladio.* Harmondsworth, UK: Penguin, 1966.

Ashbee, Charles R. *Exhibition of University Planning and Building.* University of London, 1912. Exhibition catalog.

Betsky, Aaron. "American Dream: In Form and Function, the School Campus Is Our Greatest Contribution to Architecture and Urban Planning." *Architect,* September 2010, 56–60.

Boesiger, W., and H. Girsberger. *Le Corbusier, 1910–1965.* Zurich: Les Editions d'Architecture, 1967.

Bormann, F. Herbert, Diana Balmor, and Gordon T. Geballe. *Redesigning the American Lawn.* 2nd ed. New Haven, CT: Yale University Press, 2001.

Boucher, Bruce. *Andrea Palladio: The Architect in His Time.* New York: Abbeville, 2007.

Christen, Barbara, and Steven Flanders, eds. *Cass Gilbert, His Life and Work: Architect of the Public Domain.* New York: Norton, 2001.

Conant, Kenneth John. *Carolingian and Romanesque Architecture, 800 to 1200.* 1959. Reprint, New Haven, CT: Yale University Press, 1978.

Cram, Ralph Adams. *My Life in Architecture.* Boston: Magazine of the American Institute of Architects, 1937.

Craven, Wayne. *A Monograph of McKim, Mead & White.* New York: Architectural Book, 1925.

Dober, Richard P. *Campus Planning.* New York: Reinhold, 1963.

Douglas, John Aubrey. "California and a Great American Movement." In *The California Idea and American Higher Education: 1850 to the 1960 Master Plan,* 2–7. Stanford, CA: Stanford University Press, 2000.

Farber, Joseph C. *Palladio's Architecture and Its Influence: A Photographic Guide.* New York: Dover, [c. 1980].

Githens, Alfred M. "Recent American Group Plans." *Brickbuilder* 21 (December 1912).

Hegemenn, Werner, and Elbert Peets. *The American Vitruvius: An Architect's Handbook of Civic Art.* New York: Architectural Publishing, 1922.

Hillison, John. "The Origins of Agriscience; or, Where Did All That Scientific Agriculture Come From?" *Journal of Agricultural Education* 37, no. 4 (1996): 8–13.

Huxley, Anthony, ed. "Lawns." In *New RHS Dictionary of Gardening,* ed. Huxley, 26–33. London: Macmillan, 1992.

Jenkins, Virginia Scott. *The Lawn: A History of an American Obsession.* Washington, DC: Smithsonian Books, 1994.

John, W. C. *Land-Grant College Education, 1910 to 1920.* U.S. Bureau of Education Bulletin No. 30. Washington, DC: Government Printing Office, 1924.

Jordy, William H. *American Buildings and Their Architects: Progressive and Academic Ideals at the Turn of the Twentieth Century.* Garden City, NY: Doubleday, 1972.

Klauder, Charles Z., and Herbert C. Wise. *College Architecture in America and Its Part in the Development of the Campus.* New York: Charles Scribner's Sons, 1929.

Larson, Jens F., and Archie M. Palmer. *Architectural Planning of the American College.* New York: McGraw-Hill, 1933.

Leighninger, Robert D. *Long-Range Public Investment: The Forgotten Legacy of the New Deal.* Columbia: University of South Carolina Press, 2007.

Lewis, Douglas. *The Drawings of Andrea Palladio.* Rev. and expanded 2nd ed. New Orleans: Martin & St. Martin, 2000.

Mumford, Lewis. *The City in History: Its Origins, Its Transformations, and Its Prospects.* New York: Harcourt, Brace & World, 1961.

O'Gorman, James F. *The ABCs of Architecture.* Philadelphia: University of Pennsylvania Press, 1997.

O'Malley, Therese. "The Lawn in Early American Landscape and Garden Design." In Teyssot, *American Lawn,* 64–87.

Palladio, Andrea. *The Four Books on Architecture.* 1738. Reprint, New York: Dover, 1965.

Pierson, William H., Jr. *American Buildings and Their Architects.* Vol. 1, *The Colonial and Neo-Classical Styles.* 1976. Reprint, New York: Oxford University Press, 1986.

———. *American Buildings and Their Architects.* Vol. 2, *Technology and the Picturesque: The Corporate and the Early Gothic Styles.* 1978. Reprint, New York: Oxford University Press, 1986.

Rasmussen, Steen Eiller. *Towns and Buildings.* Cambridge, MA: MIT Press, 1994. First published in Danish in 1949; first published in English in 1951.

Schuyler, Montgomery. "The Architecture of American Colleges I. Harvard." *Architectural Record* 26 (October 1909): 243–69.

———. "The Architecture of American Colleges II. Yale." *Architectural Record* 26 (December 1909): 393–416.

———. "The Architecture of American Colleges IV. New York City Colleges." *Architectural Record* 27 (June 1910): 443–69.

———. "The Architecture of American Colleges V. University of Pennsylvania, Girard, Haverford, Lehigh and Bryn Mawr Colleges." *Architectural Record* 28 (September 1910): 182–212.

———. "The Architecture of American Colleges VI. Dartmouth, Williams and Amherst." *Architectural Record* 28 (December 1910): 424–42.

———. "The Architecture of American Colleges VII. Brown, Bowdoin, Trinity and Wesleyan." *Architectural Record* 29 (February 1911): 144–66.

———. "The Architecture of American Colleges VIII. The Southern Colleges." *Architectural Record* 30 (July 1911): 57–84.

———. "The Architecture of American Colleges IX. Union, Hamilton, Hobart, Cornell and Syracuse." *Architectural Record* 30 (December 1911): 549–73.

———. "The Architecture of American Colleges X. Three Women's Colleges: Vassar, Wellesley & Smith." *Architectural Record* 31 (May 1912).

———. "The Works of Cram, Goodhue and Ferguson." *Architectural Record,* January 1911, 1–112.

Smith, G. E. Kidder. *The Architecture of the United States: The South and Mid-West.* New York: Doubleday, 1981.

Steinberg, T. *American Green: The Obsessive Quest for the Perfect Lawn.* New York: Norton, 2006.

Stern, Robert A. M. "The University Campus: An American Invention." Florida International University Honors Excellence Occasional Papers Series, 3, no. 1. Miami, October 2003.

Tate, Susan. *The University of Florida Historic Preservation Plan Report.* Gainesville: University of Florida, 2004.

Teague, Edward H. *Andrea Palladio: A Bibliography of Recent Literature.* Monticello, IL: Vance Bibliographies, [1989].

Temko, Allan. *Eero Saarinen.* New York: George Braziller, 1962.

Teyssot, Georges, ed. *The American Lawn.* New York: Princeton Architectural Press, 1999.

Turner, Paul Venable. *Campus: An American Planning Tradition.* Cambridge, MA: MIT Press; New York: Architectural History Foundation, 1984.

U.S. National Park Service, National Capital Region. *Meridian Hill Park Cultural Landscape Report.* Washington, DC, [2001].

Valance, Aymer. *The Old Colleges of Oxford: Their Architectural History Illustrated and Described.* London: Batsford, 1912.

Walpole, Horace. *Essay on Modern Gardening.* 1780. Reprint, New York: Young Books, 1931.

Williams, Kim. *The Villas of Palladio.* New York: Princeton Architectural Press, 2003.

Williams, Raymond. *Keywords: A Vocabulary of Culture and Society.* Rev. and expanded ed. New York: Oxford University Press, 1983.

Williams, T. Harry. *Huey Long.* 1969. Reprint, New York: Vintage, 1981.

Wittkower, Rudolf. *Palladio and Palladianism.* New York: Braziller, [1974].

INDEX

Note: Page numbers denoting illustrations are in italic.